THE BOY WHO COULDN'T STOP WASHING

THE BOY WHO COULDN'T STOP WASHING

The Experience and Treatment of
Obsessive–Compulsive Disorder

Dr Judith Rapoport

COLLINS
8 Grafton Street, London W1
1990

William Collins Sons & Co. Ltd
London . Glasgow . Sydney . Auckland
Toronto . Johannesburg

First published in Great Britain by Collins 1990

BRITISH LIBRARY CATALOGUING IN PUBLICATION DATA
Rapoport, Judith L.
The boy who couldn't stop washing.
1. Man. Neuroses: Obsession
I. Title
616.85'227

ISBN 0 00 215497 8

Photoset in Compugraphic Palatino by Burns & Smith,
Derby DE1 1QH
Printed and bound in Great Britain by
Hartnolls Limited, Bodmin, Cornwall

To Nancy and Margot

CONTENTS

Acknowledgements   ix

Introduction   1

PART I THE PATIENTS SPEAK:
PARENTS

1 The Car Accident That Never Was   21
2 Rituals and Contaminations:
   Zach and His Family   41

PART II THE PATIENTS SPEAK:
CHILDREN

3 Paul: Stuck in the Doorway   63
4 Arnie: The Newspaper Round   67
5 Morris: Mr Clean   70

PART III A DOCTOR'S PERSPECTIVE

6   The Boy Who Couldn't Stop Washing   78
7   The Doubting Disease   83
8   Is OCD a Brain Disease?   85
9   Unlearning to Understand   92
10 Clomipramine: A Wonder Drug?   97
11 David's Drug Odyssey   100
12 How Sweet It Is!   103
13 The Hidden   105

14 No Joke   110
15 The Music Goes Round and Round   113
16 My Mind on My Mind   118
17 Over and Over Again   123
18 The Secret Life of a Street Person   126
19 Count Me Out   131
20 Love Story   136
21 AIDS: The New Obsession   139
22 The Hair-Pulling Women   143
23 Innocent Sinners   147
24 A Thousand Commitments to God   152

PART IV ON THE BOUNDARIES
25 The Obsessionality of Everyday Life   169
26 Touch Wood   176
27 Grooming and Nesting   179
28 I Can't Get You Out of My Mind   191
29 Free Will and the Uncertainty of
    Knowing   197

PART V DO YOU HAVE OBSESSIVE-
COMPULSIVE DISORDER?
30 Making the Diagnosis   213
31 What To Do If You Have Obsessive-
    Compulsive Disorder   218

    Appendix: The Religious Perspective   223
    References and Suggested Reading   233
    Index   237

Acknowledgements

Thanks are due to many friends, teachers, and associates past and present who encouraged my writing this book.

Susan Swedo, Henrietta Leonard, and Madge Coffey, all from the professional staff of the Child Psychiatry Branch, National Institute of Mental Health, were of enormous help in sifting through and discussing much of this material. Drs Henry Gleitman, Michael Krause, Steven Wise, and Wallace Mendelson discussed the ideas and presentation at length. Dr Alan Hobson generously gave me the notes on his famous case of Sebastian. Numerous other friends and colleagues also listened to ideas-in-formation, particularly Frank Sieverts, Arnold Friedhoff, John Sabini, Alan Fiske, Daniel Dennett, Dennis Murphy, Erica Goldberger, David and Louisa Schwartz, George Valliant, Mort Mishkin, and Everett Dulit. My sister, Leda, provided the very first encouragement for starting off at all, while my husband, Stanley, and sons Erik and Stuart all listened patiently and tolerantly for more hours than they should have had to, concerning the contents and progress of this book.

The administration of the NIMH: Fred Goodwin, Hazel Rea, Sue Thompson, and Ted Colburn, were encouraging in regard to the presentation of this clinical research material in an accessible form. Indirectly, the opportunity to work as a research scientist at the National Institutes of Health provided the research background that nurtured my fascination with this illness.

But most of all, thanks are due to all the patients who told me their stories and encouraged me to share their experience with others.

In addition my editors, Richard Marek and Jerry Gross, who put up with and greatly improved upon earlier drafts, deserve my greatest thanks.

This book represents a personal view, controversial and often premature. I hope other specialists in my own and related fields will forgive my trespass.

Introduction

'Compulsive' and 'obsessive' have become everday words. 'I'm compulsive' is how my friends describe their need for neatness, balanced cheque books, punctuality, and shoes lined up in cupboards. 'He's so compulsive' is shorthand for calling someone uptight, controlling, and not much fun. 'She's obsessed with him' is a way of saying your friend is hopelessly lovesick. That is *not* how these words are used to describe Obsessive–Compulsive Disorder (OCD), a strange and fascinating sickness of ritual and doubts run wild. OCD can begin suddenly and is usually seen as a problem as soon as it starts. I have been learning about, and treating, this remarkable illness since 1972.

When the thoughts and rituals of OCD are intense, the victim's work and home life disintegrate. With severe compulsions, endless rituals dominate each day. The most crippling obsessions create absurd, embarrassing, or frightening thoughts that repeat in the mind in an endless loop. OCD is a serious disease, and much more common than we ever thought. More than four, perhaps five, million people in the United States suffer from its disabling thoughts or rituals. Assuming, since a survey has not yet been carried out, that the percentage of the sufferers amongst the population is similar in the United Kingdom, then there are over one million sufferers here. Amazingly, most OCD-sufferers keep their afflictions hidden.

Obsessive–Compulsive Disorder is also different from the superstitions of everyday life. Many people believe in lucky numbers, avoid walking under ladders, keep umbrellas closed in the house, or touch wood. My patients' rituals go far beyond these common beliefs and habits, and seem a different problem · altogether. In fact, as a group, my patients are not particularly superstitious. Everyday habits are somewhat useful and we can change them when we want. But obsessive–compulsive patients have rituals or thoughts they know are senseless, and waste hours every day using up precious school, work, or personal time. Although they have never met each other, my patients could be reading the same weird script.

I am a physician, a child psychiatrist, and a research scientist at the National Institute of Mental Health in Bethesda, Maryland. Of all of the many psychiatric studies I have carried out since 1962 and of the many unusual cases I have treated, none compares with the fascination and drama of OCD.

Senseless thoughts recur over and over again in the mind, appearing out of the blue; certain 'magical' acts are repeated over and over again. For some the thoughts are meaningless (numbers, one number, or several), for others they are highly charged ideas – for example, 'I have just killed someone.' The intrusion into conscious everyday thinking of such intense, repetitive, and (to the victim) disgusting, absurd, and alien thoughts is a dramatic and remarkable experience. *You can't put them out of your mind* – that is the nature of obsessions.

Some patients are 'checkers', they check lights, doors, locks – ten, twenty, or one hundred times – or repeat peculiar acts over and over again. Others spend hours producing unimportant symmetry. Shoelaces must be exactly even, eyebrows identical to a hair. But most often, the patient is a 'washer' who feels he must wash over and over again. All of these problems have common themes: you can't trust your ordinary good judgement, can't trust your eyes that see no dirt, or really believe that the door is locked. You know you have done nothing harmful, but in spite of this good sense, you must go on checking and counting. *You can't dismiss the idea.* The compulsion keeps coming back, and you ask yourself, 'Do I really know? I still feel something is wrong.' The compelling need to repeat small and private, or elaborate and conspicuous rituals which are irrational and bizarre is dramatic and remarkable. This is the nature of compulsions.

Our normal functioning probably consists of constant uncountable checking, a sort of radar operation, that we could not do consciously and still act efficiently. Something has gone wrong with this process for obsessive–compulsives, the usual shut-off (my hands *are* clean enough, I saw that the gas *was* turned off, the door *was* locked) does not get through. Everyday life becomes tyrannized by doubts, leading to senseless repetition and ritual.

I have come to examine in minute detail my own everyday 'compulsive' functioning through living my patients' lives with them. I too check the door, the gas, but not excessively. How do I know to stop? Socially, we all are checkers. When a friend hasn't called for weeks, our first thoughts are, 'What did I do wrong? Is he/she mad at me? Was I too aggressive/seductive/flippant (fill in your own adjective) the last time we met?' It almost always turns out that the friend has been busy, or had his own troubles. But all of us, just beneath the surface, are checkers all of the time.

The disease poses problems that call on every aspect of my previous training – an undergraduate major in psychology and English literature, and medical training at Harvard Medical School with a focus on neurology and psychiatry. At Swarthmore College, the psychologist Wolfgang Kohler taught me to look at brain functioning in terms of complex systems rather than as simple sensory or motor events. At medical school and during psychiatric residency I became fascinated by how the then new drug treatments could bring dramatic relief when other psychological treatments failed. Several months of training in London at the National Hospital for Nervous Diseases (known colloquially as Queen Square) fostered my interest (some would say obsession) in the mind and the brain. To study this disease I had to use my training in psychology and medicine, for both are essential for treating OCD.

The disease affects some of the most able, sensitive, and talented people I have met. Their otherwise normal ability to function, to become a good husband, wife, or friend makes working with obsessive–compulsive patients particularly rewarding and, when they are severely ill, very painful.

Although the disease is virtually unknown to the general public, some major figures have suffered from OCD. Samuel Johnson (1709–1784), the greatest man of his age, poet, playwright, biographer, and scholar, suffered from some version of this disorder. Miss Frances Reynolds, a friend of Johnson, vividly described his peculiar method of entering a house:

> Nor has anyone, I believe, described his extraordinary gestures or antics with his hands when passing over the

threshold of a Door, or rather before he would venture to pass through *any* doorway. On entering Sir Joshua's house with poor Mrs. Williams, a blind lady who lived with him, he would quit her hand, or else whirl her about on the steps as he whirled and twisted about to perform his gesticulations; and as soon as he had finish'd, he would give a sudden spring and make such an extensive stride over the threshold, as if he were trying for a wager how far he could stride, Mrs. Williams standing groping about outside the door unless the servant or mistress of the house more commonly took hold of her hand to conduct her in, leaving Dr. Johnson to perform at the Parlor Door much the same exercise over again.

Johnson's biographer, James Boswell, further chronicled these doorway rites:

He had another peculiarity, of which none of his friends even ventured to ask an explanation. It appeared to me some superstitious habit, which he had contracted early, and from which he had never called upon his reason to disentangle him. This was his anxious care to go out or in at a door or passage, by a certain number of steps from a certain point, or at least so as that either his right or his left foot (I am not certain which), should constantly make the first actual movement when he came close to the door or passage.

There are also descriptions of Johnson's never stepping on the cracks of paving stones, and touching every post along the street or road as he walked. If he missed a post he would keep his friends waiting until he went back to touch it.

While many felt that these behaviours were a reflection of Johnson's personality, or just the eccentricities of a great genius, Boswell felt that the mannerisms were 'of the convulsive kind', and later theorists wondered if obsessions could be *tics of the mind*. We are all familiar with simple motor tics, most often a twitching eye or facial grimace, that goes on and on and can't be stopped. But can a repeating idea be a tic?

Boswell's suggestion that Johnson's mannerisms resembled convulsions anticipated our recent biological interest in obsession and compulsions. One modern model for this disease is that it is caused by sparks, a kind of hiccup in the brain. Can repetitive thoughts and unbreakable habits be caused by short circuits of electrical activity in the brain? If so, compulsions would be like tics, which are almost certainly caused by misfiring of brain cells.

Howard Hughes suffered from a particular type of Obsessive–Compulsive Disorder in which his fanatic preoccupation with germs led to a bizarre life of filth and neglect. Hughes had feared germs since he was a child. This fear grew from simple fastidiousness to a life of sealed doors and windows, darkened rooms and makeshift 'insulations' of paper towels and tissues. His aides brought him documents or food wearing special tissue pads to avoid touching anything that Hughes might touch.

Eating and toilet rituals took up hours of each day. Towards the end of his life, paradoxically, Hughes became a filthy, unkempt figure with unwashed, matted hair, a scraggly beard, and fingernails and toenails of such length that they curled in upon themselves. He either went nude or dressed only in a pair of undershorts. Most probably the rituals of bathing and grooming became so overwhelming in Hughes's case that he was ultimately incapable of even the simplest self-care.

This awful sickness is not just the disease of the brilliant wealthy, or glamorous. My patients fight exhausting battles with invisible germs daily, even hourly. They seldom end up as neglected as Hughes, because, luckily for them, they cannot afford the indulgence or the nurturing of these rituals to the degree that Hughes could. But the paradox remains. Their hands and arms are red or even bleeding from continual washing. Their desks and drawers are uselessly arranged, the rules controlling this behaviour based on some sterile, abstract sense of order. When OCD is severe these habits become gross caricatures and distortions of useful everyday behaviour. Perhaps the most painful aspect is the insight my patients have about the absurdity and the wastefulness of the crazy thoughts that comsume their lives. Most psychiatrists don't use the word 'crazy', but that is exactly how to talk about it with obsessive–compulsives. Since they are so sane in every other way, you must agree with and understand how upset they are by how crazy it all is.

The sustained experience of obsession and/or compulsions make up what the American Psychiatric Association's *Diagnostic and*

Statistical Manual of Mental Disorders (DSM III), 3rd edition, calls Obsessive–Compulsive Disorder. It has also been called obsessional neurosis. Psychiatrists have been fascinated by this disorder for over a hundred years. Priests have described the overly scrupulous for much longer than that. Children suffer from Obsessive–Compulsive Disorder with exactly the same symptoms as adults. To a child psychiatrist like myself, an early start in a mental disorder is unusual. Other mental illnesses, such as depression or schizophrenia, often appear in a different form in young children and, in any case, are much more rare in children than in adults.

But with OCD it is the same at any age. I have seen a two-year-old start to walk in circles around manhole covers; ten years later he couldn't go to school because of his bizarre compulsion to draw Os! How these complex behaviours spring up in childhood is mysterious but suggests that some innate programme of behaviour is running wild in this disease. That each young patient has the same habits, even though they have never seen or heard or one another, is eerie. At Swarthmore, I studied how parrots build nests, how cranes dance, how squirrels hoard. None have teachers, yet each species builds the same nest, hoards food in the same way, and so forth. I think of these creatures as I meet new young patients with their bewildering tales of new patterns of behaviours that intruded from nowhere. I introduce them to each other and they are astonished that this has happened to someone else, that they are so much alike! But I am not describing a new avian courtship dance, or the rituals of an isolated primitive tribe. These are frightened, lonely people and the cruel script erupts from somewhere inside their brains.

A few individual cases of Obsessive–Compulsive Disorder have been reported in the medical literature over the past 150 years, but only recently have we learned of the large number of adolescents and adults who suffer with it – and suffer secretly.

I first became interested in this problem in children. Most other adult psychiatric patients didn't have the same problems in childhood. Obsessive–Compulsive Disorder is different: 50 per cent of all adult obsessive–compulsive patients started to have repetitive thoughts (obsessions) or rituals (compulsions) when they were young. Less than 5 per cent of adults with other psychiatric disorders had symptoms that began in childhood.

Families often don't know that they have a sick child. Many of my obsessive–compulsive adult patients tell me that they kept their disorder a secret as children, suffering for months or years because they were too humiliated or did not want to be considered crazy. As chief of a federally funded research clinic in child psychiatry I was able to study this hidden disease before an effective treatment was established, and before we realized that it was a common problem. At the National Institute of Mental Health, I began the study thinking that it would take ten years to see enough patients to get even an idea of the typical symptom patterns, the age at which they began, and what treatment worked. But just as our project was getting started, new facts exploded. First surveys showed that Obsessive–Compulsive Disorder is not at all rare – it is indeed common. Then it quickly became clear that there were new treatments that worked. Suddenly, OCD became the psychiatric disease of the 1980s. We began to see many, many patients.

The memory of Sal, the first obsessive–compulsive patient I saw in my first year of residency at the Massachusetts Mental Health Center in Boston in 1961 is still with me. A sixty-year-old labourer of Italian descent, a valued foreman, good family man, and churchgoer, Sal had developed a compulsion to pick up small pieces of trash in his home or on the street. He had a compulsion to hoard. His house grew crowded with bags full of it, which were stored in the halls and piled on the furniture. His wife's tears and threats to leave were ineffective. Over a period of a few months Sal's habit became so strong that he was unable to resist picking up even the smallest bits of paper. Picking up trash took up more and more of each day. Finally, he could not make it to work. Hospitalization during the 1940s had led to psychosurgery, a procedure rarely used now, in which all connections between the frontal lobes and deeper parts of the brain are cut. Sal had the operation and was cured, in a sense.

'You see,' Sal told me proudly, 'now I just walk by the papers, just notice them a bit more than you might – but I *don't have to do a thing.*' But because of his post-lobotomy syndrome, Sal never left the hospital.

Lobotomy had 'succeeded' dramatically in decreasing Salvatore's compulsive symptoms, but unfortunately, as often happened with prefrontal lobotomies then, he suffered personality changes from the surgery. Although Sal's disorder had been cured he remained socially disabled from the treatment. He had the inappropriate silly behaviours that frequently followed lobotomies in the early years of their use: he pinched strange young women and urinated in the street.

Sal's lucid account of the senselessness of his symptoms, whose severity had destroyed his normal life, and their sudden and complete elimination by surgery, haunted me. He had been so successful in his family life, on his job. He had been so proud of all his accomplishments. Then out of the blue, he *had to pick up trash*. The disorder just did not seem like other psychiatric disorders. It appeared to be separate from the fabric of people's lives, as if it were some outside agent that suddenly appeared to provoke the illness, and could just as suddenly disappear.

An Associated Press story on 24 February 1988 brought Sal to my mind. The headline read BRAIN WOUND ELIMINATES MAN'S MENTAL ILLNESS. A twenty-two-year-old man, identified as George, was driven to suicide by his severe washing compulsion. He put a gun in his mouth and pulled the trigger. Not only did he survive, but he was miraculously cured. The bullet had lodged in the left frontal lobe of his brain, performing a lobotomy – the same operation that had 'cured' Sal. George is now at college and leading a normal life.

The years that followed my work with Sal were occupied with residency training in Boston and with research training in Sweden. Drug treatment was just beginning to make its impact on psychiatry and with it came a new interest in the brain and the biology of mental illness. But virtually no one was applying these new treatments to Obsessive–Compulsive Disorder.

It wasn't until 1972, when visiting my old teachers and colleagues at the Karolinska Hospital in Stockholm, that I thought about Obsessive–Compulsive Disorder at all. In Stockholm, I learned of a new treatment for obsessions and compulsions, the drug clomipramine. It had just been reported by Professor Lopez-Ibor of Madrid to be helpful for obsessive–compulsive adult patients and was now being tested more systematically at the

Karolinska Hospital. My former professor Börje Cronholm, and his co-worker Dr Marie Asberg, had brought together a group of obsessive–compulsive patients from all over Sweden to test the new drug.

When I spoke with the patients on the ward (a great opportunity to practise my rusty Swedish!), several told us that they had been ill since childhood. I saw that the Swedish doctors had no shortage of patients for their study, and I reasoned that if these Swedish patients were so ill in childhood, then other children as well as adults with OCD would be found in other countries.

And so, in the 1970s, at the National Institute of Mental Health, we used our unique research setting to recruit and study adolescents with OCD. The NIMH could recruit patients from all over the country. Because clomipramine (trade name Anafranil) was not yet marketed in the United States (and still is not, although it is available in over seventy other countries including the UK), it was a timely research question to see if clomipramine would help adolescents as it did adults. This would be important to know because early treatment might be more helpful than treatment after the disease had progressed for years. Early treatment might also stop the destructive effect of the disorder on children's lives – preventing the isolation, depression, and fears that filled each child's day.

Clomipramine is a very potent antidepressant. It has a chemical structure very much like that of imipramine, a widely used antidepressant (trade name Tofranil) that has been available in Britain and America for over thirty years. But this slight difference in formula makes clomipramine especially helpful for obsessions and compulsions. Clomipramine is not free of side effects. It causes dry mouth and constipation, and it can cause drowsiness and decrease sexual function. But for many patients who have suffered from obsessions and compulsions for years, it is better to be on it despite its shortcomings.

With help from the CIBA-Geigy Pharmaceutical company, the drug manufacturer, we obtained Anafranil (clomipramine) together with a special licence to use it in our research. I confess that my group and I started the study not at all confident that the drug would work. But after a few years, we were converts. Our patients did not improve when they took placebos (which look like the drug but have no effect) or when they took another anti-depressant. But when they were on Anafranil, most did improve. The thoughts grew weaker. They were able to fight off the urge to carry out ritual activity. For some it was the end of a nightmare.

Clomipramine wasn't a perfect treatment by far. Some patients received no help at all from it. But discovery of a specific chemical treatment for obsessions and compulsions added weight to other evidence that this so called 'neurosis' might be yet another disease – like manic depressive illness, or epilepsy – with a biological basis.

Clomipramine has excited a lot of interest from researchers as well as patients. The drug does not seem to work as an anti-depressant against OCD, even though it is a very good antidepressant. But it does do somthing else – it blunts or removes the obsessions or compulsions. If we understood how clomipramine worked, what this 'something else' is, we would have a clue to understanding what causes Obsessive–Compulsive Disorder. We would know how the brain creates rituals of such a complex and fascinating sort and how it creates such a unique and powerful demon that its victim feels '*I must do this*'.

Clomipramine has a strong effect on the metabolism of brain serotonin, a neurotransmitter important for brain functioning. A neurotransmitter is a chemical substance that carries messages between cells in the brain. Serotonin is one of these brain chemicals, and is already known to be important in animals and people for many functions. Psychologically it has been related to depression, anger, and impulsiveness. Obsessive–compulsive symptoms are just the latest in the list of important jobs this chemical does in the brain.

The serotonin story itself has become extremely complicated. There are a number of places in the brain where serotonin acts, and these are called receptors. Clomipramine probably acts on certain serotonin receptors, but it is still unclear whether the net effect is to increase or decrease serotonin itself. It is still possible that clomipramine acts by influencing other brain chemicals that are affected by serotonin. Research in this area is very active at the moment and the situation changes from month to month.

We are studying other drugs with the same kind of serotonin action to see if they are as successful for treating Obsessive–Compulsive Disorder. But the effectiveness of a chemical treatment – whatever the mechanism – on the complex patterns of guilt, will, danger, cleanliness, and self-control may show us a biological basis for our behaviour at a level we never dreamed possible. A drug treatment for pathological doubting? This would seem to demonstrate a brain system operating at a level of complexity that my college psychology professors, and I, never suspected.

It is a great puzzle as to why the two best treatments for OCD are a drug and a behavioural approach. Sometimes they work well separately and sometimes a combination of the two treatments is best. Any model for this disease has to allow for both of these approaches.

Freud thought that special timing and style of parenting early in childhood might induce a child to develop Obsessive–Compulsive Disorder. For example, he proposed that very strict toilet training during the second year of life – the anal phase – could have lasting effects on personality development and make a person vulnerable to Obsessive–Compulsive Disorder. My own training had included Freudian psychoanalysis and at one time I was sympathetic to this idea. But we couldn't find any such pattern in the way the children in our study were raised, no idiosyncrasies in toilet training or measures of stress in other routines that could account for their illness.

On the other hand, we have seen the special problems that are *created* by a child's having Obsessive–Compulsive Disorder. This book shares some experiences of parents who themselves had the illness and now see it in their child. Also included are stories of the children themselves. There is no question that the disease runs in families, and that for some it is hereditary.

After only a year into our research, we were getting calls every week from parents of children and from adults with Obsessive–Compulsive Disorder. This was puzzling – we had already had more calls than we ever expected from the whole Washington, D.C., area. The textbooks had told us the disease was very rare. Later we came to see how common the problem really was. We surveyed over 5,000 students in high schools in a county school system. All of the children filled out a questionnaire about disturbing habits or thoughts. The results were startling. In these 'ordinary' schoolchildren, none seeking help, our first impressions were confirmed. There were at least twenty severe cases of Obsessive–Compulsive Disorder. The rate of 1 in 250 in the population meant that one million adolescents in America have the problem. In the United Kingdom this would mean a quarter of a million. As there are three adults for every child who has the disease, there must be four million people in America, one million in the UK, with OCD. Hard to believe. A common psychiatric disease that almost no one has heard of?

But where have the obsessive–compulsives been hiding? Freud wrote in 1907: 'Sufferers from this illness are able to keep their affliction a private matter. Concealment is made easier from the fact that they are quite well able to fulfil their social duties during a part of the day, once they have devoted a number of hours to their secret doings, hidden from view.'

As in Freud's time, very few contemporary victims ask for help, or have known that help was available. Secrecy is part of the disorder. I learned that even those few in therapy never told their therapist about their compulsions. We see new patients every week who have suffered in secret for years.

On 21 March 1987, the ABC news programme '20/20' featured several patients with Obsessive–Compulsive Disorder. The programme described cures or very marked improvement in patients who were treated with clomipramine or with behaviour therapy, the other established treatment for the disease. The national response was overwhelming. The three OCD study centres shown on the programme (ours was one) were inundated with calls and letters for months afterward. The brief stories the callers told were often dramatic. 'I was about to leave my wife. I thought she didn't care for us any more. Now I know she is sick and just want her to get help.' An eighty-seven-year-old man called just to tell us: 'I am too old to do anything about this any more, but am so grateful to know that someone knows about my problem, knows that I am not "crazy".' Part of the fascination of OCD is how it has been in our midst for so long and is regarded only as a medical curiosity. The conspiracy of silence among the patients themselves is part of the problem.

The most moving, the most powerful experience a therapist can have is to see patients gain immediate and important relief. It is one of psychiatry's great ironies that although obsessions and compulsions illustrate psychoanalytic ideas of conflict better than any other neurosis, the symptoms of obsessions and compulsions are not helped by psychoanalytic treatment. Fortunately there are now other ways to help these desperately troubled people. To start with the simplest method, we introduced children (and their families) who had lived alone with their thoughts and rituals for years to each other. They shared their pain and monitored each other's progress.

Behaviour therapists have pioneered the direct, simple, and effective approach of symptom monitoring and gradual exposure to feared or 'trigger' situations, along with reduction and prevention of the rituals. These therapists should get the credit for forcing the problem out in the open, and taking the sensible approach that it is actually good for patients to *get rid* of their symptoms! (Some psychiatrists believe that suddenly removing obsessive–compulsive symptoms without insight into unconscious conflicts only result in the substitution of new and possibly worse symptoms.) The Maudsley Hospital in London and the Medical College of Pennsylvania have carefully worked out the most effective form of behavioural treatment.

Behaviour therapy focuses on current behaviours. First the patient and therapist spend a great deal of time – hours or weeks – finding out about the rituals; exactly what they are like and where and when they occur. Then they gradually reduce the time the patient is 'allowed' to carry out the rituals. Often the therapist introduces the very situation that evokes them. A washer might be made to get his hands dirty, for example, by sticking them in mud and then go for hours without washing. Of course it is upsetting. But without the realistic exposure to the trigger stimulus, the treatment doesn't work well.

The big advances have come together: the recognition of how common obsessions and compulsions are, the discovery that behaviour therapy can be dramatically helpful, and the new fascination with the disease because of intriguing biological findings. When a drug is selectively effective in treating OCD, this too points indirectly to a biological abnormality in this disorder.

One of the more direct biological findings is the discovery, and (as is often the case in the history of science) *re*discovery that obsessions and compulsions are strongly associated with specific neurological diseases, such as epilepsy, and choreas, or movement disorders. That means that diseases of certain parts of the brain can cause Obsessive–Compulsive Disorder, at least for one group of patients. There are now new techniques for studying the brain. Computerized Axial Tomography (CAT) scans let us measure parts of the brain in living people, better than we could with X-rays. And even newer techniques of brain imaging, called Positron Emission Tomography, or PET scans, allow us to look at how the brain is working in normal persons and compare them with patients with obsessions and compulsions. These studies are very new, but the few that have been completed show abnormalities in parts of the brain, the frontal lobes and the basal ganglia, in OCD.

No one is sure of the boundaries of OCD. We have seen people with quite odd 'habits' but not quite a disorder. In our survey, one girl would get up at six every Sunday morning to spend three hours washing the walls of her room. She certainly knew that this was odd, but she just felt that she 'had to do it' but didn't really know why. She said the washing had started quite suddenly about a year before. 'I just woke up one morning last summer,' she told me, 'and I had to do this.' We would not give her any psychiatric diagnosis because she functioned well, and didn't seem 'sick'. This girl was close to her family, and a good student. She had close friends and a boyfriend. Her grades were good and she took part in extracurricular activities at school and held a part-time job. She did not seem upset, and unless a symptom interferes with a person's life by impairing functioning or causing distress, we can't say the person is sick. We are puzzled by such obsessional features and do not know if they are related to the disease or are just quirks, without any clinical significance.

We also wonder about people with many 'good' habits, whom we often think of as 'super normals'. These are people who have every minute of every day scheduled. As students, they were on every team, in every club, volunteer or community group, and they also took exercise and music classes. They were good students with high ambitions, driven, and concerned about the enormous responsibilities they took on. Super-organized, neat, and careful, such people answer 'yes' to a high number of questions in our obsessional questionnaire. Yet they feel that their habits are useful and in no way interfere with their lives. If they have a complaint, it is that they might not meet all their obligations every week of the year. Sometimes they feel frantic. But they are not complainers. They don't want anything to change – just to do it all. We have no idea if these are simply outstandingly ambitious young people who grow up to be newspaper editors, senators – or even psychiatric researchers – or if they might turn out to be what are called 'compulsive personalities'. We are following a group of super normals to find out.

In spite of the interest in individual cases of OCD in the past one hundred years, there was not much work on treatment. There is little incentive to evaluate or develop new treatments for rare disorders. So up until the 1970s, the recommended treatment was psychotherapy or psychoanalysis. Doctors made these suggestions for lack of an alternative, but many therapists found that psychotherapy was not helpful for severe cases and follow-up studies of adults could not show any advantage for this treatment.

A psychoanalytic model for Obsessive–Compulsive Disorder came from Freud's famous 'Rat Man' case, which he reported in 1909. Freud told of his successful psychoanalytic treatment of a young man tormented by obsessive thoughts of rats eating his anus. Psychoanalysis unravelled the complex symbolic significance of this horrible image, and seemed to have helped the patient. Unfortunately, the Rat Man was killed shortly afterwards in World War I, leaving unanswered the question of long-term benefit.

In the most severe cases of OCD, psychosurgery was used regularly until the 1950s. With availability of other treatments, psychosurgery is now a last resort. In some cases, however, this drastic treatment seems to work when everything else has failed. A few medical centres in Boston, London, and Stockholm, for example, will still perform limited operations using newer techniques. I have yet to send a patient for such treatment but the success of these operations fascinates me because the procedures sever connections in parts of the brain that our brain-imaging studies find abnormal in OCD. This is another clue to the biology of this sickness.

The two newer treatments, behaviour therapy and drug treatment with clomipramine, both seem to have long-term benefits. Behaviour therapists have followed up their patients for a year or two and the effect seems to last. Clomipramine has not been as well studied in follow-up, but what studies have been done show that it too is helpful over at least two years.

The first question a patient asks is 'How long does this last – will it go away?' About a dozen follow-up studies are known. Almost all of these are studies of patients who had traditional psycho-therapy or no treatment at all. In most of the studies, half of these patients did well, while about half continued having problems. Traditional psychotherapy had no effect on outcome. But these long-term studies were all done before behaviour modification or clomipramine were widely used. The few most recent follow-up studies are encouraging. It seems that the new treatments really make a difference. I hope, as yet without proof, that early recog-nition and prompt treatment will make the outcome even brighter.

As fascinated observers and students of OCD we shared our patients' astonishment in finding out that others have had the identical thoughts, images, and habits, kept secret for so long because they thought no one else could understand or believe their problem. I believe that such an unchanging pattern must come from an inborn programme in the brain, much as ethologists have described behaviours that occur in developing animals, even when they are raised in isolation.

In this Introduction, I have given an overview of my experience with this problem. Everything I have learned has been taught to me by patients and their families, for whose instruction I am forever grateful. Because they have been so silent, I thought it crucial to include first-hand accounts. When I read the patients' own accounts I learn about their attempts at self-treatment, and their ways of coming to terms with their disorder, coping with parts of it that treatment didn't cure. The first part of this book contains the stories of fathers who had the disorder and now are trying to help their sons with the same problem. Following the fathers' stories are those of the children who wrote about their experiences either when we first met, or after some years of living with the problem.

The central section of the book tells about being a doctor for those affected by this disease. These patients and I discovered each other; my practice of psychiatry will never be the same.

So much is asked about where our everyday lives stop and OCD begins, because it spills over into our religious lives, our philosophies, our romantic selves, and our ethological selves. As a result I have been forced to consider its boundaries as I have no other disease. The last section of the book comes partially in response to questions such as 'Is love an obsession?' and 'What does it mean that I like my house to be so neat?'

The basis for Obsessive–Compulsive Disorder is still not known. The evidence for a biological cause is compelling, but unfortunately it is still necessary to speak of the biology of behaviour in vague terms. The efficacy of a drug, and the relative psychological normality of many of the families, makes the importance of 'poor upbringing' as a cause of OCD uncertain to say the least. This is a disease that may be thought of as scepticism gone wild. Patients doubt their senses. They cannot believe any reassurance of everyday life: I am not dangerous, I am clean.

Reassurance does not work. The notion that there is a biological basis for a sense of 'knowing' has interesting philosophical implications. We are normally convinced that what we see and feel is what is truly there. If this is a 'doubting disease', and if a chemical controls this sense of doubt, then is our usual, normal belief in what our everyday senses and common sense tell us similarly determined by our brain chemistry?

This book is inspired by our recognition that Obsessive–Compulsive Disorder is very common. If the new epidemiological figures are true, if millions of people suffer from obsessive-compulsive illness, then a readable book about this disorder, one that's not a technical book, is long overdue and can be helpful. If you or someone close to you has OCD, keeping informed is important. New findings about the disease are now being reported every year.

Many will benefit from my profession's 'rediscovery' of this disorder. Researchers can learn about a biology of ritual or will or validation of the senses, and possibly about a biological basis for cure. Patients and their families can learn how to help themselves and each other. Through watching our patients grow in conquering their illness, or learning to live with what they couldn't change, my staff and I have learned a great deal about how people can cope when they have some help. They have shared their secrets, and still not all have been cured. As usual, our patients give back as much as they get. I hope that in the near future they will be able to get even more answers from us.

I
THE PATIENTS SPEAK: PARENTS

Everything important I have learned about OCD has come from talking to my amazing group of patients. In order to understand my fascination with this illness, you must meet these people yourself and let them tell you their own stories.

1

The Car Accident That Never Was
(Told by Dr S.)

In this chapter, a father, a psychologist with Obsessive–Compulsive Disorder, and his wife, a social worker, talk about life with this illness and about looking for help for their seven-year-old son, who suffers from the same problem as his father.

I'm driving down a main road doing 55 m.p.h. I'm on my way to take a final exam. My seat belt is buckled and I'm vigilantly following all the rules of the road. No one is on the road – not a living soul.

Out of nowhere an Obsessive–Compulsive Disorder (OCD) attack strikes. It's almost magical the way it distorts my perception of reality. While in reality no one is on the road, I'm intruded with the heinous thought that I *might* have hit someone . . . a human being! God knows where such a fantasy comes from.

I think about this for a second and then say to myself, 'That's ridiculous. I didn't hit anybody.' None the less, a gnawing anxiety is born. An anxiety I will ultimately not be able to put away until an enormous emotional price has been paid.

I try to make reality chase away this fantasy. I reason, 'Well, if I hit someone while driving, I would have *felt* it.' This brief trip into reality helps the pain dissipate . . . but only for a second. Why? Because the gnawing anxiety that I really did commit the illusory accident is growing larger – so is the pain.

The pain is a terrible guilt that I have committed an unthinkable, negligent act. At one level, I know this is ridiculous, but there's a terrible pain in my stomach telling me something quite different.

Again, I try putting to rest this insane thought and that ugly feeling of guilt. 'Come on,' I think to myself, 'this is *really* insane!'

But the awful feeling persists. The anxious pain says to me, '*You really did hit someone.*' The attack is now in full control. Reality no longer has meaning. My sensory system is distorted. I have to get rid of the pain. Checking out this fantasy is the only way I know how.

I start ruminating, 'Maybe I did hit someone and didn't realize it . . . Oh my God! I might have killed somebody! I have to go back and check.' Checking is the only way to calm the anxiety. It brings me closer to truth somehow. I can't live with the thought that I actually may have killed someone – I have to check it out.

Now I'm sweating . . . literally. I pray this outrageous act of negligence never happened. My fantasies run wild. I desperately hope the jury will be merciful. I'm particularly concerned about whether my parents will be understanding. After all, I'm now a criminal. I must control the anxiety by checking it out. Did it really happen? There's always an infinitesimally small kernel of truth (or potential truth) in all my OC fantasies.

I think to myself, 'Rush to check it out. Get rid of the hurt by checking it out. Hurry back to check it out. God, I'll be late for my final exam if I check it out. But I have no choice. Someone could be lying on the road, bloody, close to death.' Fantasy is now my only reality. So is my pain.

I've driven five miles farther down the road since the attack's onset. I turn the car around and head back to the scene of the mythical mishap. I return to the spot on the road where I 'think' it 'might' have occurred. Naturally, nothing is there. No police car and no bloodied body. Relieved, I turn around again to get to my exam on time.

Feeling better, I drive for about twenty seconds and then the lingering thoughts and pain start gnawing away again. Only this time they're even more intense. I think, 'Maybe I should have pulled *off* the road and checked the side brush where the injured body was thrown and now lies? Maybe I didn't go *far enough* back on the road and the accident occurred a mile farther back.'

The pain of my possibly having hurt someone is now so intense that I have no choice – I really see it this way.

I turn the car around a second time and head an extra mile farther down the road to find the corpse. I drive by quickly. Assured that this time I've gone far enough I head back to school to take my exam. But I'm not through yet.

'My God,' my attack relentlessly continues, 'I didn't get *out* of the car to actually *look* on the side of the road!'

So I turn back a third time. I drive to the part of the road where I think the accident happened. I park the car on the verge. I get out and begin rummaging around in the brush. A police car comes up. I feel like I'm going out of my mind.

The policeman, seeing me thrash through the brush, asks, 'What are you doing? Maybe I can help you?'

Well, I'm in a dilemma. I can't say, 'Officer, please don't worry. You see, I've got Obsessive–Compulsive Disorder, along with four million other Americans. I'm simply acting out a compulsion with obsessive qualities.' I can't even say, 'I'm really sick. Please help me.' The disease is so insidious and embarrassing that it cannot be admitted to anyone. Anyway, so few really understand it, including myself.

So I tell the officer I was nervous about my exam and pulled onto the roadside to throw up. The policeman gives me a sincere and knowing smile and wishes me well.

But I start thinking again. 'Maybe an accident did happen and the body has been cleared off the road. The policeman's here to see if I came back to the scene of the crime. God, maybe I really did hit someone . . . why else would a police car be in the area?' Then I realize he would have asked me about it. But would he, if he was trying to catch me?

I'm so caught up in the anxiety and these awful thoughts that I momentarily forget why I am standing on the side of the road. I'm back on the road again. The anxiety is peaking. Maybe the policeman didn't know about the accident? I should go back and conduct my search more *thoroughly*.

I want to go back and check more . . . but I can't. You see, the police car is tailing me. I'm now close to hysteria because I honestly believe someone is lying in the brush bleeding to death. Yes . . . the pain makes me believe this. 'After all,' I reason, 'why would the pain be there in the first place?'

I arrive at school late for the exam. I have trouble taking the exam because I can't stop obsessing on the fantasy. The thoughts of the mystical accident keep intruding. Somehow I get through it.

The moment I get out of the exam I'm back on the road checking again. But now I'm checking two things. First that I didn't kill or maim someone and second, that the policeman doesn't catch me checking. After all, if I should be spotted on the roadside rummaging around the brush a second time, how in the world can I possibly explain such an incriminating and aimless action? I'm totally exhausted, but that awful anxiety keeps me checking, though a part of my psyche keeps telling me that this checking behaviour is ridiculous, that it serves absolutely no purpose. But, with OCD, there is no other way.

Finally, after repeated checks, I'm able to break the ritual. I head home, dead tired. I know that if I can sleep it off, I'll feel better. Sometimes the pain dissipates through an escape into sleep.

I manage to lie down on my bed – hoping for sleep. But the incident has not totally left me – nor has the anxiety. I think, 'If I really did hit someone, there would be a dent in the car's bumper.'

What I now do is no mystery to anyone. I haul myself up from bed and run out to the garage to check the bumpers on the car. First I check the front two bumpers, see no damage, and head back to bed. But . . . *did I check it well enough?*

I get up from bed again and now find myself checking the *whole body* of the car. I know this is absurd, but I can't help myself. Finally . . . finally, I disengage and head off to my room to sleep. Before I nod off, my last thought is, 'I wonder what I'll check next?'

Let me tell you about myself. I'm thirty-six years old and have had obsessions, at least in mild form, since I was six years old. My son Jeffrey has had the illness since at least age two. My two brothers most probably have the disease, though less severely. There is a good chance my nephew, age eight, has OCD as well as my father and his father also. I can write this here, but families with OCD almost never tell each other about it if they can help it. I am the one who broke the silence. My brother has had a remarkable response to imipramine (which occasionally helps OCD). He said, 'I never thought I would live my life without the pain and anxiety of all my "dread" thoughts.' Perhaps my other brother and nephew will consider treatment also.

I cannot really describe the torturous pain of the anxiety brought on by an Obsessive–Compulsive Disorder attack. The checking incident I've just relayed to you used to happen to me often. Between the ages of twenty-two and thirty-three (except for one or two brief remissions) this kind of attack occurred every day. Many times it stayed with me all day long and, if it disappeared, a new attack, spawned from the old one, would quickly replace it. Later other forms of checking began. I have stayed till midnight at my laboratory compelled to check my computer's simplest calculations by hand. The work is unpublished because I can never be certain that the numbers were averaged correctly.

I do not intend to sound dramatic, nor am I soliciting sympathy or pity. It's simply a fact of life that it's the pain – the deep, searing, never-ending pain – that makes this illness so unbearable. I know the pain. So do all the other OCs out there who share this illness with me and my family members.

As a parent you must first understand this insidious disease not in terms of its origins or the bizarre behaviours it creates. Instead you begin to understand Obsessive–Compulsive Disorder in terms of the pain it causes its victims. If you can accept your child's pain, the whole illness becomes easier to live with.

Looking back, it seems that the hurt of an OCD attack was more psychologically painful than the death of my father, whom I loved. This may be hard for a normal person such as yourself to comprehend. None the less, it's sadly true. My sense of loss and grief was trivial and short-lived compared to any of the hundreds of OCD attacks I have had in my life.

While there were indications from early childhood that I had the disease, it didn't clearly manifest itself until I was twenty-two years old. My symptoms were typical of obsessive–compulsives. I would check the gas oven and door locks sometimes twenty times before I could go to bed at night. I would worry about poisoning myself and others with insecticides or cleaning fluids I may have touched. I would drive home from work, thinking that I left the light on in my office and drive all the way back to see if it was off: 'It could start a fire'. Sometimes I did this more than once in a day.

Many of the obsessions and compulsions were based on an extraordinary fear that my aggressive impulses, my anger, would, without me knowing it, leak out. I always thought I would start a fire by being negligent with cigarettes or kill someone by being a reckless driver. My vigilance was ongoing . . . and exhausting.

Each obsessive incident was accompanied by the fantasy that if I *didn't* act on it, something terrible would happen to me or someone else. Losing my job, being sent to prison, or hurting someone else were average catastrophic fantasies. Making *sure* these outcomes would not occur drove my compulsive behaviours.

The energy and time I would exert towards a hundred aimless acts has me shaking my head in disgust right now. I look back and wonder how I lived that way for over ten years. It was unbearable.

I hid my disease. I was like an alcoholic hiding his drink. My greatest fear was to be discovered. At times, my wife hated me for the illness. I hated myself. But I couldn't help it. The disease controls you, not the reverse.

A parent of an obsessive-compulsive child must understand the pain of the anxiety and also its control of one's behaviour. Your child has absolutely *no control* over what he or she is doing . . . NONE. Your child's rituals may be totally aimless. They will make no sense to you. You cannot intellectually understand why your child does what he or she does. Don't try to understand in this way because all it will do is frustrate you; normal human reasoning and logic do not exist with this disease. The only logic is your child's relentless pain, his enormous need to stop this pain and his involuntary behaviour geared to this end.

In 1973, one year after the first onset, I went into therapy. The psychiatrist was very good. Over the next three years I made some excellent progress. I learned ways to cope and adapt. If there was an emotional source to the illness the psychiatrist did as much as could be done to eliminate it.

Shortly thereafter, I went into remission and was okay for about a year or so. Not perfect, but substantially improved. After five years in therapy, it became clear that normal life-stress events seemed to trigger obsessive–compulsive episodes. After the birth of my first child, the disease struck again. This time it was worse than ever before.

I was able to work and actually perform quite well. But I had to exert so much energy managing the disease day to day that I spent much of the time emotionally and physically exhausted. Everything took me twice or three times as long to do. I'd be doing computer programming for my research and spend hours checking, re-checking, re-re-checking, and re-re-re-checking my programs for accuracy. I would consider the task done, but sure enough I was up at 2 a.m. with an attack thinking the program had one or two more errors. I would check them another time . . . each check took hours because I'd check what I'd just checked and then doubt that I'd adequately checked it. So, I had to go back and re-check it again . . . and again, and again. It was ludicrous and purposeless. I knew what I was doing made no sense at all. Yet, I had no choice but to keep checking things. These aimless acts controlled my life.

I went back and forth in therapy.

My wife couldn't stand my illness. She found it repugnant. I'm not sure I blame her, because in its severe forms it is disgusting. I hated myself for being sick, and hated my wife for her intolerance. Yet, inside both hates, I knew I couldn't help myself and she couldn't help her reaction. We coped with it in a few ways. First, she would leave me alone while I had an attack. This minimized her exposure to the illness, and my exposure to the family. Second, my therapist served a crucial function. Instead of talking about the disease with my wife, I could relate to the psychiatrist about it. This took much of the pressure off my wife. Third, I hid much of it from my wife so as not to embarrass and upset her. I learned to be a great actor. I'd be dying on the inside with rapid-fire obsessional thoughts, and be all smiles and congeniality on the outside. This was no solution for me, but I think it helped her a bit.

The first approach was best – being left alone during an attack. If I was with someone, even my wife, only my physical presence was there. My mind was so consumed by the pain and all the obsessional thoughts that I couldn't interact. The consequences were all disastrous, not the least of which was terrible communication. It was best to be left alone.

One of the amazing things about the illness was that it could go on 'hold' if I had to do something professionally or socially important. For example, if I had to teach a class, I would forget about the current obsession during the class. The second it ended, though, I was back into OC thoughts and behaviours. This was fortunate because it allowed me to function at work and with friends . . . but only barely.

In 1983, after ten years in therapy, I was on the whole better, but I was still plagued by the illness. I felt that if there was emotional etiology to Obsessive–Compulsive Disorder, we had done our best to rid me of it. My psychiatrist and I discussed various forms of drug therapy. Valium had been used for years to blunt the pain, but it was only marginally helpful. The drug made me feel tired and gave me headaches. I begged him, literally, to consider other forms of medication. It hurt so badly, and the disease disrupted my life so thoroughly, that I was reaching for any possible solution. I was desperate and exhausted.

He prescribed a drug called imipramine which has been used for many years for depression. I started on very low doses, 25 mg, because I had a history of heart disease. Over a four-month period I moved up to 200 mg.

All of a sudden, in the fifth month on medication, the OC disorder stopped. I still had OC thoughts, but I forgot them almost instantaneously! The horrendous illness fled to the recesses of my mind.

At first I didn't trust it. I thought it might be a placebo effect or that I had gone into remission again (still a possibility). But the effect kept lasting and got even stronger. Before starting the drug I had a manic quality to my behaviour – extreme highs and very low lows (mostly when I had an OCD attack). When I was on a high, I was most vulnerable to an attack. The drug seemed to minimize the variance in these mood states. With the highs gone, so was much of the vulnerability.

Imipramine seemed to stop all the catastrophic thinking. Problems became manageable, not insurmountable. It seemed to put my perceptions back in order. For the first time in over a decade the world, its risks and its potential hurts, were put back into perspective.

Attacks went from every hour of every day to once a week. I stayed this way for about four months. Then they became even less frequent, once a month. Now they occur once every two or three months. I will still get obsessional thoughts, but the pain is no longer attached to them.

How do I feel? Great! I don't mean to sound maudlin, but I have been given a new life. The most important thing was that the pain, that relentless and driving hurt, is gone.

Today, I'm on a maintenance dose of imipramine, 100 mg per day. I never thought my OCD would come to an end. But for the last two years it has. Each day I still pray that the pain will never come back to hurt me. And so far my prayers have been answered.

However, I have a new problem. Unfortunately, as I began to improve, my four-year-old son, Jeffrey, developed his own Obsessive–Compulsive Disorder.

MY SON'S STORY

I went to fathers' night at Jeffrey's pre-school. He was playing with a Fisher-Price toy, a schoolhouse, but his play was strange. He stood before the toy, jumped up and down, and flapped his arms as if excited by it. (We later labelled this behaviour 'flapping'.) His muscles from head to toe contracted and relaxed over and over again. He would grunt and contort his face as if he was exerting great effort. When the jumping stopped, he would put his arms together and wiggle his fingers just above eye level (we later labelled this behaviour 'wormies'.) The finger movement was a form of self-stimulation; the grunting and muscle contraction and relaxation sequence would continue during 'wormies' as well. He did this non-stop for thirty-five minutes. I could not disengage him. No matter what I tried, he simply would not stop.

Occasionally he would bring a person, toy, chair, or desk into the play, but these self-stimulating behaviours and the self-induced muscle contractions continued. When I tried to disengage him I was met with repeated and rigid resistance. He *had to do* this bizarre behaviour. He also had to play with the toy 'his' way. Any change I introduced was vehemently rejected.

That night I spoke with my wife. We had a strong hunch that something wasn't right.

We carefully reviewed his behaviour over the past year. We noted his excitability and extremely low attention span. He could not sit still, nor could he focus on a task. It would literally take him fifteen minutes to put his socks on because he was so distracted by other things. We discussed how he would wiggle his fingers or dangle strings in front of his eyes for long periods of time (labelled 'stringing') while doing muscle contractions and grunting. His resistance to change and new experiences were all too easy to identify. His obsessions with counting, serializing, and the repetition of questions to which he already had heard the answers a hundred times before, were also recalled. At age two he would throw a fit if an object was not in its 'proper' location on his night table and when he got upset, he would cry, 'Mummy, calm me down!'

We couldn't engage him in activity that was right for his age. When we did get him involved in some normal play – say, block building – he would bring 'stringing', 'wormies', and 'flapping', along with the muscle contractions, into the play.

As we began to identify all the puzzle's pieces, we knew we could no longer chalk all this up to developmental lag or immaturity. We desperately wanted to, but we couldn't. Something was fundamentally wrong. And he was getting worse.

Often we look back and ask ourselves, how could we have waited so long to get help? The question is really a variation of another one: 'How could we have been so negligent?' The answers can be found in several places.

Denial is one. What parent wants to face the fact that his or her child is handicapped? Jeffrey was so young – just four years old – that it was easy to rationalize away much of his aberrant behaviour: 'He'll grow out of it.' 'It's only temporary.' 'He's a boy and boys mature slower than girls.'

Moreover, he had so many healthy, positive attributes. His intelligence was apparent. His language skills were consistently improving. His attitude was generally good and he expressed a wide range of feelings – sadness, joy, silliness, boredom, and he loved to laugh. A strong need to please his parents, especially Mummy, was developing. He was insatiably curious about spatial locations: 'Kroger's is next to Wendy's? Right, Mummy?' He was gentle and kind, perhaps to a fault, and affectionate – he would hug and kiss and snuggle with us.

Yet when a child dangles strings in front of his eyes for four hours a day and tells you he can't help himself, or asks, 'Mummy, why do I play with strings?', rationalizations soon wear painfully thin. Our child was very sick. We could no longer pretend, and we also knew that we had to do something about it.

OFF TO THE DOCTORS

Many times in my life I have said to myself, 'If I only knew then what I know now!' I still say it every time I look back at our experience with Jeffrey and diagnostic medicine.

Our first contact was a bright and empathetic psychologist. His orientation was highly cognitive and developmental. This meant that he was less likely to attribute childhood psychological maladies to poor parenting and more likely to attribute them to a lack of organic or biochemical maturity in the brain, informational processing errors of the mind (due to slow growth and development), and so forth.

He was wonderful – both caring and sensitive. He felt that Jeffrey was very bright, his language adequate though not great, perhaps hyperactive and/or prone to Attention-Deficit Disorder, though he didn't fit this diagnostic category exactly. He suggested we take Jeffrey to a speech therapist to work on his low attention span and general distractability. We did this immediately. But the focus of the speech therapist's prescription was to wait. 'Let's keep on evaluating him and give him time to grow. Wait it out a while so we can get a clearer picture.'

The string play and repeated questions continued to grow in duration, complexity and intensity. The string play, now coupled with more grunting and muscle contraction, went on for as much as five hours a day. We told Jeffrey that the string play was undesirable, and that we would like to do other things with him. So what did he do? He began going up to his room. He would slam the door shut and 'string' for hours on end. He needed string play in some way. He couldn't stop it and I think he really wished he could because it made his parents unhappy.

Endless streams of repetitious questioning filled the day. He learned how to count and that became a new obsessional activity: 'Mummy, when I'm five years old, Joanne (his older sister) will be eight.' 'Mummy, when I'm six years old, Joanne will be nine.' This went on and on with everyone he knew. The psychologist was kept updated and told us to be patient. But what the hell was our son doing?

The problem was that Jeffrey, and for that matter, any four-year-old, does not possess the intellectual sophistication to accurately *self-report* what he's feeling and thinking. The guessing game as to what was wrong with our child went on. I began to wonder if Jeffrey would be able to go to school, learn to read, or hold a job when he grew up.

We made videotapes of Jeffrey's stereotypic behaviours

(stringing, flapping, wormies, etc.) This turned out to be a genuine diagnostic asset. Why? Because none of the health professionals we consulted seemed to honestly believe he played with strings all day long. Yes, they intellectually believed us, but they didn't experience the same sense of urgency about the problem. When Jeffrey was put before any health professional he was so interested in what was going on (the new room, office equipment, etc.) that whatever drove him to 'string' and 'flap' seemed to wane. So at these times he looked relatively normal during his countless professional evaluations.

Even when I told them that I too had suffered from obsessions and compulsions, they didn't take it seriously. They saw me as a well-functioning, competent professional like themselves. Also, so many parents say, 'My child is just like me', that I don't think they really listened.

Consistent with this, the child psychiatrist who saw Jeffrey next didn't seem too concerned. After all, here was a bright and inquisitive kid. Yet, when he saw the videotape he knew that something was clearly very wrong. Jeffrey's paediatrician had the same reaction. His watch-and-wait attitude turned into fast action immediately after viewing the videotape.

With the psychologist's and psychiatrist's concurrence, the paediatrician felt a neurological workup was needed. An appointment was made on almost an emergency basis. This meant that the soonest we could get in to see the paediatric neurologist was in four weeks.

When a child you love is sick, waiting is an impossible state of affairs. Time takes on a different dimension. You want answers not tomorrow or the next day, but *immediately*. Being told that your next appointment is in three weeks, that the speech evaluation is in a month, and that 'The child psychiatrist can't see any new patients until after the first of the year', adds unbearably to the parents' sense of helplessness.

Each doctor appointment represented another chance to find 'the answer'. While we were not so naïve as to think there was only 'one answer', we hoped that the *next* doctor would make the key diagnostic breakthrough. The bigger the doctor's name and reputation, the greater the anticipatory high. The more equivocal, uncertain, and confused the health professional was after the assessment, the deeper our depression. We experienced a manic high during our four-week wait to see one of the 'top' child neurologists in the world – yes, the *world*! Our medical friends, all of whom we had called weeks back for references, told us that he had 'written the book'. If anyone had seen a child play with string all day long while grunting and doing self-taught deep muscle relaxation, he had. If anyone had seen a child obsess on questions, he had. *If anyone had 'the answer', he had it.*

While the neurologist might have been a great technician, he lacked certain other crucial medical skills, not the least of which was sensitivity to the feelings of parents. He walked into his consultation room. He chatted with us for a minute or two. He barely engaged Jeffrey. Then he pronounced with the assurance of the Almighty that we had a four-year-old schizophrenic child on our hands. I wanted to know 'Why?' Later I turned into emotional jelly. But with the accusing judge before me, I wanted to know, 'Goddammit, what makes you think this? How do you know?'

In short, he said that my son might well be hallucinating during his string play. When I told him that Jeffrey relayed no fantasies during the string play, he ignored my comment.

I went further and said that during the string play Jeffrey didn't seem to lose touch with his environment. For example, I told the neurologist that Jeffrey would stop the string play momentarily to respond to a statement from his mother: 'Jeffrey, time to get your coat on to go to the doctor's for your booster shot.' That information too was dismissed.

When I told him Jeffrey had a wide range of mood and affect (schizophrenics often have blunted or dulled affect) he nodded and ploughed ahead with his diagnosis.

When I told him, as I had told the paediatrician, that I too had Obsessive–Compulsive Disorder, he smiled and moved on.

When I asked him how many four-year-old schizophrenic children he had seen, he responded that he had seen only one in the last six years of medical practice.

When I told him that I read that it was hard to diagnose schizophrenia at such a young age, he agreed, and went on to tell me with certainty that my son, nevertheless, was schizophrenic.

We learned later that Obsessive-Compulsive Disorder and schizophrenia are often confused.

When I asked him why he ruled out hyperactivity/Attention-Deficit Disorder, he said that Jeffrey didn't fit the pattern, and in particular he couldn't 'string' for hours if he had this disorder.

This just wasn't adding up. None the less, we had to find out for ourselves if Jeffrey really was schizophrenic. So we went to the library, checking out every book on childhood schizophrenia and psychosis. We called the psychologist and psychiatrist and other medical friends familiar with the case and asked them.

Jeffrey didn't seem to fit anything in the literature. But the literature was less than definitive. All the medical people we spoke to seemed to disagree with the paediatric neurologist's assessment. But they also disagreed with each other. Though there was some consensus that schizophrenia was absent, the thought of having a potentially psychotic child never left us.

THE UPS AND DOWNS OF DRUGS

Jeffrey was first put on Dexedrine, a stimulant that has been used to treat hyperactive children since the 1930s. Jeffrey had a terrific first hour of response to this drug. He stopped flapping and stringing for the first time in one and a half years. Then, two hours later, the roof fell in.

Within a few hours, his behaviour reverted back. But it was now profoundly exacerbated. Five hours of string play became all-day string play. The grunting and deep muscle relaxations were equally intensified. It seemed like he was doing this to relieve himself of enormous energy and/or anxiety.

My wife's resolve to help this child seemed to grow proportionately with each increase in the severity of illness. She would interrupt his behaviour for hours at a time – a physically and emotionally draining activity. She thought of every possible alternative to catch the child's interest beyond strings. She explored every medical alternative, working twenty-four hours a day on this problem. She also shut out the rest of her life.

She couldn't help it, but there was nothing else left for the rest of us. The only topic she would converse on was Jeffrey. The standing joke was that my wife was studying for her medical boards in child psychiatry. But, like so many jokes, it was based in a reality of hurt and suffering.

Naturally, the other children suffered. Our seven-year-old daughter Joanne didn't like the different standards of behaviour that emerged in our home. Different demands and expectations were made of her that couldn't be made of Jeffrey. 'That's not fair,' she would complain. She too felt alone. 'Daddy, why do you always play with Jeffrey and not with me?' She was right.

We told Joanne that Jeffrey was ill. She understood, but none the less felt abandoned. She wanted a brother to play with . . . yet Jeffrey couldn't really play. One day she came into our bedroom crying, 'I feel *so bad* for Jeffrey.'

Perhaps she learned best of all of us how to cope with his behaviour. Joanne learned to accept and work around his limitations. She never stopped trying to engage him in any way possible. She developed patience for his rigidity and even cajoled him to try some activities more appropriate for his age.

For me, the most amazing thing was that I never hated Jeffrey for doing this to our family. Not once did I get angry at him. Frustrated by the situation? Yes. Feelings of impotence and loss of control? Yes. But never rage towards my child, never a wish that he would die. None of this. Why? Because being an OC myself, I know all too well what it's like not being able to control your own behaviour. It's almost as devastating as the pain itself. And I knew Jeffrey had absolutely no control over what he was doing.

My illness also helped me tolerate my wife's emotional 'absence'. She too had no control over her obsessive rescue mission.

A new specialist from our local university hospital and his associates brought us crucial organization and planning. We were given a lengthy, detailed evaluation. All hypotheses were considered. They spent a great deal of time with Jeffrey. And a child psychiatry resident was available to meet with my wife and me on a weekly basis to monitor what was going on.

Equally critical was the shift of responsibility for case management from my wife as quarterback/patient-advocate to the psychiatry resident. This too was crucial. Quality medical care demands a balance between objectivity and emotion. My wife and I were too close, too involved, and too frantic to add much thoughtfulness and objectivity at this stage. The responsibility the medical resident took was both appropriate and badly needed, for everyone concerned.

The medical resident's role deserves more attention because it serves as a model for physicians trying to work with parents of handicapped children. His patience and caring for our family was remarkable. Sometimes my wife would call him with a different question five days in a row and he was there to answer each one, no matter how ridiculous it was. He would go to the library and find articles for us to read. He always had Jeffrey's best interests at heart even when it meant he had to firmly disagree with things we wanted to do. And he always treated us with dignity and respect.

The university team felt that hyperactivity was the primary diagnosis. But that in addition, a diagnosis of Obsessive–Compulsive Disorder might be also the case. They came to this conclusion after seeing Jeffrey and *before* they knew about my obsessive–compulsive history. They just felt that there was something ritualistic about the string play and they were interested in the obsessive patterns in Jeffrey's questioning. They were also willing to say, 'I'm not confident of any of these hypotheses yet.'

Their honesty, even if it didn't give us the 'answer', was better than the neurologist's dogma.

The team became especially interested in my history of obsessions and compulsions and in particular my recovery and maintenance on imipramine. However, they decided to exhaust the most fully researched and safest medication first.

The university hospital tried another stimulant – Valital (pemoline). Jeffrey's behaviour and attitude worsened. He got more anxious. An MRI (Magnetic Resonance Image, a new form of brain exam) was normal. Hearing and vision tests also came back normal.

Still, Jeffrey wouldn't stop stringing. He couldn't. He posed his question, 'Mummy, why do I play with strings?' again, and he asked us, 'Did you play with strings when you were little?' He asked his baby-sitter the same question.

The medical resident finally prescribed imipramine for Jeffrey, a drug I had been using successfully for three years.

On a Friday night exactly six months into our odyssey we gave Jeffrey his first 10 mg pill of imipramine. He became quite tired and went to sleep.

The next morning he woke up and came downstairs for breakfast. *There was no string play!* For the first time in one and a half years (save the one-hour respite from the first Dexedrine pill) Jeffrey was not doing stringing, wormies, or flapping.

The drug worked for only a few hours at a time, so we administered it every two or three hours. More amazing was how his symptoms returned, though much less intensely, about twenty minutes before the drug had fully worn off. And, twenty minutes into the next administration of imipramine, the weakened rituals stopped. Jeffrey would occasionally try to conduct his stereotypic behaviours, but he seemed less interested in them. His hyperactivity and poor attention span improved; he actually sat still for periods of time. This was a miracle in our lives.

We and the psychiatric resident began to wonder if Jeffrey had had obsessions and compulsions from birth, in addition to some degree of hyperactivity.

Adult obsessives carry out their ritualized and aimless behaviours to calm their piercing anxiety. While there may be a slim justification for each obsession, OCs in their more rational moments know that what they're doing is totally senseless. What drives me and other obsessives to do this is the pain – the ceaseless anxiety that if we don't do it some unimaginably horrible event will occur.

Might not ritualized play with a string be a four-year-old's version of a checking compulsion, hand washing, or symmetry? One form of obsession is an unreasoning preoccupation with getting things exactly even. Jeffrey could be just 'evening up' the string. Could the muscle relaxation be his way of handling anxiety? It seems much like the rituals I practised on the way to an exam. Couldn't serialized thinking, and obsessions with number sequences and relationships, be identical to an adult OC trying to create an orderly and predictable environment?

It has taken years, but I have found a number of ways to help myself and my family deal with OCD. These involve an active, almost scientific approach. Most of all they add up to confronting this sickness and putting an end to the silence.

Reading is one of the most effective ways to cope with the devastation of this illness. Anyone who is the parent of an OC child will have most of their questions answered through what is available in the literature. While there isn't a lot, there is some.

Reading buys you even more. You learn that you're not alone. You learn a vocabulary that helps you put this disease into a meaningful framework. It helps you understand. You realize that medical researchers know about this nightmare and are trying to do something about it. The availability of medications, prescription drugs that have been researched and can help some victims are vividly described. And so is the bad news. Not everyone is helped by the drugs. The disease can be so debilitating that it may require hospitalization.

One great piece of news is already in the literature. *It May Not Be Your Fault That You Or Your Child Has Obsessive–Compulsive Disorder!* Early toilet training, a rigorously disciplined home environment, an unresolved oedipal complex, and endless demands that your child clean up her 'disgusting' room may not be and is probably not the cause of this illness.

Obsessive–Compulsive Disorder, flu, and diabetes may have at least one thing in common – the cause. The disease is possibly biological; it may even be inherited from one generation to another, as suggested in my family's case. However, OCD manifests itself as strange behaviour while the other two show up as physical illness. To my wife and me this understanding that there might be a physical cause was a great relief. It brought OCD into the realm of the rational. The problem now was getting Jeffrey's teacher to understand this.

How do you tell people that your family has been struck by a serious illness? How do you explain to people that the cause of this psychological malady may well be physical?

We began with Jeffrey's pre-school teacher. She is an exceptional individual, but has her particular way of viewing the world. She has been trained to explain the majority of developmental problems in children in emotional terms – poor nurturing, sibling rivalry, and an emotionally impoverished home environment. In many instances this is valid. Yet, it made it difficult for her to accept that Jeffrey might have a physiological handicap. She also had difficulty in accepting that a four-year-old child was being so heavily medicated. In fact, she didn't accept any of this, and viewed the problem as 'emotional'.

She was correct in that serious emotional problems will result from these compulsions. But just as important is where they begin and what will bring help. By holding on to her emotional hypothesis, she made my wife feel awful, as the sole cause of Jeffrey's maladies. Having a handicapped child is difficult enough. Having someone sit in judgement of your parenting practices – when you know in your heart you have loved your child as much as possible – is unbearable.

It wasn't until the pre-school teacher learned that I have the disease that she began to re-examine her thinking. And what the pre-school teacher believed was not unique. The same pattern of events occurred with many members of our families.

We learned that the best way to tell others was to present *all* the facts. It's not entirely their fault that they don't understand the illness. It is poorly publicized and, like many emotional illnesses, denied, ignored, or hidden in a cupboard. No one really wants to be so totally candid. It means we have to reveal very personal things about ourselves which normally we wouldn't do. All of this is very difficult . . . but we have no real choice if we love our children enough to help them manage their disease, and to help friends and family understand and accept our children.

Today, Jeffrey is being maintained on imipramine. The similar experimental drug, clomipramine, is being held in reserve. L-tryptophan, an amino acid that is available in health food stores and may increase brain serotonin, seems to help him also.

Since he was put on these two drugs, most of Jeffrey's symptoms have disappeared. His language development has blossomed. He is playing with his sister and little brother. He still has a long way to go, but he doesn't have to play with strings any more.

We have also learned to manage Jeffrey better. We prepare him more carefully for changes. We give in to him on small issues, especially when the disease seems to be forcing him to behave in a troubled way. We work as much as possible with his strengths. His intelligence is a great asset and we do whatever we can to facilitate its development. He likes maps currently, and so we have put maps all over his room.

But a lingering uncertainty remains. Jeffrey has good days and bad days. I wish I could turn the clock ahead fifteen years and see how this will end. My wife is more accepting. We're all the better for this. She has come to realize that unless she keeps herself emotionally intact there is no way she can help Jeffrey or the rest of us. I take over Jeffrey's care on his bad days. Because I have the illness, it's easier for me to tolerate his compulsive symptoms. She'll never understand fully because she has never had the pain.

Dr S., his wife, and Jeffrey were pioneers during the time when awareness of OCD in America was (and still is) changing. Today they would not have had such a long wait before they were taken seriously. At a university centre today, the 'positive' family history of obsessions and compulsions would be given great weight. But at the time that Dr S. was seeing one expert consultant after another, he was talking to people who probably had never met a case of OCD. Or if they did, they probably missed it.

There are a number of good reasons for my profession's ineptitude in helping Jeffrey's family. If patients with OCD don't come for treatment, you don't learn about them in medical school or residency. But perhaps more important, until recently, the physician did not have terribly much to offer. With the discovery that drug treatment and behaviour modification therapy can really help, I am impressed at how eagerly my colleagues are now asking for information and just as eagerly applying it. Something just like that happened thirty years ago when lithium treatment was found to be effective for manic depressive illness. All of a sudden, there was new optimism that bred new interest. The rate of accurate diagnosis of manic depressive illness soared. Today, that is happening with OCD.

There are some unusual aspects to Dr S.'s story. At many centres, Dr S. and his wife would have been counselled by a behaviour therapist earlier in Jeffrey's evaluation. Probably there was no such person on the staff of the particular clinics they went to. Even more unusual was how helpful imipramine has been for Dr S. and Jeffrey. Imipramine was certainly reasonable to try – and until clomipramine becomes generally available it still is a reasonable first choice. But most obsessive–compulsive patients that I see have tried it and it didn't help suppress or eliminate the obsessions. That's why they come for clomipramine. Clomipramine was tried by this family. Imipramine worked as well or better. I have no idea why.

Probably Jeffrey had two disorders, Attention-Deficit Disorder (popularly called Hyperactivity) as well as OCD. That may have confused the diagnosing physicians. However, the tendency of many members of the medical profession to make pronouncements instead of saying 'We don't know' remains an embarrassment.

The problem 'getting through' to Jeffrey's teacher is particularly sad because it reflects a tradition – fortunately one that is fading fast – that 'good' caretakers pay attention to psychological causes while 'bad' caretakers lean towards genetic or biological explanations. The teacher's reluctance to hear Dr and Mrs S. stems, I would guess, from this unhappy split.

The S. family was lucky. This couple felt more comfortable arguing with professionals than most people. They had graduate degrees and were very smart. They were also right. My advice to other families is to be like Dr and Mrs S. If the first approach or medicine doesn't help, keep arguing – and above all keep trying.

2

Rituals and Contaminations: Zach and His Family

I met Zach, age nine, and his family years after we realized how often fathers and sons shared the obsessive–compulsive problem. (We have also seen other family combinations of OCD in mothers and sons, in fathers and daughters, and in brothers when both parents are well. But father-son combinations have been the most common.)

Zach's first day on our ward was dramatic. His father told Zach for the first time that he too had started to have compulsive rituals when he was seven and had battled with them all his life. This gave Zach his first real ally against his rituals. I asked Zach and his family to write their own stories a few months later.

ZACH'S STORY
(Dictated by Zach)

I am now nine years old. When I was six years old I started picking up things with my elbows because I thought I would get my hands dirty if I picked things up with my hands. By the time I was seven I was washing my hands thirty-five times a day. For the next two years, my fear of getting my hands dirty grew worse. Until I started on medicine my life was wrecked, unpleasant, and crippled by my compulsions.

When I was six I started doing all these strange things when I swallowed saliva. When I swallowed saliva I had to crouch down and touch the ground. I didn't want to lose any saliva – for a bit I had to sweep the ground with my hand – and later I had to blink my eyes if I swallowed. I was frustrated because I couldn't stop the compulsions. Each time I swallowed I had to do something. For a while I had to touch my shoulders to my chin. I don't know why. I had no reason. I was afraid. It was just so unpleasant if I didn't. If I tried not to do these things, all I got was failure. I had to do it, and no matter how hard I tried, I just *still* had to.

I tried to tell my ma. I told her I had to do it. She says, 'You're doing some strange things, why do you do it?' I said, ' 'Cause I don't want to lose any saliva,' and she says, 'Maybe you'll want to talk about it later.' I don't want to lose any saliva and there's no good reason. I just don't want to. I was afraid to tell anybody. People would think I was crazy or something. I didn't want to tell Dr Kaufman. I was nervous when I first came to him and then I just didn't want to talk about it. It just bothered me to talk about it. I felt ashamed. I didn't want anyone to know. I wanted it to be just for me to know, no one else.

It wrecked my life. It took away all my time. I couldn't do anything. If you put it all together I did it maybe an hour and a half or sometimes three hours a day.

I had bathroom problems too. I had to take some toilet paper and rip them up a lot of times into teeny pieces that had to be just the right size – only about a millimetre. They had to be torn perfect and then I'd flush them away.

I had to do all kinds of things with my fingers and my mouth. I had to touch all my fingers to my lips a few times if I swallowed saliva. Swallowing was one of the first things. But elbows were really first. I was afraid of getting my hands dirty. My mind said 'Wash them, they're dirty.' They *felt* dirt. After I went to the bathroom I had to wash my hands, only mine always felt dirty.

I would forget one thing after another. After I changed one pattern I would completely forget it. I remember one part of one pattern: I had to touch the ends of my thumbs to where the water came out of the faucet. Some other things I don't remember. I couldn't turn the water off with my hands. I was late for school a lot.

The medicine worked. I didn't have to do all these things. First one went away and then the next and then the next. My mom says I seem happier. I have a lot more time to do things. I'm always going to hate my sister but not as much. I don't hate her as much now. Maybe that's from the medicine.

From the beginning, I knew something was very wrong. I kind of thought, 'It's going to go away tomorrow. It's going to go away the next day or the next day or sometime.' But it never went away and I kind of gave up hope and I kept on doing them. I didn't really have an explanation. I imagined that God picked me because He gave me some gifts so He had to give me some problems too and He gave me that. I'm in gifted classes and I'm a good athlete and I'm fast and strong and I'm perfect. Well, almost perfect, as close as you can get. And I have a bowel movement problem and seven operations and my beauty marks. [*Editor's Note: Zach had operations for congenital intestinal problems unrelated to his OCD and has patches of skin pigmentation.*] Everyone has a few beauty marks, but I just have more than most people. I know a kid who had twenty operations. My mom says he's perfect now. Everyone has some problem, whether it's a stammer or they can't walk. I have a lot of things that are very good. I've had a more exciting nine years than most people. I wouldn't mind not having all the beauty marks and the bowel movement problem but I like myself the way I am. I wouldn't want to be anybody else.

CONFESSIONS OF OBSESSIONS
(Written by Zach's Father)

My name is Sam. I am a very successful professional in a very large city, involved with matters of substantial importance and large sums of money, working in a very competitive field. I have a beautiful, loving, understanding wife and three terrific, bright children. Times are good.

I am thirty-eight years old. I take 300 mg a day of clomipramine. It helps. It takes the edge of terror off the impulses. It helps me fight. So does my anger. I suffer. Sometimes my anger at my rituals is intense. Then, I remember that some people are blind, some are deaf, some are paralysed. I resist feeling sorry for myself. I fight. And I try to understand. I am a survivor. If you don't believe so, count the references to death in this account I'm giving you. In spite of my fears and anxiety, I wrote this. I will not let them control. I will fight. I am a survivor and proud of it.

My secretary doesn't know it and the other senior partners don't know it, but my days are not like the days of the others in my office who also handle multimillion-dollar transactions. They are just doing their job. I have two jobs: my profession and battling with obsessions. Come enter my thoughts as I prepare to enter that battle.

If you want to know what it's like, just try not to think about pink elephants for a while. Try to think about something else, anything else, something that will assuage the uneasiness, perhaps block out completely all thoughts of pink elephants.

Segregate your thoughts of pink elephants in a tiny corner of your mind. Surround them with other thoughts. Concentrate – *hard*.

Now, at the same time, do something else. Read a book. Drive a car. Ride a bicycle. Concentrate on both things at the same time. Oh, and if a random, uneasy thought of a pink elephant – or of death, perhaps, though one never knows for certain what the thought will be – should come barrelling into your consciousness, ward it off, blot it out. Hold up a cross to the Dracula – Ritualize.

Quick, think of something pleasant. Think of good times. Repeat in your mind those mantras you say to yourself over and over: Life. Life is good. Concentrate. Wait! Don't stop pedalling your bike. You'll fall. Life is good. Say it over and over. Say it in your mind until you get it absolutely right. Life. Life is good. Look where you're going. You're coming to an intersection. Life. Life is good. I am alive. Faster. The light is red and you haven't got it quite right yet. Life. Life is good. Life, life is good! The intersection.

Red light, almost. Life, life is good. Say it over and over again. Got it! Stop! Made it! I'm okay, for now, for a few seconds until it starts again. See what I mean? And it gets worse.

I once saw a juggler who got a dozen or so plates spinning on the end of narrow sticks. He started with one and then he added more and more, always being careful that none of the plates stopped spinning and fell, racing from one to the other to re-spin them, all the time trying to start more and more plates spinning. He must have gotten tired doing that. Fighting my obsessions tires me like that.

I am very careful as I read a book or newspaper or magazine. I never know what terrible things lie on the next page or the next paragraph or the next sentence. I read slowly. I concentrate on the mantra.

Damn! 'Death'. There's that awful word. All right, start to offset it. Be careful. Better to go backwards over what you've already read. Try to remember where the words are. You can't go forward anyway, because forwards is the future and you don't want to contaminate the future with eyes that have just beheld a word of such terrible consequence. Go back over what you've just read. Go to the past. You can't really harm the past (you don't really believe that) – use it to your advantage. Would anyone in my office believe this if they saw it? Of course not.

I saw the word 'death'? Yes. All right, careful. 'Life' must be here somewhere. Go back more pages. Where did I see it? 'Life', where are you? There's 'living'. No, that won't do. It would work for 'dying', but not 'death'. 'Death' is the most terrible word. It can only be appeased with 'life'. And if 'death' was capitalized, try to find 'life' capitalized also, or find two or three 'lifes' to even things out.

Careful.

No-ooo. Damn! 'Died'. Now I've got to find 'living' or 'alive' or 'lives' or some such word to offset 'died' before I can go back to the first problem. What about 'lived'? It's not much better than 'died'. Implicit in 'lived' is that what was alive is now dead. No, it must be one of the others.

Shit! 'Deceased'. Now I've got to offset that before I can offset 'died' and then offset 'died' before I can offset 'death'.

I want to scream out in anger and frustration. This is silly. This is stupid. Why am I doing this? Why am I doing this? Stay calm. Work through it. Carefully. Slowly. There, 'alive'. And there, 'lives'. All right one left to go.

Shit. 'Corpse'. I can't go on like this. Why am I doing this? Wait. 'Life'. Okay. I'll use that for 'corpse'. Now, just one more 'life'. Just to be sure.

No! I can't believe he asked me for a sheet of paper, interrupted me, just when I was coming to the end of the search. When I only had one to go. Now I've got to start over. Be calm. He doesn't know what you're doing. Hide it. Don't let on. Why can't I be normal? All these other people don't have to do these things. I'm tired. I can't keep this up. What was the order in which I saw the words? Maybe I just won't do it. But I *have* to do it. Try not to look up with my contaminated eyes until I'm finished with the good words. What time is it?

Damn! Now I've looked at the clock – time, the future – I've contaminated it. Now I've got to offset that against something else. But what? The past. That's it. Find a calendar or a book. Here, this old textbook. At the front, there should be a copyright date. Yes, a year long before I was born, so I can use it to free myself of the contamination I created by looking at the clock without affecting myself. I stare at the year, and get ready to zap it with my eyes. Wait. What do the numbers in the year added up to? Nineteen. No, I can't believe it. Nineteen was the age of my ex-secretary's son when he was killed in the car accident that night she called me at 2 a.m., hysterically crying. Block it out. Think mantras. No, find another year, one that adds up to eighteen, to *chai*, to 'life' in Hebrew. Yes, here's another book, another year – eighteen. Relief. Now, don't look at the clock. Don't look at –

I think you have the idea by now.

'Just stop,' my mother would say, in a cajoling fashion. 'People are looking at you. They're wondering why you're doing those things.' What things? I'm not doing anything. Just leave me alone, I'd answer. But I knew they were watching me, talking about me, belittling me. And I felt like a jerk. I know I looked strange. I'm weak and it sickens my stomach. I can't stop. There's a feeling of constant uneasiness.

Maybe I'm crazy. Unlikely. I'm too logical. Twisted as all this is, it's so logical, like religion.

I get no comfort from religion. My God is stern and demanding, as unforgiving to me as I am of myself. My gods are hard, insisting on perfect penance constantly. Shape up boy!

I have no tolerance of religion. I have my own magic. It's strong. It's demanding. It's up to me to do what must be done, to faithfully ritualize. I must protect those I care about. I must ward off the incessant evil contamination that is everywhere.

It's so primitive – religion, so childish. It's what I do on a mass scale. Offer sacrifices. Zap people and then write them off. That girl in graduate school never did understand why I never asked her out. I had even asked my friend to test the waters, to see if she was interested, and she had been. He told her I wanted to ask her out, to expect it, and I had wanted to, had looked forward to it. Ah, the anticipation of something pleasant. It's dangerous. I'm walking on eggs. I barely got by with the other rituals. Don't tempt fate. She is pleasure.

An attractive girl. Just the thought makes me ritualize – just a small one, just to get rid of the feeling for a few moments so I can fantasize. A little zap, maybe. A small denial.

Okay, I won't listen to the radio today. Not quite right. Okay, I won't listen to the radio today *or* tomorrow. Still not enough. Increase the power. I won't listen through a week from today. Not enough. Okay, for a month from today. How am I going to remember that? I'll forget. I'll absent-mindedly turn it on before the month is up. Then, I'll really have problems. I will undoubtedly go somewhere that a radio is on. Won't that blow the ritual? No, it must be an affirmative action on my part. There must be intent. If I just walked into a store where a radio was playing, that would be passive, not active. Still, a month to remember the ritual.

Most of the time, no one is watching and no one knows what I'm going through. No one *can* know. The rest of them are normal. I usually feel that I'm the only one cursed like this. But I can do something. I have the power to ritualize, to make a difference, if I just appease the feelings.

I'll decide to deny myself bicycle riding. No, I realize, it is winter. That won't do. One really can't use one's bike in the winter.

Television. I decide not to watch television today. No, that only works at night, when I'm at home and all the blinds are closed so

I could not possibly accidentally see a television on through a neighbour's window, and I'm about ready to go bed, and the television's off and I can be sure it won't get turned back on. When the clock will hit midnight, the day will be over, and the ritual will have been successful. For a few moments, before it starts again, I'll have relief.

Too much risk in accidentally seeing a television on at some time during the rest of the day.

Elevator. I won't use the elevator. That makes things easier. It sort of brings pleasure. I'll deny myself elevators. I'll walk up and down the seven flights to my apartment. But there must be something easier. What about escalators? Fuzzy area. Too close to elevators to use freely. Not far enough away to be decreed a separate denial category. Must be included with elevators, same function. A policy decision.

You see, even when I had one that would work, I ruin it. I took away the efficacy of denying myself the use of elevators. I have marred the ritual with doubts. It doesn't 'feel' right any more. And all because I'm lazy. Shit!

Okay, I won't use the car. But I need to go to the store later.

I'm running out of things to deny myself. Maybe I'll use elevator denial after all. No, too late. Once you take a pass on a denial, it's not available again until the next ritual. Panic. I'm running out of things. Easy. Concentrate. There must be something else. Board games, maybe. Hold that one. Music boxes. Close to phonographs and tape recorders but different enough to work. Hold that, too.

How did I get started on this in the first place? I didn't see a trigger word like 'death' or hear such a word, for that matter. Doing so, of course, would have required that I see someone, preferably the person who uttered the first word, to cleanse the act by saying the word 'life'. All I did was have that feeling, that uneasiness, that almost physical need to assuage, to keep things under control.

What else is there? Think! The zoo! But could I really get there today? Is it still open? It would be difficult, but yes I could. Okay, use that for now, but to be sure, late tonight, when it's almost midnight, use reading-denial. I close my eyes so I can't possibly read, and then deny myself reading for the rest of the day. I don't open them until I think it's at least fifteen minutes past midnight. I can't be sure our clocks aren't a few minutes fast.

The rituals are so unforgiving. I've got to work so hard and they won't give me a break. If there is more than one way to view something, the rituals insist that I take the hardest. The gods – the rituals – demand strict obedience. If I don't quite get it, I must do it over.

Even good feelings cause problems. They disturb the carefully balanced status quo. I begin 'looking around' inside to see whether I'm at liberty to indulge. Perhaps I should appease the gods first. After all, I can't be sure that all my ritualistic penance has been accepted. I should perform a few precautionary, anticipatory rituals, to prepare the way.

Neutral. Unfeeling. Calloused. Cold. Hard. Impervious. It's the only way to maintain my equilibrium. I try to feel nothing. Not too good. Not too bad. Control. If I have control, I won't have to ritualize as much. Strive for numbness.

I suffer from Obsessive–Compulsive Disorder. I cannot remember ever not being an obsessive–compulsive. I cannot imagine life free of obsessive–compulsive behaviour. It is as much a part of me as my blue eyes. It is as if I had been born with a birth defect, like the baby that cannot hear that knows no life of sound.

It is with me every waking and every sleeping moment. I ritualize in my dreams. It is my master. There is no escape. I am the legislative, judicial, and executive branches. I 'make' the rules, interpret them and enforce them – strictly, brutally, incessantly, without remorse.

My first memories of obsessive–compulsive behaviour centre on the age of seven. I was playing with a group of children in front of my house. We were playing a variation of a game of 'It'. We called it 'Cooties'. One person 'had the cooties' and all of the others tried to avoid being tagged and 'getting the cooties', being contaminated. I remember the feeling. It was more than just a game. It was a matter of desperation for me. I just could not allow myself to be tagged, to have all the contamination flow into me. I ran very fast to escape.

My family called them 'superstitions'. I don't know if I coined the word or if my mother did. 'Just stop,' she would say. And I would want to stop. And I would hear the wistfulness in her voice as she ordered/begged me to stop. 'Just stop . . .'

Drug abuse starts out as a choice. It may be no easier to stop than obsessive–compulsive behaviour but at least the drug abuser has exercised free will. I did not. I did things because I 'had to'. I did not understand. I still don't. And now it is thirty-one years later.

I remember thinking, at the age of seven, that by the time I became fifteen years old, an incredibly long time in the future, I would stop these things. I would have outgrown them.

I remember my mother telling me about her oldest brother who did similar things, who just finally 'outgrew them'. I don't know how she knew he outgrew them. She probably thinks I outgrew them, too. I thought about her brother from time to time. I thought more about it when, to my dismay, my son began exhibiting obsessive–compulsive behaviours. I recognized it. I understood it. And I, of all people, was as frustrated and angered by his behaviour as my father probably had been over mine. I just wanted him to stop.

There has always been a compelling logic to the rituals. I was always trying to assure or avoid some outcome by my ritualizing. The professed focus would change. But the behaviour persisted: Protect myself from contamination. Protect my grades, my sports prowess, my masculinity, my life, my success, people I cared about.

With a change in my focal point would come changes in the stimuli of the rituals. There was a point, for example, when my need was to protect myself from stupid people. I could not even look at certain people – those who had already failed a grade or were doing poorly. I would prop a book up on my desk at school and put my head down on my arm behind the book so I would not even accidentally catch a glimpse of an untouchable. For every glimpse was a new stimulus, a new invitation for a command performance of rituals. If I finished one ritual and saw an untouchable, I would be required to start again. Over and over and over. It was so tiring.

An eight-year-old cousin of mine died when I was seven years old. It was sudden. It was frightening. The details were always shrouded in mystery. To this day, I don't know them. I never really wanted to know too much. It was traumatic.

It was also, as I think about it, concurrent with my first memories of ritualizing. I don't know whether there was a sort of symbiosis between the rituals and my cousin's death, but it would not surprise me. I dreaded going to my cousin's house – the empty bedroom, the sadness, the unspoken words. The house seemed antique, shrouded. I did not want to touch anything there. I just wanted to get away. Being there upset me. Thinking about it upset me.

My cousin's very name became an anathema. A classmate of mine with the same name became, *per se*, odious. I could not look at her, touch her, think about her without associating it with my cousin.

As a young graduate student, an older married woman, the wife of the head of a small company where I worked part time, made a pass at me. I was on the rebound at the time, vulnerable. I probably would not have done anything even if her name had been different from my cousin's. That her name was the same, sealed the decision. Better to avoid a moment's pleasure for the terror I would have felt thereafter. Ritualistically, it would have been the union of sex and death. Forever. Avoid it. Better to deny myself than to suffer such egregious consequences.

I was never exactly sure what the consequences would be – death, eternal damnation, stupidity, failure, errors, contamination. I was not about to tempt the fates to find out.

One distressing aspect of my situation as the great ritualist was my certainty that I was the only person on earth who suffered, had ever suffered, would ever suffer as I did. I could not talk to anyone about my rituals or my fears. I was scared and mortified. That I could not stop ritualizing only served to make me feel more helpless, more ridiculous, more detestable.

I remember once seeing a very good friend of mine doing some things that to my ritually attuned mind seemed oddly akin to my rituals. Could it be? A comrade in arms? I could not ask him. I would have died before I would divulge my secret. To this day, I still wonder.

I do not think it would have made much difference to me anyhow, though I will admit that my recently acquired knowledge that perhaps 2 per cent of the population suffers from Obsessive–Compulsive Disorder had a liberating effect on me.

Suddenly I was not the only crazy person around. On the other hand, that knowledge struck me rather like the news that my ex-fiancée and my best old ex-friend had called off their engagement. There was vindication but no joy.

What are they, these rituals? Sometimes I fantasize that they're like a virus, a foreign invader that simply needs to be expunged. Occasionally, more bemusedly than sadly, I would imagine myself being the controlled pawn of observers from outer space. How else could one explain the inability to fight the compulsions that I knew were so senseless?

What are these rituals? My chemistry, I think. Why such chemistry? Genetics, I think. Did the ritualizing cause the self-hate? Or did the self-hate cause the rituals? Why do I do so much cognitive ritualization while others wash their hands? What can washing one's hands do? If I see the word 'death' it makes eminent sense to me to negate it by countering it with a glance at the word 'life'. Do others try to wash away self-hate?

I have a theory in the embryonic stage. My theory makes serious presumptions, based on the earliest of memories. I cannot remember very many events, only shards here and there, impressions which make a bell in my mind ring occasionally.

My theory is that, as a child, I could find little solace or comfort in my fears. I strongly resist foisting blame upon my parents. My first years are but a black box. It violates my sense of justice and responsibility to lay my troubles on others' doorsteps, like an abandoned child. That is a cop-out. I will take responsibility.

Perhaps someone at home was too stern. Perhaps my parents had such pervasive fears of their own that they were incapable of, and uninterested in, dealing with the fears of a little boy. Maybe I was met with stern looks, or with blame for the world's ills. Maybe I had a sense I was being manipulated. Maybe I decided I could find no comfort from others. Maybe I was chemically genetically incapable of being comforted. Maybe I became very afraid.

But how can a little boy cope with his fears by himself? How indeed? Maybe I tried to impose an order on things. Maybe I convinced myself, in desperation, that there is an order of things, because I was my own last resort. But that's ridiculous. There is no order of things. Ah, but there must be an order. It makes sense.

It is logical. It is beautiful in its logic. It's simply a matter of uncovering the order; working it out one must simply learn the rules. It's a great leap of faith, but then I was a very scared little boy.

The rules. What are they? Simple. Counter bad with good. Offset. No one will help you. You must do it yourself. Others may not even be aware that the danger exists. Do good.

And the good must be good enough to offset the bad because I am on my own against terrible forces. My efforts must be powerful enough to triumph. I must border on omnipotence.

Genetics. Predisposition. Activate the right buttons. Anxiety. Order. Ritualize. Twitch, twitch. The rituals must be comprehensive. They must be strong. To be strong means they tend to be complicated, tedious, taxing. The more serious the danger, the greater the required salutary effects. No one said this was going to be easy. Be strong. Fight. It is a huge responsibility you've got. Such power! Brook no weakness. If you're weak, the forces of evil will triumph. Resist. Fight. Survive.

Power. My magic is powerful. It *must* be powerful. Look at what it's up against. I must be careful. Always so.

Sam is one of several extremely successful men I have met with Obsessive–Compulsive Disorder. I have seen bank presidents, a congressman, judges, and corporate lawyers (along with plenty of ordinary folks) with crippling forms of this illness. Amazingly, there seems to be a kind of double-entry book-keeping that permits efficient, even brilliant, performance virtually at the same time. Except when the illness is so severe that the rest of life comes to a halt.

Sam has a particular form of OCD that involves endless ruminations, but which can be remarkably hidden. We have seen a number of men and women in high-powered jobs whose mental lives are agony, but who function superbly. Some have told me that the very act of keeping intensely busy dispels the nightmare treadmill of thoughts.

Sam has had many years of psychoanalysis, during which time he and his doctor worked hard together to reconstruct the psychological factors in his illness. While I think Sam's relationship with his therapist was very supportive, I believe that Sam's formulations about his childhood came as a desperate way to make sense out of his senseless rituals, not the other way round. Sam too is not sure. Psychoanalysis helped Sam's depression a great deal. It did not affect his obsessions or his rituals. What is clear is that clomipramine finally helped the obsessions. After Zach responded to the drug, Sam tried it too. The results were slow and not without problems. At first all he experienced was the unpleasant side effects of the medication, but he persevered, and slowly over the months that followed the thoughts faded. Not completely, but they are better than they have been in years.

Obsessive–Compulsive Disorder is more compatible with professional success than with personal happiness. Wives and husbands are alienated. Over the years, what first seemed like admirable reserve and self-control wears into suspicion and guardedness. The husband or wife of someone with OCD feels isolated and rejected. That is clear from what Sam's wife wrote me.

LIVING WITH THE SECRET OF
OBSESSIVE–COMPULSIVE DISORDER
(Written by Sam's wife)

From our first meeting, Sam seemed very intense, terribly afraid to 'let go' and strangely secretive. I often thought, however, that I was imagining peculiarities that weren't really there, that I was trying to put together pieces of a puzzle when, in fact, there was really no picture to assemble. But there was an indefinable 'something', and as time passed I knew it was true, illusive but truly there. It *was* like a puzzle.

It was usually easy to find reasons, or at least excuses for Sam's behaviour. I believed he was very nervous. Twitches would come and go. But there's nothing criminal about a twitch. Sam never acknowledged their existence; I assumed he was embarrassed and chose not to say anything. But there were other strange eccentricities. Sam would page through a book or magazine as if looking for a certain word. He would look with an obsessive intensity. If I asked him what he was doing, or even spoke, my inquiry would be met with silence. But I also detected a controlled rage. Why?

I often noticed that Sam would write something down on a piece of paper and then throw the paper away. I thought he believed I didn't see him doing it. This was always a very determined act. If I pointedly asked, he would ignore me or try to make a joke of it.

My curiosity became overwhelming. I thought the words he had written held the answer to his strange behaviour. Twice I went into the garbage and collected all the paper scraps. I put them together like a jigsaw puzzle. What I found only mystified me more. The first phrase was 'past, past, past'. The second said, 'Zeus is worthless'. I never told Sam what I had done. Nor did I ask what it might mean. I was sure he would respond with anger.

The strange behaviours would come and go. But if one disappeared it seemed to be replaced with another. I kept hoping it would all just go away. Sam was often depressed. Sometimes he would go into an intense deep depression. Those seemed to come at times when we had no serious problems. When, in fact, we did have a serious problem to deal with, Sam always pulled himself together and coped. This made me wonder if he really could control all of this if he wanted to.

I believed that Sam and I had a solid, happy marriage. I believed that we communicated well and we shared our feelings and problems together. But there was always this dark secret, this vague unapproachable subject hanging over us. It was there in happy times and sad times, on vacations, anywhere, everywhere, always.

To me, it constituted a kind of selfishness. I was expected to live with it and never question it, never acknowledge it, never understand it. But I knew it was there and often it took over; that it would raise its head and I would never know what precipitated it. It also represented to me an involvement with oneself that was self-centred, egocentric, and selfish. Sam was so introspective, so involved with his own 'craziness' that I often felt neglected, left out, forgotten. I am a patient person. I waited. I sensed that this was all beyond Sam's control. I just hoped for some confession, some explanation of what was going on.

We had been married ten years. I was pregnant with our third child. I had watched Sam ride his roller coaster and I had learned to adjust to his needs, his moods, his peculiarities, his secretiveness, to his anger and his self-loathing. I had entertained the thought that he was having an affair and couldn't deal with the guilt or that he hated me but couldn't deal with a broken family situation. But I knew that really it was 'something' coming from inside. He had reached a new low. He was terribly depressed and angry. He was totally involved with himself and seemed to withdraw deeper into a shell each day. He was almost totally noncommunicative.

I was frightened both for myself and for our children. I was angry that we were expecting another child, but Sam's spirit was not a part of our family. It was somehow totally involved with himself. He was possessed.

I thought of people to go to for help: his parents, our rabbi, our family doctor. I dismissed each and every thought, knowing Sam would be furious if I spoke to anyone about him. I finally decided to write down all my thoughts, all my feelings, and give them to Sam. I also demanded that he go for professional help. I threatened to leave him if he didn't co-operate. I had hit a brick wall. I could no longer ignore it, excuse it, try to understand it, or believe it would just go away. I couldn't stand the secrecy, the exclusion, the self-involvement, the peculiar behaviour or the depression and anger. I was angry and frightened. I felt helpless and I felt I was watching Sam drown without trying to reach for any lifeline. I was afraid he might commit suicide.

Sam consulted with a psychiatrist and entered psychoanalysis. His illness was given a name. Doors began to open and little by little some light shone through. Slowly, Sam opened up. I began to learn the history of his behaviour and how it controlled him. At times, knowing made it no easier to deal with. He would still get depressed and angry. He still seemed self-centred and I still felt excluded. I believed that he would improve and the psychiatrist would help him to learn to live with his affliction. I hoped that the psychoanalysis would help Sam to understand and deal with his anger. The depression no longer reaches the depths it used to. The rituals have become as familiar and natural to me as my husband's face.

I only now am allowing myself to hope that the drug is really working, that our lives could become more normal. It is almost impossible to believe, and a superstitious part of me will not let me count on the change yet.

ZACH: OUR SON WITH OCD
(Written by his parents)

When we saw Zach trying to pick things up without using his hands, we both felt a growing fear, almost a panicked feeling. This feeling was soon accompanied by anger against fate. He was only six years old.

Our new baby was one month old and so I was seeing our paediatrician regularly. He encouraged me not to assume the worst. It might be a reaction to the baby. As the rituals increased, like ripples from a stone dropped in a pool, we all agreed he needed help. We consulted a child psychiatrist.

Zach was dealing with his obsessions and compulsions with total denial. He seemed to believe that no one saw anything. At times, he couldn't use his hands, might touch the ground after so many steps, or would take a little back-kick after so many steps. One time, he lay down on the floor of a shopping mall and drew a line around his body with his finger. He seemed to be defining his territory, protecting himself from some unseen danger or evil. And Zach washed his hands. He washed and washed and washed. He wouldn't touch his shoes or his glasses. His sleeves always hung down over his hands. He used the sleeves as a protective shield when he had to touch something. And then he washed some more.

The washing of his hands began to take longer. Sometimes it was a minute, sometimes two or three minutes. He developed a routine that involved sticking his thumbs up into the faucet and then swinging his hands back and forth under the water until his whole body was moving with an uncontrolled force. Then, he wouldn't dry his hands. They would be raw and chapped, but he wouldn't dry them. Often he would finish washing his hands, then turn around and start all over again. Sometimes this behaviour would cause Zach to miss the school bus or an activity or even a party.

Zach began to exhibit many of Sam's characteristics. He was angry, tense, and often depressed. They both are perfectionists and show anger if they do anything wrong or imperfectly. All of these symptoms saddened me. I felt at a loss to help Zach. The psychiatrists said that Zach was continuing to totally deny the OCD. I believed I was doing everything I could to help him, but I still felt frustrated and saddened by his inability to control his own mind and his own body. And really I could do nothing to help at all. I knew what not to do to make him feel worse. I didn't question his behaviour, demand that it cease, or tease him, badger him, or otherwise shame him. But that provided little satisfaction as I watched him suffer. I watched two people I love so out of control and so unhappy.

I worried about Zach's sister and brother. I especially worried about his sister, who was old enough to sense that something was not right. She watched all the strangeness around her without understanding. She asked why Zach washed his hands so much. I tried to explain that it was something he *had* to do, that he had a special feeling he couldn't make go away any other way. She accepted it. But Zach's strange behaviour made her uncomfortable. In moments of anger she would tease him about it. A terrible gap existed between Zach and his siblings. He was a loner even at home. He developed a loathing for his sister because she didn't share his problems. As his brother grew older, he resented him as well. He blamed everything on them.

Zach grew afraid of everything, stayed close to home. He chose to be alone a lot. He became very dependent on me. I felt I had to protect his secrets. This wasn't the family life I had planned!

We were fortunate to hook up with the OCD clomipramine study at the National Institute of Mental Health. We had reached an impasse. Although the psychiatrists might help Sam and Zach to deal with their lives, they were unable to 'heal' them of their OCD.

When Zach left for Bethesda, Maryland, to be hospitalized for evaluation for that programme, two and a half years after we had noticed his first symptoms, Sam shared his own story with Zach. Zach was elated at having a comrade. I think it took away much of his shame and maybe even some fear.

In looking back over the last fifteen years I am amazed at how living with rituals has become a natural part of *my* life. I try not to get angry, frustrated, or impatient. I am glad to have an understanding of what is happening. I hope – believe – that major progress in helping OCD sufferers is close. Zach has had a good response to the clomipramine. His rituals are still there, but they have been greatly reduced. Zach is not nearly as depressed as he used to be. He has begun to play with his friends and to accept imperfections within himself. This, of course, has made me very happy.

Sam's response to the drug has not been as clear-cut. But, we patiently await changes. We now talk about his response to the clomipramine, side effects, and about rituals and OCD. Just lifting the veil off 'the deep dark secret' has given us a new relationship. It has made us much stronger as a married couple. And it has given us much greater strength, too, to deal with Zach's problems and to propose solutions to new problems as they come up.

It is now two years later (1988) and Zach is still doing very well. His father had a slower response at first to the clomipramine, but gradually, over a year's time, showed steady if slow improvement and now admits that things are much better. Like most of our patients, Sam had not got much help for his obsessions from ordinary antidepressants, even though they helped improve his depressed mood. The clomipramine is not an ideal solution for Sam. The most troubling side effect of the drug for him has been a decrease in sexual potency. This has been helped partially by lowering the dose, and by adding small amounts of L-tryptophan.

It has been known for a long time that OCD can run in families. Now that we have seen a great many patients, we can say with certainty that at least 20 per cent of our patients have a close relative (parent or sibling) with the same problem. In a way these children are lucky – they are more likely to have understanding families once the secret is let out. The genetic nature of OCD supports our biological theories about the illness.

It could be argued that if something runs in families, it could be just because the children copy the parents or conceivably vice versa. It doesn't have *to mean that it is transmitted biologically from generation to generation. But this is not likely. Parents keep their habits secret from their children as they keep them secret from everyone else. But a more convincing argument against a 'modelling theory' of OCD is that we rarely see a father and a son with the same symptoms. But 'modelling' means that a behaviour is simply copied from another person observed to do the same thing. Sam had mental rituals while Zach was compelled to wash. In the earlier story, Dr S. 'checked' while his son Jeffrey did his 'stringing' rituals. So we don't find any support for a modelling theory and instead believe this is an important clue for the biological basis of OCD. Zach's mother validates Zach's and Sam's accounts. I included her story because for those unfamiliar with OCD the accounts can sound so peculiar, so unconvincing, that it is tempting to say, 'Why don't they just stop it?' It helps at first to hear from someone entirely normal and unsuspecting who had to see for herself how terrible and unyielding these 'trivial' habits can be.*

But perhaps the most important lesson of all is how important it is for the family to be open with each other about the problem. Sam's wife was incredibly relieved finally to have some clue and some validation for her unhappiness. Zach became almost a new child overnight just learning that his father had faced the same problem. The secrecy that seems to be inherent in this disorder is the first and sometimes the greatest enemy to overcome.

II

THE PATIENTS SPEAK: CHILDREN

HICCUPS OF THE MIND

The first patients I met with OCD will always be special to me. They had to work the hardest to explain to me what the disease is all about. As a result of this, they have made a particular effort towards describing their problem in a way that an outsider might grasp. They are special, too, because I have followed them the longest and so can include their perspectives over several years.

The following 'odd' stories recur in our clinic every day as fresh waves of patients appear. The doorway rituals, checking, and washing repeat themselves endlessly in each patient's life. In fact, almost every new case is some slight variant on these major themes.

3

Paul: Stuck in the Doorway

Paul, aged sixteen, was transferred to our ward from a local psychiatric hospital. They were stymied. Paul 'got stuck in doorways' and they weren't sure how to handle him. At almost any hour, Paul could be found in a doorway, slightly swaying back and forth, with his eyes fixed at the upper corner of the door frame. 'What are you doing?' a ward attendant would ask. 'I'm stuck,' Paul whispered back, without moving. 'I have to do it over again to get it right; I have to do it a certain, a special way.'

'Have to do what?' the attendant would ask.

'Get through the door right,' Paul would answer.

At the NIMH Paul settled into his new room quickly. He politely admired the view, and was pleased with the TV. But Paul's large brown eyes stared out anxiously from under long uncombed bangs, and his brown beret never left his head. After introductions had been made and his mother had left, we came back to talk with Paul. He was no longer fiddling with the TV. Paul was standing motionless in the doorway, looking up and towards the right-hand corner of the door frame. He looked as if he were concentrating terribly hard. But when I spoke, he was completely and adequately in contact. He was surprised when we asked if he was seeing things. 'Of course not, Dr Rapoport. I just have to do this.' I tugged at his elbow, and he came along with me with, I thought, a certain relief. We sat down to talk.

Paul looked disconcertingly like my younger son. He liked talking to me, was comfortable with my curiosity. He exuded a gentleness and respect that made him special. But Paul was stuck: the thoughts were repeating over and over in his head and his story was hard to follow. He stuttered a little as he told me how glad he was that we had other kids like him. He wanted to meet them. But it was hard for him to explain *how* he got so stuck. During his whole stay with us, he never could get across just what he was going through. Words were hard for him; we could see he was trying to explain. School was hard too. He had tried to write about it, but writing was not easy for him. Something stopped him from getting through doors. I couldn't get a coherent explanation because the situation wasn't coherent for him.

Ten years later, Paul came back and wrote his story, trying to describe this maddening disorder that never could be fully explained. These are his words:

It's hard to put an exact date on when it began. When I was about five, I remember coming downstairs and telling my parents that I was bothered by the way I had to put on my pyjamas. My parents told me not to worry about it. So I might have had rituals when my father was still alive. But after he died, when I was six, they got worse.

I was seven, and the school bus would drop me in front of my door. We have a white fence in front of our house. I couldn't get through it. *Something* made me go back and do it again. My sister was behind me, and pushed me through. It was okay until I had to go through it again.

Then, I was about eight, the thoughts came. I would think a bad thought, then I would have to think the name 'Jesus Christ' to stop the bad thought. I would do this more when someone made me scared, like the big kid in the class who said he would beat me up after school. I still can't figure out why I was the kid everyone picked on. I was shy, not so good at school, but in the beginning nothing of my habits showed. Maybe it was just that I didn't fight back.

By the time I was twelve, I was always doing rituals. I had to spin around in class and the kids teased me. I never got to be a fighter. When bigger kids teased or threatened, I got scared. I would be in the coat room, and had to spin around eight times before it 'felt right' to come into class. Everyone began to think I was crazy. I've never been crazy. (I should know, I've spent time on hospital wards with people who were really crazy!) This was the first time that it was noticeable to other people. I had kept all of this secret pretty much for seven years. But now it was terrible, because I was shy anyway. After I got out of the hospital my mother got a psychologist to help. He was pretty nice, we played games and stuff, but it didn't help.

By seventh grade, I was skipping school. I only had two friends.

I hated being teased. My rituals got worse and worse. I stopped seeing my doctor and stayed home. I was immobile. I spent a day getting from one room to the other. The yard was the worst place. That front gate with the two posts was the biggest hurdle – to go through those perfectly enough. The cracks in the sidewalk were also big problems. Not the little way they are for some kids but in a very big way.

I would make movements with my arms, make noises, to get bad thoughts out of my mind. I stayed in my pyjamas because it was so much trouble to get into the dressing rituals, since I had to do it over and over. This was part of why I stopped going to school. Because getting dressed was so much work.

After months of this, I was giving up. That is how I got into the hospital. My mother told me I had to go, and I didn't want to. My family didn't understand, but at least they didn't tease me. My sisters would yell at me if I was in front of the television. They didn't understand: *I couldn't move.*

Actually, the yelling helped a little. When I was stuck in the gate in front of the yard, my mother would yell at me to come inside and sometimes it seemed to help.

Paul's story is as clear as I think it ever can be. We, he and I, simply don't understand much more. But when he was sixteen he couldn't put it together even that much. He just knew he got stuck. The familiar themes are all there: He got stuck. He gradually came to know he was different. He kept it secret for years. And even though he looked 'crazy', which to most people means schizophrenia, Paul was never 'crazy' in that way. And that made it worse: he always understood, always knew how weird he looked to others.

Paul was one of the first group of children I met with Obsessive-Compulsive Disorder. I marvelled that anyone could look so 'sick' and yet be so reasonable. Once, when Paul was going home for the weekend, and it was late on a Friday evening when his taxi didn't show up, I drove him home.

On the way to his house, we chatted about his weekend plans. We came to the front gate of his house. I promised I'd wait in the car while Paul went through the gate and into the front door, a distance of perhaps thirty feet. But Paul had to cover this route in seventy-four steps. And he had to do it right. With his entire family watching from the window, eight pairs of eyes shifting from one side of the yard to the other, like spectators at a tennis match, and with me in the car also watching, Paul tried his seventy-four step pathway, zigging and zagging across the front lawn. The family signalled me just to wait, it was better that way they mouthed. We all watched together like naturalists witnessing the dance of some new and exotic bird. It took two hours for Paul to get inside. Miraculously, his weekend went well.

It is this combination of normality surrounding the most severe and strange compulsions, these parallel tracks, that fools everyone and that hypnotized me. I am fascinated by the way such bizarre rites can be so debilitating; yet the rest of the victim's mental processes is spared, and he can go on with his normal life, capable of deep and caring relationships. This unique situation permits my patients to suffer secretly. What particularly intrigued me was the extraordinary reasonableness with which my patients get on with jobs and school. But they live with pain. Their very sanity makes covering up feasible. It is this unusual 'packaging' that keeps everyone from realizing that the disease is much, much more common than had been thought.

Just as puzzling are the different forms the disorder takes. For Paul, the strongest compulsions were to carry out 'entranceway rites'. Why was Paul stuck in doorways and not washing all the time – the most common of the rituals? Are there a variety of primitive rituals with 'control centres' in the brain? How does this pattern get 'chosen'? What turns it on? So far, no model of Obsessive–Compulsive Disorder – whether from a psycho-analytic, behaviourist, or biological point of view – explains the specificity, the selectivity of the symptoms. A related puzzle is what makes patients change over time – and most of them do. A washer will turn into a checker after years of washing.

I still see Paul; he is as reasonable and as nice as ever. He thinks that he may never be entirely rid of his rituals, but they have got much better. He has had years at special schools where he wasn't ever teased, and made good friends. He's had some trials with medicines, including clomipramine, that never worked for him, and years of psychological therapy that helped him better accept himself and his rituals. Behaviour therapy was tried, but did not help much.

At school, a local community college, Paul seems to his teachers and classmates to be just another student, a little shy, doing well at mathematics and economics. But his inner world still differs. Recently he wrote down some thoughts on his present condition and sent them to me.

'I still try to walk through only one side of doorways and will try not to look at certain spots; if I do think of bad thoughts or look at certain spots, I will have to back up and do it again. But a lot of the time I only have to do it once.

'I also sometimes have trouble walking through my kitchen because when I see knives or other sharp objects I usually get bad thoughts of the knife cutting me and I usually try to walk through the kitchen without looking at it.

'I also feel I have to read things over and over in the books I have to read for school. I read the paragraphs over until I think of a good thought instead.'

Paul wants everyone to know that he has *tried* to stop. He says telling a compulsive to 'just stop' is like telling a fat person that they should lose some weight. It never seemed to help. Like many other compulsives, he is depressed a lot.

But still the most remarkable part of Paul's story, as with the stories of most of the children and teenagers I have come to know with this disease, is its unremarkable ordinariness. These kids who just wake up one morning with awful, sterile rituals and phrases stuck in their heads. Can there be tics, or in effect, 'hiccups' of the mind? I was seeing something that nothing in my training had prepared me for. I had to see more.

4

Arnie: The Newspaper Round

Arnie started having the thoughts when he was thirteen. We met him then, a thin earnest boy with very good manners. He had the unusually adult manners that are so common in children of much older parents. His father, a minister, had just been assigned to a new town. Arnie hated moving. 'I'm shy,' he told me. 'Moving is really awful.' As with his last few moves, Arnie had found a neighbourhood paper round right away. He had just started, with over a hundred deliveries to make. One particular night, he missed a few and the customers called to complain. This had happened before and Arnie had simply gone out later and delivered the papers to those houses he had missed. The complaints hadn't been particularly nasty, just simple requests: 'Where is my paper?' or 'Can you bring one by?'

But this time Arnie couldn't get the calls out of his mind. He berated himself, repeating the callers' complaints to himself.

The next day was worse. After Arnie had finished a block, he had to go back to be sure that there was a paper on each and every doorstep. As soon as he had checked it, and turned to face the new work, the feeling came over him: 'I had better make sure.' Back he went to re-check, and then to check again. The job that once took one and a half hours now took him three or four. Anyone who has had a paper round can tell you that occasional misses are inevitable. Delivering papers is a balance between care and speed. But speed is exactly what obsessive–compulsives cannot bring to a job. For a checker, a paper route is a nightmare. As Arnie and his parents remember it, that was how his illness began.

He had been sick for a year when he and his family called us. By this time Arnie, an only child, completely preoccupied his parents. They had tried at first to help him with dressing and showering. After they couldn't help any more, Arnie had spent a year in a psychiatric hospital. Most of his problem was checking. But as it often happens, counting and washing and unwanted thoughts entered and joined the attack on Arnie's life.

During the week he stayed at the National Institute of Mental Health, Arnie got better. No one knew why. It can happen that way with OCD; perhaps the interviews helped in some way. Perhaps he was already starting to improve. As far as we are concerned, we were just getting to know Arnie and had given no treatment at all. Nevertheless, Arnie and his parents were delighted. In spite of my disclaimers, the Reverend and his wife shook my hand with tears in their eyes as they left, saying 'God brought us here, Dr Rapoport. We can never thank you enough.' They never could believe that we had nothing to do with this remission.

Eight years later, when Arnie was twenty-one, he came back to see me. Like Paul, he had written about those bad times, and told us to let the new kids see it:

'I started to doubt *everything*, whether I was doing things right or whether I had done them at all. I stood in my room at night, mentally reviewing the day to make sure I had done everything I was supposed to do. I had to think over every event of the day, including whether or not I had read the paper or watched TV. *Then the compulsive thinking spread to compulsive actions.* It started to take me much longer to brush my teeth, or take a shower. I got to bed very late at night. And then I was late for school. After a couple of months, I wasn't late any more, I was missing school instead. At its worst, a shower took sixty minutes. Dressing took over an hour. If I put on my socks, I had to check the bottoms of my feet for dirt.

'Eventually I just dreaded getting up in the morning and facing all the compulsive actions associated with showering and dressing. At one time, I was getting up at 10 a.m. and not getting dressed until 8 p.m.'

For a while Arnie was able to cope. He graduated top of his high school class, and stayed free of his compulsions until his third year at college. Then his life, up until then calm and pleasant, low-keyed and orderly, started to come apart. His compulsive reading came back. His grades dropped, and he came back home. Arnie left college without finishing the term.

Arnie began to have thoughts. From time to time, thoughts of violence, killing his parents or gouging out his own eyes with needles crossed his mind. Arnie knows he has not harmed and would not harm anyone deliberately. 'I know they are crazy ideas,' he told me, 'but that doesn't keep them away; they're much stronger than regular thoughts.' Most troubling for Arnie were the curses against God. Arnie considers himself a strong Christian, yet the more he tries to repress them, the more the thoughts come back.

Arnie is back in college. Like Paul, he's doing well again. But the effort to perform, to keep up a normal life, exhausts him, because he still has to fight with the thoughts and rituals.

Arnie writes now: 'My summer job as a stock clerk in a shoe shop brought back my checking rituals. I had to sort shoes by size and style, and with the checking, I worked much more slowly than

I liked. The other clerk at first told me to hurry up, and then he left me alone and didn't speak to me at all. But, Dr Rapoport, at least I got the job done, and my boss was satisfied.'

Sorting shoes was not the summer work Arnie would have hoped for, but he has learned to take pleasure from small accomplishments. As if the burden of checking isn't enough, Arnie has to battle additional symptoms. As he tells it: 'My newest problem is numbers. I was never superstitious before, and I don't really think I am now. But numbers have come to be terribly important. I must make sure that I do not repeat something 6 or 13 times, or 60, 66 or 130 times. Even numbers that add up to 6 or 13 or 130 must be avoided, such as 42, 33, 85, or 76.'

Behaviour therapy was not available and he was reluctant to try it in any case. Clomipramine seemed modestly helpful, but after about six months its usefulness wore off. Increasing the dose brought a slight decrease in counting but drowsiness and nausea were unpleasant side effects at this dose.

Arnie, thin, shy, and nervous, tells me how important it has been to keep hoping. The doctors, he says, have helped by keeping up his hope. He thanks them for this, but regrets the years and years of talking about the habits he couldn't change.

'My psychiatrist helped me understand how my father was under a lot of pressure, but how he really cared a lot about me. I got much better at communicating with my parents. But I still don't know why I do what I do. It never changes these habits.'

Arnie has learned to expect little and take what little he can from life. Making do, he says, gives him his greatest strength.

5

Morris: Mr Clean

Each morning for one hour, eighteen-year-old Morris washes his hands and arms with either Flash or Ajax. He scrubs his hands so hard that they have become raw; they sometimes bleed from the intense scrubbing. On a trip with his family, Morris will suddenly feel trapped in the station wagon. It's better if he drives. It keeps him busy and that seems to help more than anything else.

Morris can remember exactly how it started even though he was only three. He was nervous, in a new house his family had just moved into. Pulling a chair up to the sink, he climbed onto it, turned on the tap and washed his hands. For two years it just made him feel better. He felt he had to do this over and over again, but then the washing need faded out.

He went without compulsions – miraculously, he now thinks – until junior high school when the compulsions and thoughts came back. He started to picture his mother, a healthy woman, in a wheelchair. He tried to ignore or suppress the thoughts. He saw a psychologist who told him it was all right to have angry feelings against his mother. Morris knew that it was all right, but he didn't think he had any angry feelings against his mother – and anyhow it didn't seem to help or to matter if he did or didn't. The wheelchair idea still haunted him, and it had a crazy, terrible force to it.

When the thought hit especially hard, Morris would wake the family and they would sit together – father, mother, sometimes his big sister – and try to figure it out. But they weren't able to – not one of them.

Other symptoms grew stronger than the wheelchair picture. His father and Morris would go riding sometimes, and he would picture his father and the woman at the stables having an affair (they weren't). There was another thought he couldn't get rid of. More meetings with the psychologist about his interest in his parents' marriage, about his sexual fantasies about his parents. He *was* interested in his parents' marriage, he *did* have sexual fantasies. By this time, the psychologist and he were good friends, but that didn't help.

And then the paralysing compulsions started in school; his worst symptom came at college. Morris had to rub out words over and over again, so that he got very behind in taking notes, and if a rubbing out attack came during written exams or quizzes, he received 'incompletes'; he couldn't finish.

There was one bright spot at college. Morris fell in love with a girl in his class. She became a strong support in his life. They made love. But she never knew about the obsessions and compulsions. These anxieties seemed more private, more difficult to share than any of the intimacies they had had together. Morris also felt it was humiliating.

The recurring obsessions made Morris withdraw from the girl and his friends, then drop out of college. Because he never told his girlfriend the truth, she thinks he stopped caring for her. But nothing could be further from the truth. His time with her is the only really happy memory Morris feels he has. His life is full of overwhelming bursts of obsessive doubting – two months of wondering if he had a venereal disease (he didn't). The washing comes back and lasts a month; in fact it has never completely gone. Clomipramine has been no help at all.

But Morris still hopes it will get better. He jogs, lifts weights (somehow exercise helps), and he keeps very busy. When things get better, Morris says, he will go back to college.

Once when Morris was very sick, his father came to see me. He was very upset and asked for a private appointment. A well-dressed, handsome man, he was embarrassed and hesitant. Years before Morris became ill, he in fact *had* had an affair. 'Could this have caused Morris's problem?' he asked. I didn't see how, I told him. The stresses in his marriage were not enough to explain his son's illness. We were seeking a very particular sort of answer – why people handle stress, even if stress *is* important, in this *particular* way.

Paul, Arnie and Morris were among the first children I met with Obsessive–Compulsive Disorder. They taught me a great deal – and just as important, helped me unlearn a lot. Outside their habits, they're not unusual kids. They are a bit shy, but not so much that, if otherwise well, anyone would have worried about it. Their illness began insidiously, during everyday trivial activities, activities they had carried out countless times before: walking through the front gate, washing, delivering the neighbourhood papers.

The teenagers described the progression of their symptoms with an objectivity that at first seemed strangely adult to me. But they were not 'hypermature', just so much more willing, more co-operative, than the patients child psychiatrists usually see. And that is my point. My first important shreds of knowledge about this disorder came from talking with large numbers of compulsive patients – children, adults, their families. I found them 'normal' and easy to deal with. In the beginning, my 'understanding' was just an impression, based on how it felt to sit and talk together, and what it was like to watch these astonishing rites.

Now, ten years later, my 'understanding' has become a conviction that this disease is more like a tic, more like a medical illness than we in the medical profession have believed. Yes, these are ordinary children but with bizarre 'hiccups' of their minds.

III
A Doctor's Perspective

The patients' stories came first. Their astonishingly lucid accounts made me realize that these people in some fashion had a 'foreign body' in their otherwise quite sensible minds. A mind splinter, a cinder of thought that 'irritated' their mental processes and wouldn't allow them any rest.

Half the time, Obsessive–Compulsive Disorder starts in childhood. The children are usually boys, but when it starts later in life, men and women are affected equally. Their most common rituals are washing, counting, and checking. The word 'obsession' comes from the Latin obsidere, to besiege, and indeed these patients are besieged, truly possessed.

The children all ask me in one way or another: 'Can you make them go away? Can you get them out of my mind?' One bright fourteen-year-old girl told me: 'I wish I could go back in time to where it first began because now it seems so out of control. What was once myself and my rituals is now my rituals first, and then myself. What distresses me the most is that I know they are unnecessary and unreal, however, I still do them.

'I've really lost touch with myself and that's really frightening. I wish I could get the ''old Sally'' back. I keep hoping it's just a dream and that I'll wake up and everything will be normal. I used to like who I was a lot, but now I feel I don't even know myself any more. I have so many goals and dreams I want to accomplish, but I know I will never accomplish them with OCD. I feel like I'm in a mental labyrinth from which I cannot escape. I hope I can get better.'

My alliance with these children is immediate and warm, as it is among friends dealing with a mutual concern. These children do not treat me, or anyone else, in a 'neurotic' way, not like other self-critical or suspicious people with lives of failed relationships and self-destructive acts. They do not cast blame, don't tell me why the teacher didn't like them, or why their families just don't understand. They come with parents who support them, and friends who miss them. They come to say, 'Something weird and crazy is happening. Please make this go away!' This book is not a recipe of a special technique for talking to patients with OCD. It is about what I learned by just listening and watching, and from the remarkable coincidence of several lines of research, on the frequency of the disease, on the new drug treatment, and *on abnormalities of the brain in OCD, that came together while I was doing this.*

The symptom that occurs more than any other, in whatever country OCD is seen, is washing. Our clinic staff with its insiders' slang reports new cases in terms of how many washers, or 'thinkers', and so forth. We know now that at least 85 per cent of our patients have performed excessive, compulsive washing at some point in their illness. Why washing? Is there some vestigial centre in the brain for grooming behaviours that is activated in this disease? For a while I wondered if this symptom were some artefact of the American preoccupation with bathroom fixtures, deodorants, and 'personal hygiene' which so bemuses our European associates. But the cross-cultural data on OCD, although not perfect, suggests that cultures less obsessed with cleanliness, for example rural Nigeria and rural India, also have patients preoccupied with contamination and ritual purity as their most common form of OCD.

Washing, depending on the context, means animal grooming patterns, good health habits, kinship acceptability, rites of purity, and group ritual to protect against danger. But I hadn't thought much about that in 1976 when Charles's mother called me for the first time.

6

The Boy Who Couldn't Stop Washing

Charles, then fourteen, spent three hours or more in the shower each day and took another two hours to get dressed. This strange behaviour had been going on for a couple of years.

'I hear you have a new study, Dr Rapoport,' his mother said. 'The other hospital didn't know what to do. They stop him from showering *there*, but when he comes home, he just starts up again.'

'What does *he* say about all this?' I asked.

'He just tells me he can't help it. He says he just *has* to.'

Psychotherapy had not helped, nor had a variety of standard psychiatric drugs, or months of the hospital's behavioural treatment programme. Charles kept trying to wash off 'something sticky' from his skin. As military dependants, Charles and his family were entitled to care in military hospitals and the doctors had done their best. But they had seen few patients with such a problem before. Most psychiatrists see a handful at best in a lifetime. At about the same time, they read about our new study at the National Institute of Mental Health. They were calling from North Dakota.

Now we are flooded with patients much closer to home. At the time, though, I still thought OCD was rare. So Charles and his family came to Bethesda as part of our study in 1976.

Until he had to leave school (or more accurately, couldn't get out of the shower in time to get to school), Charles had been an eager student who loved biology and was interested in plants, genetics, and chemistry. His biology teacher was encouraging him to plan ahead for an out of town college, and to think about becoming a teacher or a doctor. Charles had shown a great ability for observation in the laboratory experiments, and in drawing logical conclusions from these observations.

Now he could not trust his own 'good sense' or his senses. There was no such thing any longer as 'knowing it was okay' or 'seeing for himself' that his hands and body were clean. His mother was desperate; life had become a nightmare of invisible contamination. Charles 'knew', he 'felt sure' that there was some sticky substance on his skin. He thought of nothing else.

In her futile efforts to help, Charles's mother joined in the rituals. She knew they were crazy. But it was hard for her to see him so miserable if his rituals weren't carried out. So she cleaned everything he might touch with rubbing alcohol. She helped him scour his room over and over again. She kept people out of the house to prevent 'contamination' from the street. Charles's father spent more and more time at his job, and came home late to avoid the whole bizarre scene.

I saw how OCD can distort family life, splitting it into warring factions and eliminating ordinary routine. This is familiar now, but at the time, watching a family act out the rituals without understanding was weird. As Charles's mother told me: 'He had never been unreasonable before; he really was no different from most boys. So when he cared so much for something, even though I didn't understand it, I felt I had to go along. And he got so upset when I didn't.'

Talking with Charles alone was easy and pleasant at first. He was bright and he could be fun. He was hopeful that the study could cure him. But a problem came up almost at once. He was terrified to have an EEG, a brain wave test, because the test involves putting electrodes on the scalp with a very sticky paste. It is fairly easy to wash off. But, as Charles shouted, *nothing* was easy for him to wash off! Suddenly this poised, bright boy was feeling his horror of stickiness with a bizarre intensity, 'Stickiness is terrible. It is some kind of disease, it is like nothing you can understand,' he told me. The worst thing he could think of was to touch honey. Once started, Charles couldn't stop. Stickiness was danger, was annihilation.

His condemnation of viscosity was a page that Charles hadn't read from Jean-Paul Sartre's essay on 'stickiness', Sartre's personal metaphor for annihilation of the self. Stickiness, Sartre said, is halfway between solid and liquid. It is soft, yielding, and a trap. It clings like a leech and attacks the boundary between oneself and it. 'Columns of stickiness falling from my hand,' he said, 'suggest my own substance is flowing into a pool of stickiness.'

Water was different, water was no threat to solidity. Charles always felt the sticky threat on his skin. It meant dread, an insidious attack, the worst feeling he had ever had. Without any provocation he had just spent two years washing. He shrieked that putting something really sticky there would be terrible. 'I can feel it,' he'd scream at us, 'it's really there. I can't stand any more.' This was in the heat of the argument. He knew and he didn't know that the stickiness *wasn't* there. We insisted: no EEG, no study. The EEG was done. Charles was up all night washing.

The discomfort of going along with our study was worth it for Charles. A month later, he and I took part in a strange, but to us wonderful ceremony. I watched as Charles poured out honey onto a knife, and then grasped the honeyed blade smiling. The ward cheered. He was our first patient to respond dramatically to the new drug clomipramine. (But more about that later.)

I know now that Charles was a typical child with Obsessive–Compulsive Disorder. But at the time, he was one of the most curious cases I had seen.

Because he was one of the first children I ever saw with OCD, he and I spent hours talking over 'why' he couldn't stop washing. He described what he felt – the urgent insistent sense of 'I have to' that was inside him. He didn't hear voices telling him to carry out these odd behaviours – 'Everybody asks me that, doctor!' – that would be *really* crazy. His eyes were teary when he said: 'Please don't say I'm crazy. That's been the worst part, the other kids and even my sisters teasing me and calling me nuts.' He knew it *sounded* crazy, but he didn't feel crazy. He just knew he *had* to wash, that's all.

It became easier to talk to Charles when he saw I didn't think he was crazy. The very ease of getting to know each other was deceiving: it all seemed so normal, so simple. So much of my psychiatric training had been geared to interviewing suspicious, angry, isolated, and irrational patients. It took me a while to realize that for most of this new group of patients, that kind of skill wasn't needed.

On our ward, Charles became the nurses' favourite. He was open, appreciative, and friendly. When we first met Charles, he had only one friend. Rituals left him no time to leave the house. Many of our patients say that one friend stuck by them through years of isolation. I want to meet these friends, but that's another study.

I asked Charles what would happen if he *stopped* washing. He looked perplexed and could come up only with some vague notions that 'maybe some sickness would come' or 'it could be bad luck'. His insights did not really begin to explain how his life could have become so drastically limited by his ritual washing. The psychological explanation about washing might suppose that Charles felt guilty and ashamed about masturbation. I certainly heard sexual wishes, fears, and impulses from other adolescent patients, but not from Charles. That theory isn't enough to explain the disease. Now that we have seen so many patients over many years, we find even more complexity. Symptoms can and usually do change over the years. When patients start before adolescence, they often count, check, or repeat movements. In adolescence, they wash. After adolescence, they may ruminate. But at some stage, almost 85 per cent of our patients have some grooming or washing ritual. A useful explanation of the symptom pattern in OCD must be one that predicts who will get sick, why there is all this washing, and why it comes and goes.

Charles remained free of all symptoms for a year. And then, gradually, they returned even though he was taking the medicine regularly. He had developed some tolerance to the drug.

Charles still isn't completely cured. In spite of dramatic improvement with clomipramine, he can hide his ritual activity by performing in the evenings when he's alone. But the pressure to carry out the ritual washing and dressing never completely went away. He still can't go through a door without being compelled to turn around and walk through it again. When taking a shower, he still has his particular soap ritual. He holds the soap for one minute in the water in his right hand, and out of the water for one minute with his left hand, repeating this process over and over again for up to an hour. Charles now has little response to clomipramine, and only modest improvement with behaviour therapy. But he continues to fight these urges, and remains optimistic that help will come.

Charles's rituals and inner calls for symmetry could be a page from an anthropologist's notebook on the rites of a primitive tribe, or a caricature of a nonexistent religious order. *But he had had no teachers for these rituals.* Although he is 'typical' of obsessive children and adults, he has never met anyone else who does anything like this. I ask: 'Why do you do these things?' He just shakes his head. 'I don't know. I really don't know.' He means it.

Since Charles, I have met and treated more children and adults with Obsessive–Compulsive Disorder than most psychiatric hospitals see in twenty years. But it was with Charles that I began to respect the illness as a common and terribly destructive affliction. What makes some patients so memorable? With Charles, perhaps it was his trusting gratitude that I was trying to help. Whatever the reason, I was determined to find out more about his problem.

Darrel was altogether different from Charles. He never understood why other kids in our study cared about washing. He was never compelled to carry out any ritual. The day his problem began, Darrel woke his parents early in the morning; he was in terror. He asked them, begged them, to lock him in his room. He said he was worried that he might go out on the street and kill someone. How? Perhaps push them in front of a car. Or something. They were astonished. Darrel was a quiet boy, who played the piano well and liked school. He had never been a problem child. Darrel had never even needed much discipline and did not have a bad temper.

Was he mad at anyone? 'You don't understand,' he said (a phrase I have heard almost every day since I began studying this disease), 'I just am not sure, I think I *might* do this. Or electrocute someone.' His parents tried to distract him. They were wasting their energy. *He couldn't get the thought out of his mind.*

Darrel's parents did what he asked. They locked the door. A few hours later, they brought him downstairs for breakfast. He was crying. And asking the strange question: 'How do I *know* if I am going to kill someone?' All the 'right' answers didn't work – 'You're a good boy, you are gentle, you would stop yourself, you would never hurt anyone,' and so forth. Darrel listened patiently to these useless phrases. They provided only a few seconds' pause before he started up again. 'But how do I know if . . .' 'How can I tell?'

I met Darrel while he was still on very high doses of haloperidol, a strong tranquillizing drug that is used for schizophrenic patients, and after he had been on a ward for violent patients for several months. He walked stiffly, and spoke in a monotone. But he could describe his curious state of both knowing and not knowing his innocence. He kept on asking, 'How can I be sure if I killed anyone?'

This sort of philosophical discussion took up most of the time I spent with Darrel. In fact this was all he would talk about. 'Knowing' was the subject. Darrel could not believe his memory, his eyes, his thoughts. In one way or another, every patient with OCD wants to know how to know.

7

The Doubting Disease

A major feature, and a strange one, of Obsessive–Compulsive Disorder is the inability to be reassured by the senses. Obsessives have lost their ability to 'know' certain simple things that we all take for granted, things that we all constantly check for by some mechanism of which we are unaware, except when it doesn't work. This mechanism is not working for these patients at a level that astonishes me, for they are asking 'How do you know' about things that we find oursleves hard put to explain: Is the grass really green? Are my eyes blue? 'Why,' I say, 'we just *know*, that's all.'

Obsessive-compulsive patients literally come to doubt their own senses, at least in a selective way. The younger children get demoralized, bewildered, that their parents don't help them, can't help them, and struggle with their families who can't understand why they 'just don't stop' their rituals. 'When you write your book,' they tell me, 'be sure to explain that *we just can't stop.*'

Then there is the content of the rituals. Compulsives (our term for patients who mostly ritualize) and obsessives (those who mostly ruminate) rarely have rituals or thoughts about neutral questions or behaviours (although this can happen; some of these curious 'neutral' obsessions are described later in this book). What are their rituals about? There are several possible ways to list the symptoms of OCD. Everyone agrees that the most common preoccupations are dirt (washing, germs, touching), checking for safety or closed spaces (cupboards, doors, drawers, appliances, light switches), and thoughts, often thoughts about unacceptable violence, sexual, or blasphemous behaviour ('I have killed someone', 'I am a lesbian'). These thoughts are virtually never acted upon. But in all these preoccupations, a basic function is out of control.

Our patients all believe that their thoughts are odd or crazy; they are embarrassed by their habits and teased by their friends. They keep their ideas and actions secret; indeed some become brilliant actors at hiding their thoughts or rituals. (Thought: Can such a disease prepare one for a stage career? I wonder if there are actors who suffer secretly from OCD?)

When it gets bad, the patients hide. Avoidance of others and of situations that set off these odd patterns is a major complication of OCD. Even the most neutral compulsion – straightening drawers, or counting to 32 – is embarrassing because these too have the inner compelling force that marks the disease. The most trivial gesture looks peculiar when it is repeated over and over and over again.

My patients' secretiveness takes the most inventive forms. I have learned some of their tricks. Marion, now twenty-six, used to pray briefly before hopping into bed when she was twelve. Her grandmother, who slept in the next room, heard the noise from the bedsprings and assumed her granddaughter had finished praying. After her grandmother began to snore, Marion crept out of bed and prayed for three more hours.

During our study at the NIMH, two boys with severe washing rituals would shower for five minutes on the hospital ward to avoid suspicion. Then they sneaked off to a ward under renovation elsewhere in the hospital. The ward was empty, but the showers still worked. They washed there for hours until their rituals felt completed.

When I started the study, I was much too impressed at how well my patients could function in spite of their disabling rituals. Some had top jobs. Others were the pride of their schools. As I've said, these are the world's greatest actors and actresses. Over the years, I saw how this had its bad side. They might have found help earlier if they weren't so good at 'passing'. I know too many stories of public success and private hell; the ability to 'pass' now calls up my admiration *and* my alarm.

8
Is OCD a Brain Disease?

The clues that patients with OCD have something wrong with their brains were too strong, too numerous, and too important to ignore early in the study. First, of course, were the lucid accounts from the majority of my patients saying 'This is new, this is *not me.*' Then there was the minority, an equally impressive group of patients we saw who *did* have other neurological problems, and with them, had come OCD.

Steven had never had any signs of Obsessive–Compulsive Disorder until the week following his eleventh birthday, when he had his first seizure. The problem was epilepsy and his parents were relieved to learn how epilepsy could be managed with drugs. They were even more relieved when they found that the anti-epileptic drugs were medicines that Steven tolerated well.

But epilepsy was not to be Steven's biggest problem. In fact the day before his seizure, Steven had asked his mother: 'Do you *have* to have numbers in your head?' She dismissed his question as whimsical. But after Steven's seizures were under control, he was left with the numbers. The next time Steven saw a doctor it was because the number 4 dominated Steven's life, ruining school, ruining any chance of fun.

Jacob was rushed to the neurosurgeon at our local university hospital in the middle of a sunny afternoon. An athletic eight-year-old, he had been playing football with his older brothers in his backyard. Jacob had suddenly collapsed in a coma. After four hours in surgery, a bleeding cerebral aneurysm (a hole in a weak part of a blood vessel in the brain) had been repaired. Jacob's recovery from the bleeding into the brain was amazingly fast (not unusual for a healthy eight-year-old boy), at least as far as his neurosurgeon was concerned. But when Jacob woke up, he was trapped in a nightmare of ritual. The expected post-op questions: When can I go home? When can I walk around? weren't heard. Instead, there was a list of acts: Jacob had to touch everything seven times. He swallowed seven times and asked for everything in sevens. Multiples of seven and, worst of all, the *time* it took to do everything by sevens, filled his day in the hospital. Months after his successful neurosurgery, Jacob's life was still a treadmill of ritual gestures. He could only go back to school when the touching-counting compulsion was stopped by treatment with clomipramine.

Steven and Jacob were unusual cases. Most obsessive-compulsive children and adults have never had brain surgery and do not have epilepsy or any other neurological disease that we can find. But nevertheless, a much greater number of such patients than should be expected by chance were joining our study.

Steven and Jacob had neurological diseases that did not affect one simple part of the brain. But over a period of time, a specific pattern of brain disease, together with obsessions and compulsions, began to be seen. These brain structures, called the basal ganglia, are buried deep within the brain; their name means literally 'lower nerve knot'. They serve as relay stations between all of our senses, our motor functions, and higher cortical centres.

As we saw more and more patients with obsessions and compulsions, we noticed what a high proportion of them had, or had had, minor tics or twitches of the face or hands. You wouldn't notice this sort of thing seeing just one patient, and tics appear rather frequently in the general population. But as we recruited more and more subjects for our drug study, and as we realized that OCD was a common disease, the pattern of obsessions and compulsions together with these tics and twitches stood out very clearly.

It is humbling to read what others have said about tics and compulsions. Indeed, I find that few of my own observations are original; the connection between obsessions and compulsions and the basal ganglia was not a new idea at all.

In 1894, Sir William Osler, then Physician in Chief at Johns

Hopkins Hospital, wrote 'On Chorea and Choreiform Affections'. His description of a girl described as 'Tic of the Muscles of the Face and Neck; Fixed Ideas; Arithromania' will be immediately familiar:

A.B. aged 13, seen Sept 6, 1890. The child is well grown and well nourished, though rather stout for her age. For a year or more, she has had occasional twitching of the muscles of her face and neck noticeable in the sudden elevation of the eyebrows.

A short time after the onset of the twitchings it was noticed that she began to have all sorts of queer notions and practices, many of which persisted for some weeks or months and were then changed for others not less anomalous. Some of her vagaries are as follows, nearly all being modifications of the fixed idea known as arithromania. Before getting into bed at night, she lifts each foot and taps nine times on the edge of the bed. After brushing her teeth she has to count one hundred. For a year at least she has always entered the house by the back door, protesting that she can never enter by the front door again. Lest her mother should prevent her from getting in by the back door, she for months carried the key herself. On reaching the door, she knocks three times on the edge of the window near by, and three times on the door before unlocking it. She will not under any circumstances button her shoes. In drinking water she will take a mouthful, then put the tumbler down, turn it once or twice and repeat this act every time she drinks. Before putting on clean underclothes she has to count so many numbers that there is a great difficulty in getting her to make the change except under the strongest threats from her mother.

The patient was sent to the country under the care of her aunt, who was urged to control and train the child. The patient recovered completely.

A connection between obsessions and motor tics was observed by Georges Gilles de la Tourette in his original 1885 description of the syndrome that bears his name today. Gilles de la Tourette, a Parisian neurologist, had been studying hysteria, and was also interested in hypnosis. But he is best known for Tourette's Syndrome, an extraordinary condition in which multiple motor movements are accompanied by uncontrollable sounds which in more advanced cases may be offensive words or phrases. Like OCD, individual case histories had been described since medieval times, but it took Tourette's fine report of nine cases to crystallize this now well-recognized syndrome.

Obsessions and compulsions like those of my patients appear in about one-third of the cases with Tourette's Syndrome. These occur in addition to their tics and sounds. In his first report, Tourette wrote: 'The more revolting these explosions are, the more tormented she becomes by the fear she will say them again, and this obsession forces these words into her mind and to the top of her tongue.'

Since that study, many reports have documented a relationship between Tourette's Syndrome and compulsions. For example, families of Tourette's patients are more likely to have a member with OCD. Tourette's disease is almost certainly a disease of the basal ganglia. I have come to believe that Tourette's disease and Obsessive–Compulsive Disorder are two sides of the same neurobiological coin.

But the best description of a neurological illness – that is, a known disease of the brain – that can produce obsessions and compulsions came from Professor Constantin von Economo (1876–1931), a most colourful physician of Greek extraction whose family had emigrated to France. Most of his education and his professional life were spent in Vienna, where he studied medicine. Von Economo's famous monograph of 1917 on *Encephalitis Lethargica* (an English translation became available in 1931) gives some of the most elegant description of the psychological effects of brain disease ever written. Because von Economo was both a clinician and a pathologist, he could link the clinical picture of the more than five hundred variants of the sleeping sickness he described with his studies of brain abnormalities.

During the years 1916–18, Europe was plagued by a severe epidemic of viral encephalitis that left thousands dead, and thousands of others in a stuporous twilight state, combined with a movement disorder like Parkinson's disease, except that it tended to attack young people. Von Economo devoted his life to studying this infectious neurotoxic agent and its effect on the brain, which, he demonstrated, was for the most part in the area of the basal ganglia.

Most medical historians are more interested in von Economo's observations about Parkinson's disease because, as our elderly population has increased, the number of Parkinsonian patients has risen. Von Economo's observations helped to forge a connection between the basal ganglia and Parkinson's disease. But what I find interesting are not von Economo's observations on the terrible and constricting alterations in motor movements that his patients suffered, but their many psychological changes, most particularly the alteration of *will*. In discussing the mental state after *Encephalitis Lethargica*, which the disease came to be called, von Economo wrote:

> These patients do not say 'I have a twitch in my hand,' but rather as a rule say 'I have got to move my hand that way.' The frequent subjectivization of these processes, experienced as compulsory by the patients, is, I believe, one of their characteristic attributes . . . but for instance, in . . . epilepsy . . . the patient says 'I have a twitch in my arm'; that is, the movement does not become subjectivated, though it has its origin in the cerebral cortex.

Von Economo went on to worry about how a 'lower' part of the brain, the basal ganglia, could be responsible for such a complex function as that of 'will' and 'intentionality'. His own work had shown that the cerebral cortex, which he and other neurologists of his time assumed was the part of the brain that controlled higher functions like these, was intact in *Encephalitis Lethargica*. He concluded that the shift to the higher centres must only be partial as far as will is concerned. He believed that there must be an 'intimate relationship of frontal brain and brain stem [by which he meant the basal ganglia] as far as utterances and will and emotional activity are concerned.'

The neurology of obsessions and compulsions cannot, unfortunately, be simply deduced from these post-encephalitic patients. As Oliver Sacks, a neurologist and writer who has written eloquently about how brain disease affects the mind, points out, there are many other small viral 'attacks' on the brains of post-encephalitic patients that affect several of its parts: the thalamus, hypothalamus, diencephalon, and central grey matter. Interestingly, for the connection I am making here, all of these structures integrate emotions, sensory information, and motor behaviours.

As I have already mentioned, our obsessive–compulsives often had peculiar small movements which are hard to describe. Some are tics or twitches of the face or hands, and look like mild cases of Tourette's Syndrome, while others have simple tics. Still others have fleeting jerking movements of the hands and feet. Some have complex, odd mannerisms such as touching the nose, pulling their hair, reaching out to twist an arm backward. I hadn't seen that since medical school in connection with a post-infectious brain disease called Sydenham's Chorea. So here was OCD again in connection with a neurological problem.

Since our patients become accomplished actors, they can disguise these movements brilliantly. A woman showed me how she could embellish her 'arm twitches' to look as if she were stretching. Another compulsive toucher showed me how she can simply appear vivacious and affectionate.

The rituals and the thoughts themselves in Obsessive–Compulsive Disorder have a tic-like quality, out of context and uncontrollable. The repetitive thoughts, perhaps as the French psychiatrist Pierre Janet believed, represent a form of neuronal discharge – just like the motor tics or jerks. Janet believed in a kind of 'psycholepsy', tics of the mind. Like epilepsy, where someone can be seizure-free for months or years and then suddenly begin again, obsessions can be dormant for weeks or months and then something sets them off. My patients ask: 'Why did the thoughts disappear?' and inevitably, 'Why did they come back?' I usually can't answer either question.

I too was struck by the tic-like quality of the obsessive ideas. Can they result from some electrical firing of diseased brain circuits? Do these unreasonable, recurring patterns of movements and feelings suggest that thoughts can have 'fits' just like movements? Are there 'electrical' mini-storms of thoughts (like the electrical discharges in epilepsy) that produce obsessions?

I feel extraordinarily lucky to be doing my research at this time, when new methods have been found to study the human brain in action. Brain-imaging techniques now can monitor electrical or biochemical activity over the entire surface of the brain and, with some techniques, for deeper parts of the brain as well. These are all done while an alert human subject performs various mental activities. The deepest probe into the living brain has become possible with a technique called Positron Emission Tomography. PET scans take advantage of the fact that the brain uses glucose and oxygen the same way that other parts of the body do. Chemicals normally used by the brain are first labelled with a radioactive isotope. When the isotope decays, it emits positrons (positively charged electrons) and they give off gamma rays which are picked up by detectors outside the body.

PET, along with other new brain-imaging techniques, has been applied to Obsessive–Compulsive Disorder. There is now evidence that part of the brain (one portion of the basal ganglia, called the caudate nucleus) and portions of the frontal lobes behave differently in patients with this illness. Two independent laboratories have found this unique pattern of abnormality in OCD. The evidence grows for the neurological basis for this abnormality of thought. Specifically, the evidence points to the parts of the brain that Osler and von Economo were studying. The parts of the brain that seem abnormal in the PET scans of these patients are the *same* parts that are affected by the encephalitic type of Parkinson's disease and by Tourette's Syndrome. The pieces of a puzzle are falling into place.

It is remarkable to be able to study how the brain works as it carries out the complicated and subtle thoughts and ideas that OCD patients have. Can we localize 'doubt' or 'will'? These notions preclude attempts to study the illness in animals. We must work with human patients to understand OCD.

I went to medical school (instead of going on in experimental psychology) with a particular goal. I wanted to study abnormalities in thought and behaviour in relation to abnormalities in physiology. But in Obsessive–Compulsive Disorder, the thoughts are abnormal in areas so refined that philosophers have considered these functions in more depth and detail than have physicians. Obsessive-compulsives have problems with 'will' and with 'knowing'. New discoveries about this illness reveal a biology of the mind at a level I never thought possible.

9

Unlearning to Understand

The expectation that every neurotic phenomenon can be cured may, I suspect, be derived from the layman's belief that the neuroses are something quite unnecessary which have no right whatever to exist. Whereas in fact they are severe, constitutionally fixed illnesses, which rarely restrict themselves to only a few attacks, but persist as a rule over long periods or throughout life.

SIGMUND FREUD
New Introductory Lectures
on Psychoanalysis

Unlearning came fast. I had to discard most of what I had been taught as a psychiatric resident about Obsessive–Compulsive Disorder. I was taught that patients with the disorder would usually have a special 'obsessional' personality profile: individuals with compulsive personalities are people who are perfectionist, punctual, cold, neat; they are this way about *most* things, and have *always* been this way. Maybe 20 per cent of our patients fit this description, most don't. Many are quite sloppy, even messy when younger, and careless about their appearance, their room, and their possessions. Most curiously, many with perfectionist strivings or rituals are highly selective in *what* to be perfect about or *where* to clean up.

This contrast between an island of fanatic neatness, surrounded by a sea of mess, can be striking. Today I take this rather for granted, but the first time I saw what a mess my patients could stand, it seemed astonishing. I had come to visit the ward to see John and Richard, both sixteen and both with washing compulsions, who were on our paediatric ward at the NIMH for observation. They showered incessantly and one of them also changed his sheets several times a day. The nurses learned to institute some unusual nursing procedures. First they locked the linen cupboard in order to keep the rest of the ward supplied with clean towels and sheets. Then they rationed the boys to two bars of soap each day. Next they had to stop them from bringing their hospital bedsheets to the patient laundry room so that the other patients would be able to do their personal laundry.

In spite of this, and on these same days, the nurses could not get John and Richard to pick their clothes up off the floor and hang them up! Instead there was a dialogue one could have had with any teenage boy, and certainly a familiar scene around my house:

'Please hang up your clothes in the cupboard. Please take your books off the floor.'

'We'll get to it later.'

The selectivity was just as surprising in other ways. When they meet each other, my patients relate best to those with the exact same symptom. But one who washes usually has no sense of why someone else, for example, would want to check. They are of course sympathetic and support each other because they recognize the waste, the sense of compulsion, and absurdity of each other's symptom. But there is no general urge to do any of the other common OCD behaviours outside the few specific obsessions or compulsions that a given patient happens to have. So a 'washer' will be most sympathetic to a 'checker' in a general way, but shake his head just as I do and say to himself, 'Thank goodness I don't have to do *that*.'

Most puzzling is how these movements are 'sort of' under the patient's control. They can be stopped for minutes, or sometimes for hours, but they always return. This quasi-control is not unique to the movements; it is true for the thoughts or rituals too. For years this 'voluntary' aspect of obsessions has been used to support the idea that they are primarily the result of an emotional problem. But a number of neurological symptoms can also be controlled for a time. Patients with Tourette's Syndrome, for example, can temporarily inhibit their jerks and tics, even their vocal outbursts.

Psychoanalytic training had convinced me that special ideas

and fears were enacted symbolically through compulsive rituals. The paradigm was Freud's case of the 'Rat Man'. This young man had been plagued with obsessions since childhood, and when he consulted Freud in 1907, he began analysis centring around his recurrent thoughts of rats eating their way into his anus. Freud's psychoanalysis involved elaborate and imaginative connectings, through his patient's dreams and associations, of the young man's rat fantasies with his feelings towards his father, towards money, and towards his sexuality.

From reading classical cases, and from supervision by experienced clinicians, I hoped that I would learn to do the same. After I got to know a patient well and had gained his trust, sooner or later I thought that, as Freud had with the Rat Man, I would come to know the guilty wish or fear behind the patient's washing, checking or counting. If the patient could not identify these, it was because our work together had not been 'deep' enough.

But now I know that most of our patients will never find the 'hidden' thought. Of course, obsessive patients, as do others, eventually come to share thoughts that they were at first too embarrassed to talk about. But in spite of increasingly good rapport, and sharing of other very intimate thoughts and feelings, at least half our 'ritualizers' can never come up with any real concept of the 'idea behind it'. Others have ideas that sound more like theories to explain the repetitive behaviour itself.

Obsessive–Compulsive Disorder was like some pattern within being released, a pattern normally kept in check. Compulsions and obsessions can be neutral acts or thoughts that must simply be repeated; they are done without fear or in any related context. No theory I had learned explained this.

For example, Stanley, now sixteen, was compelled to repeat actions over and over. These habits had begun suddenly, when he was fifteen, and he hated them. An athlete and star basketball player, he dreaded the slowing caused by the repetitions that, even though he could disguise them, 'threw off his game'. But as hard as he tried to 'co-operate' with our research and with me, he didn't have a clue about why he did everything twice. The best way he could describe his motivation was as an urge to repeat and a vague discomfort if he didn't. The most salient feature was the insistent force behind that 'dumb' act making everything else unimportant.

Much earlier in my training, if a mother would spend hours washing his room with her son, or parents would lock a child up to keep him from 'killing' others, or a mother would walk out of a restaurant because they had not 'walked in right', we would have nodded knowingly at our diagnostic conferences and spoken of 'intrusive parenting' or 'problems with boundaries'. We had a lot to learn about this disorder! The old formulas didn't apply.

I had learned to be careful about 'taking away the symptom'. This could cause 'symptom substitution', one professor of psychiatry insisted, so that 'depriving' the patient of his symptom would prove too superficial an approach. Once we removed the 'chosen' symptom, a new one, or even several new ones, would spring up in their place. The training that most psychiatrists received, until very recently, regarded this disorder as perhaps the best of all disorders in its capacity to reveal the symbolic significance in abnormal behaviour. Surely the 'washers' were clinical embodiments of Lady Macbeth. Clearly, the checkers wished some danger to their families and needed to deny it. Certainly, their symptoms must represent a way of handling these forbidden wishes, these unspoken grievances and guilt.

What Sigmund Freud actually said about obsessive–compulsive neurosis is far less doctrinaire. His writings included speculations about genetic and other biological influences. While Freud speculated on psychological influences in obsessive–compulsive neurosis, he also wrote: 'As to what factors can bring about such disturbance of development, the work of psychoanalysis comes to a stop. It leaves that problem to biological research.' He also acknowledged how difficult it was to make the meaningful connections with obsessional neurosis compared to other neuroses, such as hysteria.

It remains one of the great ironies in psychiatry that Obsessive–Compulsive Disorder, the illness most cited to illustrate the fundamental principles of psychoanalysis, should be the disorder that benefits the least from this treatment.

Behavioural psychologists created the first revolution in the treatment of OCD. In the 1960s and 1970s a learning theory approach to this disorder seemed very appealing. If the symptoms were seen as conditioned connections between a fear and something that would reduce this anxiety then a ritual would be born. Learning theory models of OCD are still debated, and for many the treatment works. But in the last few years, the new biology of this disorder generated by the unique response to drugs and abnormalities in brain scans has had a greater influence in the thinking about this illness. Despite this shift, the most important benefit of behaviour therapy cannot be overestimated. During the 1970s I read about its efficacy in treating phobias and OCD. For patients willing and able to use its precepts, behavioural treatment should be the first approach.

My view of obsessive–compulsive patients as otherwise normal individuals developed as I listened to person after person tell me about his or her disorder. But it was the process of treating my patients with drugs or behaviour therapy that finally convinced me that they never 'needed' these symptoms to maintain balance or control over some internal psychological conflict.

The psychopharmacologist, the doctor using drugs to change behaviour, has a powerful tool for relieving OCD. Each time I give a drug, I actually conduct a mini-experiment. Most of our patients had tried other drugs that hadn't worked and other treatments that hadn't worked. Through using the new drug, clomipramine, I became convinced that getting rid of these symptoms as quickly as possible is the only rational treatment for my patients.

When the drug did work (and it did not for at least a third of our patients), the unwanted ideas and images faded away and no new symptoms developed. Parents turned to us with relief. They stopped following their children around; they were pleased to get on with their own lives. Charles's mother returned to helping her husband with his work. Paul's mother saw more of her sister again. Often parents' behaviour, even quite odd and unreasonable behaviours, are a reaction to difficult demands from a sick child, demands that they are only too glad to leave behind when the child stops suffering.

10

Clomipramine: A Wonder Drug?

I had been studying psychiatric drugs, conducting psychopharma-cological research since 1964. The study of clomipramine began in 1975 with academic interest but considerable doubt. It was hard to believe that such a specific treatment for OCD was possible. My own training took place just as drug treatment began a revolution in psychiatry; it was the new biology of mental illnesses. The revolution has created an explosion of information about brain sciences and the application of this information and new treatment techniques to the study of mental illness. The discovery of effective drugs was the most important force in bringing psychiatry back towards the mainstream of medicine.

Psychiatric drugs work best for general mood states, like anxiety or depression. Obsessions and compulsions were such selective problems that it seemed unlikely a particular drug would be uniquely helpful.

But my scepticism changed to belief. Patients in the study started to improve after three weeks on clomipramine. They did not improve with placebos, which we also gave every patient in what we call a 'double-blind' trial. A placebo is an inert substance that looks like the real medicine but has no action. In such a trial, a patient will have a month or two on one and then on the other; neither they nor we know which phase is placebo and which is the real drug until after the study is over.

Gerald, for example, aged fifteen, was a junior in vocational high school where he was learning to assemble and repair complex electronic equipment like his electrician father did. The future seemed secure for Gerald. The electronics firm, the largest employer in his small Indiana town, had promised him a good job when he graduated. But two years earlier, following a seemingly minor event – an electric blanket had caught fire, and was quickly extinguished at no harm to Gerald or to his room – Gerald had begun to brood about ideas of harm coming to his family or friends.

To ward off these thoughts, he felt compelled to wash. The washing lasted two to three hours each day when thoughts preoccupied him. His work at school started to slip; he avoided school and finally was unable to get there at all.

Gerald's family had heard of our study with the new drug from a local television programme. Gerald was shy and uncomfortable with the large-hospital atmosphere. During the first five weeks he received a placebo (as we found out later). During his time on placebos, Gerald was discouraged and could hardly keep up with the ward routine, often staying alone in his room to avoid anything that might set off his washing rituals.

During the second five-week treatment period, the clomipramine part of the trial, there was an unexpected change in Gerald. At first we thought perhaps he was worse. He was telling us about more symptoms than he had ever had and he seemed much more concerned about the way these symptoms got in the way of his real life. He spent much more time trying to explain how he felt. But this, paradoxically, was a sign that he was getting better. He had started to take the study seriously; he had started to tell us what was really on his mind. Over a period of a few weeks, it became clearer that Gerald was getting much better. He emerged as an enthusiastic, hard-working, attractive young man. His student-volunteer work in the hospital electronics shop was exemplary, and he was given a glowing recommendation by his supervisor. He warmed to the ward personnel. It was a pleasure to see Gerald come alive. He became interested in life in Washington and took trips into town to visit museums. Gerald joked that the guys back home would think he was a sissy, but he liked seeing that stuff, so he didn't care. Amazingly, his rituals faded. He still had some fleeting scenes of family harm, some bursts of washing, but these were weak, minor footnotes in his thinking, hardly noticed unless he was asked about them.

My enthusiasm for the medication was raised by the dramatic response of several other very impaired teenagers like Gerald and by the relief of their families and therapists. When a new drug appears, you want to know not only if it works, but whether it is better than other drugs already available.

Since we treated Gerald, we have found out just how good

clomipramine is. It is much better than another antidepressant, desmethylimipramine (DMI). DMI is like its 'parent' compound, imipramine, a good antidepressant, just as good for depression as clomipramine. But for OCD, clomipramine is much better. To compare two treatments, the patients took one for five weeks and then took the other. To keep the comparison unbiased, studies were done double-blind. The results of the comparison between clomipramine and the other antidepressant were clear. DMI, our comparison drug, was no more effective than the placebo. Whatever clomipramine does in the brain, it is something very specific: it fixes compulsions and obsessions.

When such a special treatment is found we have taken a big step closer to understanding the physiology of a disease, perhaps to understanding the physiology of the mind.

While clomipramine and its selective positive effect on obsessions still fascinates me, it is not a panacea. What looked like a 'miracle cure' at first may offer only a partial improvement. For at least a third of our patients, it gives no help at all. We don't know why that is. First we looked to see if the non-responders had built up lower blood levels of the drug and hadn't got into some therapeutic range, but that was not the case. Nothing that we see clinically seems to predict who will be helped by clomipramine. The drug can work in very severe cases or in mild cases. There are some early research findings from research laboratories in Sweden and in our own country that show that patients with higher serotonin (measured in blood platelets or in cerebrospinal fluid) may be better responders. That fits with the theory that the drug acts on the serotonin system.

No one really knows how the drug works and why it works for one person and not the other. But it *has* catapulted this obscure and dreadful disorder into a new importance: a problem that might get solved.

Clomipramine is available on prescription in Britain but is still not available in the United States. Since pursuing this treatment, I have had the unlikely job of helping people bring an unlicensed drug into America. Customs sometimes intercepts, but the frustrations of getting approval for good new treatments is a subject for another book.

My drug study brought me into many lives that had been crippled by OCD. The stories of my patients' struggles with this modern day possession are important to understand. Whether you know it or not, you *do know* someone with this disease.

11

David's Drug Odyssey

The amazing selectivity of a drug's effect provides some of psychiatry's best clues to understanding the biology of a mental illness. Sometimes these clues come from unusual sources. A patient named David gave us a remarkable account of the biology of obsessions and compulsions based on his experiences with illegal drugs. His story was a 'natural' experiment.

David, a darkly handsome eighteen-year-old, was sophisticated and streetwise. Two months earlier, David had turned himself in to a Baltimore drug and alcohol treatment programme. For a year, he had drunk half a case of beer every day and, since the age of fourteen, he had used and abused speed (amphetamines), angel dust (PCP), cocaine, barbiturates, Valium, as well as LSD and something David called 'shroom' (psilocybin). He had used each of the drugs at least twenty times, and some hundreds.

David missed so much school that he was expelled in his last year. He had been in several driving accidents and his licence was revoked. Surprisingly, David had kept up a façade of 'togetherness' at home that completely fooled his parents, two harried lawyers who were often out of town. But when he was arrested for theft, they finally became involved.

Only after he began the drug rehabilitation programme did David tell his counsellor what he had hidden from everyone more carefully than he had hidden his drug habit: that he had had 'crazy thoughts and things he had to do' – mostly counting up to 22 over and over again. He had had these thoughts for years before the drug problem began. David was also washing his hands, an hour at a time. But it was the counting that ruined his days. When the 'counting fits' came on, he had to stop whatever he was doing to tap on the wall 22 times, or in multiples of 22. He had to walk in and out of doorways 22 times, or get up and down out of his chair 22 times.

The counsellor sent David to us. David was very interested in our study and, because of his own experiments, accepted more readily than our other patients the notion that a particular drug could improve his obsessions.

David had made a distinction in his own mind between three classes of drug effects, based on what they did to his obsessions and compulsions. Amphetamine and cocaine made his rituals worse. Much worse. Because he was 'hooked' on these drugs, he took them often, and when he did the rituals increased so much that he spent his 'high' tapping out 22s all over his wall. Alcohol, Valium, and angel dust made him feel better in a general all-over sort of way, but the rituals just went on as usual, neither more nor less intensely. What mattered to David was that two of his drugs, 'shroom' and LSD, made the rituals and thoughts disappear completely for five or six hours after he took them. By now each drug was completely predictable.

David wondered if we could explain how this happened. We thought that we could. Psilocybin and LSD act on a chemical system of the brain that regulates a neurotransmitter – the serotonin system. Neurotransmitters are chemicals that are released from nerve cells and carry messages to other cells or other parts of the brain. Nerve cells are highly specialized and one particular type of neurochemical may carry a particular message to one particular type of cell. The other drugs on David's list do not affect the serotonin system. What impressed us so much with David's story was how the drugs fit together with how we think that clomipramine works. Both clomipramine and David's 'good' drugs have specific effects on the serotonin system, and probably increase serotonin, at least in some areas of the brain.

Amphetamine and cocaine made David worse. This made sense too. These drugs have a strong effect on the dopamine system. Dopamine is another neurotransmitter, but one which acts *against* the serotonin system. We think that clomipramine increases serotonin and amphetamine increases dopamine in the basal ganglia. These are the parts of the brain that we believe don't function well in Obsessive–Compulsive Disorder. The drugs with no special effect on David's obsessive symptoms don't do much to either the dopamine or the serotonin systems.

The next question was, of course, would clomipramine help David? David's self-experimentation had told us he should be a 'serotonin subject': he should improve on the drug that increased brain serotonin.

The first five weeks in the study (which turned out to be on DMI, the 'control' antidepressant drug) didn't do a thing for David. But in the last half of the study, he had the first relief from his counting that he had had in four years, with the exception of his few hours of freedom on LSD.

Cases like David's are one of the most valuable parts of a clinical researcher's work. The leap from a particular clinical case, from one patient's story, to learning how the brain works was what tempted me into medical research in the first place. The unique aspect of the clinical researcher's life is the opportunity to go back and forth from real life to the laboratory.

Because they also have their effects mainly on the serotonin system, newer drugs are now being tried for Obsessive–Compulsive Disorder. Two – fluoxetine and fluvoxamine – seem promising. Fluoxetine has just become available in the US but has not yet been well studied for OCD. Fluvoxamine is not yet available in the US but is on the market in Britain and several other countries. They may be as good as clomipramine, although it is too soon to be sure yet.

A postscript about David: At the end of his treatment with us, he said it had been harder to tell his family about his obsessions than about his drug problem. 'You see,' he said, '*everyone* was doing drugs. But I didn't know anyone else who had to count.' A recent national survey of psychiatric disorders found that patients with Obsessive-Compulsive Disorder (compared with the general population) are more likely to abuse drugs. It is possible that they, like David, were trying to treat their own illness.

12

How Sweet It Is!

After the television show '20/20' featured OCD on 21 March 1987, we were flooded with calls. It took months to respond to them, and in the process we heard some remarkable stories from patients with OCD and from their families. I and my staff met weekly to sift through the two thousand calls; volunteers (patients and their families from our previous studies) sent out information to each caller. Most were referred to the treatment centre nearest them. We met a few who were appropriate for our studies. But the call I found the most intriguing was about sugar:

The woman's voice quavered over the telephone. 'I saw the programme about compulsions on "20/20", but I don't think anyone has ever heard of a problem like mine.' She then related a version of this illness that I had never come across, and one that in its way was as devastating as any form I had seen. She *did* have OCD, of that I am sure. I never saw her – she got lost in a paper deluge during that month when our (usually well-organized) staff was overwhelmed by telephone calls. But we spoke at length, and the conversation still haunts me.

Miss X began her compulsions in mid-life. In that aspect she was already different from the rest of my patients, most of whom start their disorder before the age of forty, the age at which Miss X began to have her problem.

Miss X was born to be a spinster, she told me, always liked a neat house, and loved to cook. Men were trouble, always messing everything up. So far, she sounded ripe for being a 'straightener' or possibly a 'checker', perhaps even a straightforward cleaner or washer. But that was not her story.

'Dr Rapoport, please don't laugh. My problem is sugar, confectioners' sugar.'

'Sugar?' I said.

'That's right, sugar. You know, the fine powdered kind.'

'What about it?' I asked dubiously.

'Well it happened suddenly,' she said. 'About twenty years ago, I got the urge to see how it would be, I mean to see how it would *feel*, if there were confectioners' sugar sprinkled about in my flat. You know, the way you put it on top of a cake.'

'You put it around your flat?' I asked.

'That's right. I have the sprinkler for putting powdered sugar on my baked things. It's a little can with a handle and tiny holes on the top. I used that.'

'Where did you sprinkle it?'

'Oh, just about everywhere. It just *didn't feel right* if I didn't get the sugar everywhere. It had to be even. I put it on the floor, on the furniture. I only stopped when I ran out of confectioners' sugar. The regular kind wouldn't do. Somehow I knew that.'

'What happened then?'

'Well, it was a mess of course. But at least I could rest. It was better having the sugar there than not having it and not being able to concentrate. If I didn't do it, I'd feel awful.'

'You've been doing this for twenty years?'

'On and off. That's the point. Sometimes the feeling goes away for months, and then I can clean up. That's a relief too. I can invite people to the house, and get everything unsticky.'

Miss X promised to write. As I said, this was during our busiest month. I was certain I had filled out one of our clinic mailing forms before we said goodbye. I promised to put her in touch with a colleague in New York (where Miss X and her presumably sugar-filled flat were located).

I never found the form and she never called again. All the questions came to mind the next day: What about ants, cockroaches, and so on? Were there other culinary compulsions? Did she still cook? What did the flat look like? Had anybody seen it at its worst?

I like to think that the information I gave Miss X was useful. Perhaps she tried behaviour therapy (my first suggestion) or clomipramine (my second). I hope she now holds her sugar sprinkling can over cakes.

13
The Hidden

Psychiatrists survey a whole community to understand a population and its health. Patients in clinics may not be like patients 'out there'. It could be that doctors see a problem in only one particular form or only in certain combinations. Perhaps only the most complicated or the most ill cases show up. For some treatments, only the least sick, the most able to pay, or those who keep appointments are seen.

Epidemiology is the assessment of how often what illnesses affect a population as a whole and in parts at different times. The last ten years has seen a revolution in American psychiatry. Psychiatric epidemiology has come into its own. With the development of more standardized ways to make psychiatric diagnoses, diagnostic interviews were developed that were suitable for surveys of whole communities. We were luck to be studying OCD in the 1980s. We could start to answer the question: If you say there are so many 'cases' of OCD, where are they and how are they getting on?

I usually do most of my work at my desk. I meet with staff, see patients, talk on the phone, edit medical reports, and so on. But in 1985 I took part in an epidemiological survey that got me out of my office. I went on a strange hunt, looking for obsessive-compulsive patients who weren't looking for help. It was an epidemiological survey, a survey of a community, which meant *we* had to go to *them*. The point was to see how common the problem was and to see how people with 'undiscovered' OCD got by.

For twelve months, I was back in high school, or rather, high schools. I sat in school 'health rooms' and talked with pupils. When I was a kid, the scale and the cabinet with the red cross on it meant Medicine and Science to me. Now it was strange to sit in these overheated, poorly painted (green was still standard) health rooms as the teenagers shuffled in. One interview every two hours. It was a rural school system, five hours drive from the National Institute of Mental Health. My team and I were sometimes displaced to libraries or corridors (a busy high school is a terrible place to conduct a private interview) when the school nurse needed her space. We were tolerated outsiders, administering a 'health survey' to politely bored pupils.

On slow days we asked ourselves: 'What are we doing here?' Unemployment was high; kids were more worried about finding a job than about finding a date. Most looked blank when we asked about 'habits' like washing or counting that wouldn't go away.

It felt naked to work without an office. It was peculiar to walk into a building each day where no one knew you. But we wanted to know about the cases that weren't looking for us, and this was the only way to meet them.

The unlikely experience of going back to high school proved worth the trouble. For one group of pupils, the interview wasn't at all boring; in fact for them, our questions were amazing. They had never expected to talk about their problem with anyone. Here were these people asking about the 'other life'. This was exactly what we were looking for, cases 'out there' in the community. Most obsessive–compulsives never tell anyone about their symptoms. We wanted to find out why they never tried to get help. What had they told themselves about these peculiar thoughts and habits? Did *anyone* know?

Fred was the first case our survey found. He came twenty minutes late for his appointment.

'I'm always late,' he apologized.

'How come?' I asked.

'I just do everything slowly, so I'm always late, that's all.'

'Doesn't that make trouble for you?'

'Sure. My friends don't like to wait. I never get through with my work.'

'Is the work hard at school?'

'Not really. It should be easy. But I have to check it so much. Over and over again. I'm never finished.'

Fred had never known anyone else who took four-hour showers or who washed their hands one hundred times a day.

I asked him why he thought he did these things. He answered: 'I'm just different. I guess there is something wrong with me. But no one would understand. When I was little, I used to believe that God put these ideas in my head. I'd fall asleep pretending I was picked out for some sort of special test by God. I'd say to myself, "God is going to come and explain why he made me so different. Everyone will stop teasing me then." '

Fred recited the same odd list of symptoms I had heard for years in my clinic. They had been there almost as long as he could remember.

'I'm tired of having to do these things,' he confessed. 'Like the numbers, everything in fours, avoiding sixes, and having to look at things just a certain way.'

'What way?'

'Well, like I look at the clock in my room, and then look at the door. And I have to see the bottoms of my feet and that looks silly to my friends.'

'Do they make fun of you?'

'No, they're pretty nice. But they ask if I'm okay, and know when they have to leave me alone.'

Fred was still pretty upbeat. He knew he could lick this, or learn to live with it. He knew he'd like himself no matter what.

Fred's grandmother had died a year ago. Now he had no one to talk to. His mother had all she could do to manage two shift jobs since his dad left. 'Everyone has so much on their mind,' he said. Most of the children in that rural school system had worse troubles in their families. They kept these habits to themselves. I gave Fred a number to telephone. He promised he would, but I knew he wouldn't.

The twenty teenagers in our high school survey who had Obsessive-Compulsive Disorder had never talked about these problems. Most had been suffering for years. As we 'hit' true cases, we heard stories of lonely and odd childhoods. A plump teenage girl named Debby admitted that she counted certain numbers for hours each day.

'This is really wild. I never told *anyone* about the numbers. They keep going over and over. They've been there for years.'

'What did you think they were?' I asked.

'When I was six I heard about the cricket that followed Pinocchio. I thought I had a little voice in my head like Cricket who put numbers there. But Cricket was supposed to be a helper, and I never could see what good this did. I waited to find out what Cricket was going to do. I told myself, ''Any day now he'll get round to fixing it.'' '

Debby was one of a dozen children I met who had their own 'science-fiction' story to explain the 'planted' thoughts.

Three of these students had in fact gone to see a psychologist. But they went to talk about *other* problems, not about ritual washing or the weird thoughts. Those were too private and too humiliatingly crazy. They never considered talking about them. These kids were terrific actors. They devised gimmicks, movements, and excuses to hide their rituals or preoccupations.

'How do you keep your friends from finding out about the habits?' I asked Debby.

She took on a wide-eyed, scatterbrained, Goldie Hawn-type look as she told me: 'I'm always late for dates, and running to the bathroom. My friends think I am such an air-head, and I let them think that. But I'm very organized and serious. Nobody knows me at all. No one knows about my counting and checking.

'When I have to check something, or wash, I bat my eyes and say ''I just *must* do my hair. It's *such* a mess,'' or something like that, and they just laugh as I go off. Maybe some actors get started because they have something to hide.'

Stories like this made the trips worthwhile. Our findings from our clinic were valid; the clinic cases were like the untreated cases. Twenty doesn't sound like so many but to find this number in an ordinary high school system supported the surveys done previously. Those surveys were with adults; now we were repeating the findings with teenagers.

From the number of cases we found, and from the way we chose those to interview, the epidemiologist on our team could calculate the probable percentage of teenagers with OCD in the country. Their calculations surprised all of us. There were more than a million teenagers and many more adults in America suffering from this disease. Why hadn't anyone known? The answer is that obsessive–compulsives usually don't go for help. Perhaps because they never thought there would be any help.

No one had looked for them, either.

We went back to see all of our cases in 1987, two years later. I sat with Fred on the front steps. I had phoned the day before to get directions and he had set the time. But it was half an hour before he came downstairs. From the way his mother apologized I saw it must happen a lot; he was stuck doing something over and over again. Fred finally came down. The housing project was crowded, a TV and, for some reason, a police radio were both blaring inside.

We sat on the concrete steps. Fred looked simply terrible. He had lost twenty pounds.

'Did you get here all right?' he asked. 'I was worried the directions weren't clear.' I told him they were fine.

'I don't do a good job giving directions. Not at anything else either,' he added. 'I remember you. You came to the school and asked about how things were going.'

'How have the last couple of years gone?' I asked.

'Fine,' he said. 'I don't have a problem any more.'

'How do you mean?'

'Well, I realized that this is how God made me and how I am supposed to be. I just *should* be cleaning all the time. When the other kids tease me, and call me Mr Clean, I just ignore it. Now I *want* to do these things. I make myself want to, because it's something I can't change.'

Things weren't going well. Fred still took four showers a day, each lasting half an hour. He had thoughts that frightened him about his parents dying. And he checked his homework over and over again so he couldn't finish. He was barely passing. When I was ready to leave, he told me he didn't sleep well, that he lay in bed for hours until he fell asleep and a few hours afterwards he was up again. He would think about how he felt lonely and upset all the time, about whether he did anything wrong during the day.

'But I've got to live with this, there isn't anything else to do. So I'm learning to like it.'

I started to argue, but it wasn't going to help.

14

No Joke

A lot of people like to tell jokes. Most don't do a very good job of it, but can telling jokes be a compulsion? A little while ago I would have answered, 'Of course not.' Now I have met someone for whom it is. Sometimes it is very hard to tell what a compulsion is. We have been able to recognize the 'classical' patients: the ones who wash and check, the children who are sure they have killed someone, and those with terrible unacceptable thoughts in their head. But the boundaries of the problem still puzzle us. Murray, it turned out, was a compulsive joke teller. But he, or rather his problem, wasn't funny, and had a lot of people fooled.

We almost did not see Murray because his parents could not agree on anything, even Murray's appointment time. He lived in one state with his mother and stepfather; his father and stepmother lived in another state. The fights between his natural parents were remarkably intense when one realized that they had both remarried, apparently happily, five years ago. Before we even met Murray, we were being telephoned each day by one parent or the other. 'Do you see children who have to tell silly jokes?' they would ask. 'Of course,' we said, 'but not in this clinic.'

We finally set some rules about who would bring Murray, when, and how. That helped us deal with Murray's parents, but still left him with a most unusual and, it turned out, most troublesome problem.

We weren't sure if we should treat Murray. Some years earlier, when he was twelve, he had started to wash excessively, and to check that his wardrobe door was closed. This had taken up hours of each day, but all by itself the problem had faded without any special treatment. Now Murray's main complaint, and that of his school and his family, was that he had to tell jokes. He had to tell bad jokes in the middle of class, and in spite of angry teachers, irritated classmates, and threatening principals.

This still did not sound like any of the rest of our patients. This unhappy family, or rather families, had travelled long distances for us to hear very silly jokes from an otherwise very smart fourteen-year-old boy! I thought this *was* a bad joke. We wondered whether Murray could be so fed up with these squabbling adult caretakers that perhaps he was creating a diversion – anything to stop their bickering? But when Murray started to explain, we saw that this was not a silly child.

Murray, a pudgy boy, with a slight tic, a kind of wincing movement in his right eye, explained, 'I'll be sitting in class in my school, and I am paying attention, and know the answers. Then, the thought "joke" comes into my mind, and I *have* to start. You see,' he said in a rush, hardly able to talk fast enough, 'it just hits. I raise my hand, start to giggle, and *have* to tell the jokes. It's a kind of an attack or something.

'I know there is no discussion allowed in class, and the teacher will get angry, but I still can't help it. So I say, "I have a joke to tell." The teacher says, "Not now, Murray," but by then, I've started.'

I interrupt, 'Didn't it get you into trouble?'

'Yes,' Murray nodded miserably, 'I have been suspended about a dozen times, and now I can't go back, and I had good grades, and wanted to go to college and now I don't know what we'll do.' He started to cry. Once he started, he just let go and sobbed. This was no joke.

'Okay,' I asked, after he was calm again, 'can you show us? Will you tell us the joke?' At this point, Murray got a fixed look on his face, a far away silly stare like Lou Costello in the old Abbott and Costello movies. He started, mechanically, to tell a 'joke'. 'Lemme tell you a joke,' he insisted, but the joke consisted of a silly two-year-old's sentence, 'A man put his head in a pail of water,' and Murray clutching his sides, laughed convulsively. Another 'joke' followed. This time about someone getting covered with mud, 'A man falls in the mud.' But this was not a two-year-old, but a worried, scared fourteen-year-old.

By now anyone could see that Murray didn't really think it was funny. When the 'spell' was over, he said, 'Good, it's gone now!' He was truly forced to act like this. The joke telling had got him expelled from the best school in his town. Murray saw his life collapsing. Worst of all, he hadn't met anyone who understood anything he was going through. The teachers, his friends, and most of his family thought he was disobedient and crazy, and most of the time everyone was furious with him.

Since Murray had had earlier periods of washing and counting, we at least knew that he had had Obsessive–Compulsive Disorder. It just wasn't clear if the joking was part of the same problem. I was sure we had never seen anything like this. So were the three neurologists who had seen him before he got to us.

I gave Murray clomipramine for a month. The jokes went away. The school took him back: a success! His family is still fighting but his work on the school newspaper and soccer practice keep him busy and, as far as we can tell, no longer in the middle of the family fights. When he stopped the medicine, some months later, the jokes started to come back.

The best sense we could make out of Murray's case was that his problem might have been related to another disorder, Tourette's Syndrome which, as I have said before, is related to Obsessive–Compulsive Disorder. In that disease the victims have tics and make noises. Sometimes the noises are words, particularly four-letter words, insulting or obscene words, or phrases that are unacceptable for the patient's particular situation.

The type of words and phrases vary with the background of the patient and the particular situation he or she is in. For example, one patient of mine in polite company had to use four-letter words, but once, on a plane to Miami, he had to gag himself to stop from shouting out 'Hijack!' This was right after a number of planes had been hijacked to Havana from this route. There were warnings on the plane that even joking about hijacking was a punishable offence. Whatever the 'programme' in the brain is, in this disease the instructions to the patient from this sick ritual are: 'Say or do the most unacceptable.' In Murray's school for gifted, mature boys, the 'unacceptable' was being silly. *Obsessing about doing* the unacceptable thing is more typical of OCD; *really doing it* is more like Tourette's Syndrome.

Murray is well now. He has no tics and no more impulses to tell his jokes. He only took clomipramine for a year and it has been three and a half years since I first met him. Murray is sure that the drug 'fixed' him. He plans to be a doctor and do medical research. I am not so sure any more how much the drug really did. Usually, when clomipramine really helps, people have to stay on it for a long time. And both OCD and Tourette's Syndrome can go away on their own – again, no one knows why.

15

The Music Goes Round and Round

Don was standing by the window talking intently on the telephone. Aged sixteen, he was a thin, articulate boy who, in typical teenage style, became irked at my interruption.

He seemed even more like the suburban high school pupil he was when he started to tell me about the rock tunes in his head. 'They stay with me, Dr Rapoport, and I can't get them to go away.'

'Yes, yes,' I said, 'we *all* get tunes in our head. Just the other day, I saw a new show, and I have been humming the tune for days now,' I said agreeably. 'I was talking about it just this morning.'

'No,' said a now uncool, serious Don, who looked as if he would cry. 'That isn't how it is at all. This is what I'm in the hospital about. You see, the tunes chase everything else away. It's awful.'

There must be a mistake, I thought to myself. What is this boy doing in our study of Obsessive–Compulsive Disorder? 'Don't you wash or check or count?' I asked.

'Sure, I *used* to do that, but only a little. I did everything twice, and only even numbers were okay. I washed my hands seven or eight times a day.' Don seemed bored and impatient recounting this.

'But none of *that* was what really got me in trouble. It's the music that goes around and around. It's over and over again.'

'What kind of music?' I asked.

'Well, sometimes it is a frightening sort of background music, like in the old adventure movies when the villain is walking towards you, and you have this sort of droning.'

Don had talked to a psychologist for four years, about being anxious, and having trouble getting on with other kids. But he had *never* mentioned the tunes in his head. Why not? Well, at first he had thought that this was like everyone else. Later he wasn't sure if other people heard music like he did. He never thought it was important. It had been there for so long, he was used to it.

'You have to see how it is with these tunes,' he pleaded. 'Other people joke when they complain about tunes stuck in the head, but basically they *enjoy* it. Mine are never enjoyable. They continue for hours, days, weeks, months and years. They cannot be blocked out, these songs are like free spirits who come and go whenever they please.

'For example, last summer [the summer of 1985], the rock group Tears for Fears had a hit song called ''Everybody Wants to Rule the World''. It wasn't such a great song. But it was in my head for a year. This has been happening really badly since I was nine.'

'Trying to adjust to these songs is very hard. I have to put in two hundred per cent of the effort other people do just to do everyday things. The songs cause chaos in my mind, tiring me, and wasting most of my time. And the songs are each connected to a memory.'

'But aren't songs connected for everyone?' I interrupted.

'Not the way they are with me. It's a sequence that has to be thought. I hate moving, and the songs are each connected to particular places I've been. But they aren't places I care about so much, just places that the songs are attached to. The songs are like labels for places and it all could be a list of names. Instead it's songs.'

Don did have obsessions – they were tunes. While there are some very rare kinds of epilepsy that can include brief fugue states in which music is heard, there is *nothing* else that makes music stay for years. There are rare brain tumours, in the temporal lobe, that might conceivably cause such an experience for a while, even for months, but Don's CAT scan of his brain did not show any such tumour. And the tunes had been with him for years. A tumour would have shown up by now.

In Don's case, we were also sure that the tunes were obsessions because Don had had the other symptoms – washing, counting and checking – that were typical. The tunes in some way felt sort of the same. There was nothing pleasant in these tunes: they were senseless, just stuck in his head, a relentless repetitive force that is the essence of any obsession. He had to fight against the music just to get on with his day.

Most of the images in obsessive–compulsive experiences are visual. There are, however, infrequent cases of images that are other than visual. Textbooks have referred to tunes in the head. One medical journal reports a twenty-three-year-old student who could not rid his consciousness of a currently popular tune. Another medical journal discusses an elderly man who heard a senseless phrase – 'These boys when they were young' – in his own voice over and over again. Shortly after I met Don, a second person asked me to help get rid of a tune.

George K., a farmer from Maine, telephoned after he learned about our project on '20/20'. He had had at least six notes of a fiddle tune playing in his head for thirty-one years. No one in town knew; he had kept it secret from his wife for the early years of their marriage.

George's wife had died a year ago. He wasn't well now, and couldn't get to Washington, but when I was in Boston a few months later, he came to the clinic I was visiting and I heard his story.

As a young man, when it first started, he had wondered why this had happened to him. Never one for introspection, he hadn't come up with much. He liked music on the radio, but wouldn't go out of his way to listen to any. There had been a pretty good fiddler at a party he went to when he was younger. But that fiddler played good tunes, and a lot of different ones, not like this dull, short, sort of jig that was stuck in his head now, repeating itself over and over again.

George and his wife didn't have secrets from each other and he finally had to tell her. 'I just blurted it out one day, when I was so down about it,' he told me. 'I was scared she'd laugh at me, but never expected her to just sit down and cry like she did. Then she came over and thanked me. She looked happy. She told me she always saw me looking so serious and bothered and had always thought I was angry with her, or else bored with everything she said because I never really listened like I should. I should have told her a long time before, but I thought she'd think I was crazy. After that she was so much happier, and I worried a lot less about it.'

George didn't like leaving his farm, but twice had travelled to a famous Midwestern medical centre to get help. Twice they ran tests, examined his hearing, interviewed him for other 'hallucinations', consulted neurologists, psychologists, and inner ear specialists and conferred. Twice he was told that they didn't know what it could be.

George's wife died of a stroke; she had had hypertension. He was sixty now, and he had high blood pressure too. He felt pretty sick from the medicine he had to take, though he still worked his farm, and never planned to do anything else if he could help it. He had come to accept the tune as a constant unpleasantness, a bore, and an irritation. But he was used to, as he put it, 'living my life through the noise'. But since he had seen the television programme, he had started hoping, for the first time in years, that he could get rid of his tune, 'just to see what it would be like to spend a day without it.'

I gave George only a small amount of clomipramine, because of his other medical problems. He also took some L-tryptophan, the amino acid that is a precursor of serotonin, which may make a small dose of clomipramine more potent. His own doctor followed up on him, but George and I kept in touch. After two weeks, the tune had grown weaker. It was still the same tune, though fading out, he said, like a radio programme with the reception going down as you drive along a road away from a town. Finally, after more than three months, it was really gone. George said he'd never be off the medicine. He looked thoughtful. 'The silence is so restful,' he told me, 'I only wish my wife was here. I could really listen to her. She said I never listened.'

These specific musical types of OCD are quite rare; visual images are also relatively uncommon among our patients. But because OCD is so much more common than we ever believed, it is likely that there are several thousand others like Don and

George walking around who think that only *they* have the tunes, who don't know that they might be helped through drugs and/or therapy. Unless you spend time talking about such things (something our patients avoid most of their lives), you never will find out about help. Repetitive tunes in the head are hardly an everyday topic; and anyway, obsessives are a secretive group. Possibly only musicians would have trouble concealing this affliction, as the repeating tunes could influence their composition.

Have there been musicians with obsessive tunes? A candidate is Erik Satie (1866–1925). Although he lived alone in Paris and at times in great poverty, he dressed fastidiously, and his personal trappings were typical of OCD. No one was allowed to enter his room during his life. When he died, his wardrobe was found to contain a dozen identical new suits, shirts, collars, hats, walking sticks, and a cigar box was found with several thousand pieces of paper with the same symbols and inscriptions, all of them, for some unknown reason, about Charlemagne.

Satie's OCD may have also influenced his music, though this is less clear. Satie's 'trinitarian obsession', as musicologists refer to it, was manifested in his works, which were frequently conceived in groups of three. Within his music, Satie wrote, he intended to present different views on a theme. Almost always, three were offered, the three 'Gymnopédies' being the best known.

The images in Obsessive–Compulsive Disorder are concrete and detailed. They are not hallucinations; they are seen as definite projected images recurring in the same form, down to the same detail. Obsessive images come from 'inside', unlike hallucinations which are seen 'out there'. All that obsessive images have in common with hallucinations is that neither patient wants them around!

In spite of the many psychological studies on imagery, there remains a controversy about the nature of the mental image. It has been suggested that images have no true pictorial quality. Images have been proposed to be vague, more a scheme for representations than truly representational. But OCD patients' images were, in fact, the *tune*, the *entire literal* tune, with never a variation. Obviously then, at least some mental images have great detail, vividness, and concreteness.

Again I must end with puzzlement. These odd manifestations of OCD do not fit well with any of our models. We are certain that they *are* part of OCD because, typically, patients such as Don with tunes in his head had other periods of washing, checking, and so on. And, too, these cases respond selectively to clomipramine. But what fixes these tunes or phrases so firmly in their minds? What force keeps the tune going? Is hearing a tune a ritual, a form of compulsion? Or is it more like an obsession, an intense preoccupation with a particular sequence of notes? When I can't get a tune out of my head – and this *has* happened to me for a few hours each day for a few days at a time – is this a minor hiccup of *my* mind?

I am the doctor and still I wonder about myself . . .

16

My Mind on My Mind

The neighbour of a friend telephoned. Arthur, his sixteen-year-old son, was having problems. Would I see him? Arthur wasn't going to school any more, wasn't talking to the family, and now wouldn't get out of bed. His father told me about doctors Arthur had seen for more than a year and medicines he had tried. But the boy just seemed to get more and more morose; he was no longer the happy-go-lucky kid they had known.

Arthur, plagued by acne, red-eyed, miserable, was not happy to see me. 'The last thing I need is another shrink! No one would understand. It's crazy.' He knew, he told me, that if he even opened his mouth I would pronounce him insane, and that anyhow nothing ever does much good. 'It just goes over and over again in my head. I don't even want to play soccer any more, and I was the star of my school team.' Homework was never terrific, but 'I can't ever finish anything now because the words get in the way.'

Arthur didn't quite make sense. Not because he was hard to

follow, but because what he described didn't quite fit with any of the disorders I was used to treating. I wasn't thinking about obsessions and compulsions then; the research at the NIMH was just starting. But as I listened, the pattern became clearer.

First we spent hours of verbal fencing while he tried to find out whether I thought he was crazy. 'Do you talk to people who are *really* crazy?' he asked. 'Sometimes,' I said. 'Can you not be crazy, but have thoughts that are *driving* you crazy?' he asked. 'It sounds to me like that's what's happening to you,' I told him. Saying this convinced him that I might understand and help. And so it was that I finally heard about what was bothering Arthur so much, what had kept him so miserable for two years.

'How do I know,' he asked, 'how do I know if there is something wrong with my mind?' I started to say something sensible but he stopped me. 'I know, I know,' he said, '*everyone* says that. But how do I *know*? And how do I get the thought out of my mind that there is something *wrong* with my mind? The thought goes over and over again.'

By the fourth 'over and over again', I had begun to catch on. I had been slow because this conversation was taking place in my other office, and not the NIMH, where our work and my mind were focused on this problem. But I finally saw that Arthur had an obsession, and his obsession was *his mind*.

'You're not crazy,' I told him. 'I do think it's likely that you have obsessions; they're much more common that we ever thought. But start from the beginning.' And Arthur, still quite reluctant, began.

Two years earlier, at a school party, Arthur had taken some LSD. He felt 'weird' for a few hours, but was fine the next day, fine until the thought began: *Did the LSD do anything to my mind?* The thought never went away; instead it got more and more complicated. *There must be something wrong with my mind if I am spending so much time worrying about it. Is there something wrong with my mind? Was this from the LSD? Will it ever get better?* Once his school-work started to drop off, everyone treated Arthur as if there were indeed something wrong with his mind. This preoccupation dominated his thoughts, preventing him from studying and having fun.

The family was surprised by my announcement at our next

family session that Arthur suffered from obsessions. He had seen several doctors, and they had been told that he suffered from depression, schizophrenia, drug reaction, but this was a new diagnosis. Moreover, I wanted to start him on clomipramine, a medicine that wasn't even on the market! It sounded like science fiction to them. But they had tried the standard treatments for the other diagnoses and they hadn't worked. At least this was something new. Arthur's father bought the drug in Paris (his work involved frequent travel, so for Arthur's lucky family obtaining clomipramine from a country where it is marketed was simple). Six weeks later, Arthur was back with them, back at school, and back on the soccer team.

The improvement came gradually. First Arthur's mood got brighter, but he still spent most of his time thinking about his mind. Then he told me that even though he thought about 'the mind thought' just as much, it didn't have the importance, the power it did before. He could even shrug it off a little. Finally, the thought would just pop into his head and then pop out before he could even react to it.

During this same period, I learned more about the rest of Arthur. I learned that his father came from an old world culture, unlike his American-born mother, and had always been disappointed in Arthur's easy-going, fun-loving style. It was all right for his sisters to like sports, and to be so close to their mother, but Arthur somehow didn't measure up. I learned, too, that taking LSD that one time had meant risking harsh judgement, and that some of that judgement was self-imposed.

What was unusual about Arthur was that his obsession was so pure: only that one thought! He had no other thoughts and no compulsive rituals. So not only did he have a problem that often is missed by doctors, but he had a somewhat unusual form of it. Ruminations, as Arthur's obsessive thoughts are called, have been known for as long as compulsions; they are not rare. The combination of pure ruminations and their single-thought content had led everyone to miss the diagnosis.

Later, Arthur had a chance to talk with other children in our study, and found a few with the same sort of ideas – ideas that went around and around and took on a life of their own. Over the next few years, Arthur became happier, and there were other changes. He had never liked to bat around ideas before; he couldn't see why some people spent so much time discussing what 'could be'. He tells me that now sometimes his college friends tell *him* their troubles.

Arthur (and I) became complacent for a while, but the complacency didn't last. Every six months or so, it strikes again! His college life will be filled with soccer, skiing, exams, and meeting girls, then out of somewhere, what he calls the 'mind thought' comes back and I will get a call late at night: 'Dr Rapoport, I can't sleep. I *know* there is something the matter with my mind.' He has no more theories to offer about why it happens. Arthur has stayed away from drugs; he has no visions or odd ways of thinking. He has even got some good grades at college.

During these attacks, Arthur 'knows' something is about to snap. Terrified, he can't get his mind off his mind; the old memory of his only experiment with LSD preoccupies him. Worrying about his mind crowds out friends, family, work, everything. Talking to his family, to me, is only faintly reassuring. Medicine, that is, clomipramine, is the only treatment that works, but it only works after a few weeks. Before that takes effect, Xanax, an anti-anxiety drug, seems to help. Until relief comes, Arthur says the wait is the worst time of his life.

'How do you know what I really have?' he asks me over and over again. 'What if you're wrong about my being obsessive–compulsive. What if I'm really schizophrenic?' Arthur is not schizophrenic. He is starting to be somewhat more 'typical' in his obsessions as more general doubts, such as 'Am I doing the right thing?' creep in. The only time he has cried since he was a little boy is during his attacks. With the medicine, however, the doubts always fade within a few weeks.

Arthur wrote from college: 'I think the best thing an obsessive person can do for himself is to attempt, even for brief periods, to not think about it, which is of course what people suggest. It varies from day to day, hour to hour, minute to minute. Part of my obsession now is to constantly search for a common theme in my worries. So even when I'm feeling better I am forced to reflect, which in turn starts the process all over again.

'The guilt is something new. I am doing OK at college, but when I begin to take a few hours off to see an old friend, I start thinking, ''I should be working – I will let down everyone if I don't go back to work.'' So I turn the car around and don't go to see the friend.

'It is better than it was. I don't really worry that I am going crazy, but now there is this feeling of disaster. My thoughts tie themselves into knots. The worry about the worry will make my mind break so then I *really* will have a worry.

'My instinct tells me that it will be very bad for me to let myself go on thinking like this. When I am bad, I withdraw from everyone and then I have that much more time to get into my thinking maze. Then I am back saying to myself: ''Well if you are trying not to think about something, this proves how abnormal you must be so there must be something really terribly wrong with you.'' And that is what I was thinking about anyway. So around and around it goes. This is the best I can do to describe a feeling that must be impossible for someone else to understand.'

In the autumn of 1987, a few months after he wrote this, Arthur became severely depressed while taking clomipramine. The obsessions were no longer his problem. He took a term off from college, and went into psychotherapy. Depression is the most common complication from OCD. For many obsessive patients, the problem of depression is secondary to the handicap caused by the rituals. In Arthur's case, it's puzzling because his rituals were helped by clomipramine. There may be a form of OCD related to depression, but that relationship isn't clear here. When Arthur stops the clomipramine, the obsessions come back. His depression continues. Although psychotherapy seems to help somewhat, it is still to soon to tell if it will cure his depression completely. Meanwhile Arthur copes as best he can. It will probably never be easy for him in this life.

17

Over and Over Again

Stanley's adoptive parents, the Armstrongs, were both research scientists. Raising an adopted child had been easier than they expected: none of the problems they had been warned about had occurred. But now they were upset and bewildered. Stanley had to repeat everything twice – twice, that is, on good days; sometimes it was more often than that. He couldn't stop. The Doctors Armstrong agreed that it had started suddenly, but it was difficult to learn much more than that.

Stanley was a typical 'jock': muscular, crew cut, and with little to say. To the neighbourhood kids, Stanley Armstrong was 'one of the boys', spending free time tossing baskets with friends in his driveway. But that was not the boy I met. He just shook his head and said, 'I have to do things over and over again.' The thoughts and repeating compulsions just wouldn't stop; they took the pleasure out of every sport. Part of the problem was that Stanley was overwhelmed and couldn't talk about it. He had lived for sports; that was where he excelled. The worst part of repeating everything in twos, fours, sixes, or eights or more was how it threw off his game. He could barely compete, much less manage the time and concentration to win.

Stanley and his parents didn't have to say much to convince us he had Obsessive–Compulsive Disorder. He had already spent many futile months trying to talk about his problems with his psychologist. So we gave him clomipramine.

But we weren't able to help Stanley. The drug didn't seem to work for him and the side effects of the medicine – in Stanley's case, muscle tremors – severely limited how much he could take. The compulsions kept on growing, but Stanley was a fighter. All the energy he had put into sports, he told me, now went into fighting the repetitions. He wanted to be a scientist like his parents. He wasn't going to give up anything. I told him if he had that much grit, he'd win whatever fight he fought.

Stanley kept in touch. Seven years later, as a pre-med college student, he called asking for a summer job. He wanted to help us with our study of OCD. We agreed and he was a terrific help in contacting other former patients in a follow-up study. He'd phone and introduce himself and say he had been in the study too, that he hadn't got much better but was still working on it, and what had happened to them? The response was terrific. More than 90 per cent of the patients Stanley phoned co-operated with that follow-up study. That summer, I asked him to write about how his compulsions began. This is the story he told:

All of a sudden, one day in sixth grade [when he was about eleven], placing my shoes down on the floor perfectly became a necessity. 'Perfectly' is the key word for the beginning of my illness. I had to put my shoes down perfectly. I had to write using perfect penmanship, talk perfectly, without any slips of tongue, variations in speech tone, or rate. My steps had to be in perfect cadence with arms as they moved machine-like alongside my body.

Tests on computer-scored paper were a menace: the circle had to be filled in so perfectly that the tests were never finished.

At this stage I had no idea that something was wrong. I thought my slowness was just a part of me, how my personality was. In junior high school, I started delivering papers and then I realized how different I was. I had to look back constantly to see if any papers had dropped off my cart (they never had); I had to go back to each house to see if I had missed a delivery (I never missed). It took me two hours to deliver forty papers; it took other kids one hour. Something compelled me to check, to make sure.

These obsessions were like 'mosquitoes of the mind'. I couldn't make them go away. They wouldn't stop: always there, insistent, itching, a force.

Thinking about cleanliness was part of it too. If something was near me or touched me that I thought was 'impure', I felt uncomfortable. For instance, in Social Studies, in eighth grade [when he was about thirteen], there was an 'unclean' air conditioner next to my seat. Don't ask me why or how something got to be impure; I don't know why, it *just felt that way*.

By high school I was counting numbers. A day would start out being ordinary, and then the only thing on my mind would be '6,

6, 6, 6' or '8, 8, 8, 8'. I had no control over these numbers, they had a mind of their own – *my* mind!

Our Marching Band had a competition during my numbers time, and I got confused by the numbers and didn't keep up with the steps. We lost the competition and I always felt it was my fault, and maybe it was. I was also in the Symphonic Band and during one competition I couldn't play my clarinet because I had so many numbers in my mind that I couldn't concentrate on or 'hear' the music. I only pretended to play. Maybe no one knew about that time, I still wonder if they did.

I tried out for the school golf team, but the cleanliness obsession made me uncomfortable. Hitting the balls would spread the dirt and make things, including me, 'unclean'. I knew that to hit the ball in a clean iron stroke you had to dig into the ground and create a divot. But I couldn't make myself do it. I missed the ball a few times and didn't make the team.

Later on in high school, sexual thoughts became part of it too. I felt guilty that I masturbated, but what was really bad was the obsessive thought that perhaps the neighbours had looked into my window and had seen me. I said to myself that they couldn't see me because of how my bedroom window was placed. But this disease gets ridiculous at times. *I felt sure that they had climbed the roof in order to look in my window.* My mind had to work out how that could really happen because the idea wouldn't go away.

I thought about dying and what a relief it would be. I could never be really *sure* that the neighbours *didn't* see me masturbate. Everything had to be clear-cut, but life never is. Now that I am in college, I know that.

My obsessing has evolved and keeps changing. After the perfection, the numbers, and the sex there has been a more general feeling of depression. My obsessions extended them-selves (I think about them as independent agents) into other areas of my life. I worried about what I said to people, the position in which I kept different features of my face, like my lips and tongue, and about how I appeared to people.

But the worst part, the part that is now hurting my college life, is the way the obsessions take up so much time and mind space that there isn't room for friends, or girls. I don't initiate any kind of relationships. I must force myself to start to talk to people – I can't stand feeling so passive. I know it would pay off. I'd be happier.

I have had times when I was perfectly okay so I do have a perspective on how much I am missing when I am sick. At least I try to learn how to live with the pain, the one that only obsessive–compulsives know. Others can't understand how awful it is, but this story may help some. I hope so.

Stanley's struggle against this disease is successful, as far as external accomplishments go. But every day is a secret war. In a sense he is right; no one will ever really understand, even his doctors. Like several other of our young patients he is applying to medical school; he wants to study OCD. Stanley is a fighter. I'm counting on him for our team.

18

The Secret Life of a Street Person

Since I met Tim, I no longer take for granted that street people are all unemployed alcoholics or schizophrenics. Now I look at the people sleeping on park benches and wonder if some of them really do have a place to go, but can't bring themselves to go there because that's where their rituals hold them prisoner.

Tim looked and sounded like the thirty-five-year-old country lawyer he was. When he talked about his fascination with the law and his interest in becoming a public defender, the soft Georgia drawl had the curious effect on me, a New Yorker, of making him sound particularly clever. In presenting his case, he had an engaging way of summarizing his own story. Looking at this man with the close-clipped red hair, in a well-fitted summer suit, I never would have guessed I was talking to a man who had slept for two years on park benches.

Tim called after he had seen the television programme about OCD. He was interested in our research and in trying the new drug. At first, his story was just more of what I had come to expect in our clinic: he couldn't stop washing. Tim had always been neat even as a small boy. His mother died when he was thirteen, but he thinks in retrospect that she may have been an obsessive–compulsive because, before the family would go on a trip, she would stay up all night and work for days just to make sure that all the clothes – those being worn on the trip and those staying at home in the wardrobe – were washed and ironed, and that all the floors and walls were scrubbed, the patio washed, and the house made spotless. Tim remembers his mother saying about her pre-trip routine, 'We might have an accident and people would come into the house, and it should look neat.' A younger brother used to wash his hands for hours, but Tim didn't know if he still did.

At high school and college Tim kept up the excessive washing. By now we had seen more than a hundred young men in our study and heard endlessly about their struggles with endless showers. Tim's style of talking went with his drawl, low-keyed and slow, but he built up a story so that it got more and more peculiar.

In spite of his struggles with ritual washing, Tim did well at his state university and for a while got the washing down to a manageable amount. His father, a busy local veterinarian, never understood his son's odd habits but was proud of his good grades. He was particularly proud when his son got into law school, where Tim's good study habits and organized mind got him top grades in the class.

Tim's dad told his son: 'I solved my own problems with drive, just drive.' And he had. His grit had overcome poverty, a drinking problem, the death of his mother, and later his wife, at an early age. This tenacity, this determination, was what he had to offer Tim. When Tim tried to explain his habits to his father, his dad would be sympathetic, worried, and puzzled, but his advice finally came down to: 'Why Don't You Just Stop?'

Tim tried at first to explain why he Just Couldn't Stop. 'I lose myself in this,' he'd say. 'There gets to be nothing else and I don't make sense to myself. It isn't something I can stop. Honest.'

'Of course it's hard, Tim, but let me tell you about stopping the drink. It was the hardest thing I ever did. But I stopped . . .' The usual story followed.

Eventually, the father-son conversations stopped. Tim got better at hiding his rituals, as my patients almost always do. But the rituals got worse. By staying up most of the night and napping after school, Tim got in hours of washing and his schoolwork, too. His dad boasted about what a help it was having a son at home, a great help for a busy widower like himself. Tim went off to Atlanta to law school, got a small flat for himself, and for a while he thought his problem was gone.

But at the end of the first year of law school, the rituals took an ominous turn. During the following months, the washing and, now, flat cleaning took over. And one day, the worst and most bizarre chapter of his life began.

'If I started to clean the flat,' Tim told me, 'I could never stop. *The only way to keep the flat clean was to go in it as little as possible.* Once I had got it dirty, I'd have to stay and clean up and I'd never get to college. And I was on the law review! Once I started cleaning, I wouldn't get out of the flat till noon. I had to vacuum until it felt right. Just being there in the room made it feel dirty. As soon as I stepped through the door, the cleaning had to begin. I started missing classes and my grades were starting to slip.

'That summer, I worked at a law firm that knew me from the summer before. But this time it was awful. I'd be late because of the cleaning, and didn't like being criticized for lateness. The result – I received no job offer.

'By my second year, I was desperate. I realized that I couldn't go to my flat during the week or I would never get through college.'

'So where did you stay?' I asked.

'Well, first I tried motels,' Tim answered. 'For some reason, motels were okay. But they were expensive. Besides, I had an awful experience. I think it was the most humiliating thing that ever happened to me. I got stuck showering one night and was in there for twelve hours. The motel manager turned off the hot water. I was just getting the soap off when he also turned off the cold water! Then he was banging on the door and I was out on the street. I offered to pay double, but he just wanted me out of there. He threw me out in the middle of the night and I had no place to go. I spent the night in the street and I realized it was a *big relief.*

'So finally,' Tim went on, 'I took to sleeping in the streets. Park benches were a relief after that. I studied in the library. It was the best sleep I had had in a year.'

'Wasn't it worse – I mean dirtier – sleeping outdoors?' I asked.

'No. That's the funny thing. It was all right in places that I didn't have to take care of. So college, park benches, anywhere away from my flat seemed okay. Of course I felt dirty, and pretty peculiar. It was the strangest thing I ever did at first.'

'That's a lonely life,' I said. I asked Tim what about the police. 'Didn't they bother you?'

'Mostly not. The campus people knew me. The city police hardly ever came around. But once they did.

'It turned out later that they were looking for someone else who looked like me, a man about my age with red hair who was supposed to have sold drugs or something. It was cold that night and I was sleeping in my sleeping bag on a bench on a blanket. It was cold, but I finally got to sleep. The next thing I knew was that someone was shining a light on me in the middle of the night. I woke up to see a gun pointed at me. I saw a policeman behind the gun. He took me down to the station for questioning.

'At the station, they saw from my I.D. that I was a student and that I had an address only a few blocks off campus. They were sure at first the licence was stolen. They phoned around, checked it, and there were no charges. Of course they asked, "Why were you sleeping on the bench?" I thought up some kind of excuse, told them I couldn't sleep, had gone for a walk, and fell asleep on the bench. They were suspicious of me and my sleeping bag but dropped the whole thing. I still have bad dreams about being woken up by a policeman shining a light in my eyes.'

But in spite of these hassles, Tim's compulsions were so potent, he couldn't have done it any other way. The dirt, the loneliness – he had never expected to live like this. But he had hit on something that worked, and there was no way he was going to give it up.

Tim's story is unique. Most severe washers cringe at the start of their routines, and experience a kind of lethargy at the prospect of getting up and beginning their day of tedious routines. But they usually don't discover such a 'dodge'.

Avoidance is a chronic problem for patients with OCD. Tim, however, is the only one I met for whom the need to avoid was so strong that he actually lived in the streets rather than face his flat and 'get it all started'.

Tim graduated from law school and is now working as an attorney. He has done so for more than ten years. He married a classmate. She cleans the flat – not a sex role stereotyping here – because if Tim starts he may not get to do anything else. Marriage and a supportive boss have helped Tim through some rocky years. Sometimes, though, their system has stopped working. Tim has been hospitalized a few times. He and his wife separated once for six months when his washing worsened. At those times, he also got depressed.

This story has a happy ending. Tim has slowly got better, though we could never be sure why. At first it seemed to be the clomipramine. But he had to stop taking the drug because he couldn't tolerate the side effects (sleepiness and nausea), which were unusually strong for him. I thought Tim would relapse but so far he hasn't. While he was taking the drug, Tim saw a behaviour therapist (at our insistence) who made him deliberately and gradually cut down on showering. The therapist also had Tim's wife do less for him.

It's been a few years now, but the last time I saw Tim, he told me that he volunteers some time for legal aid, and never turns down a case if it involves defending a street person. When he passes a man sleeping on a park bench, he always turns around and wonders.

Some patients with OCD can hide from the stimulus that 'turns the OCD on', the way Tim did. Most cannot avoid the switch so effectively. Yet almost every cleaner or washer tells me that being outside or in some public room is almost always easier because those places are *already* dirty. Does this response reflect some atavistic tendency to keep one's nest clean?

19

Count Me Out

I met Laura when she was twenty-two. I had been seeing OCD patients for more than ten years, but the story of her childhood was the saddest one I had ever heard. As a child, Laura had preferred to be treated as mentally retarded rather than tell anyone about her counting. It took the system a long time to find her out.

Laura came to our clinic asking for help with her checking, presently her most disturbing symptom. (Like most of our patients, her rituals had evolved over the years. In fact, she now had several.) Her plain broad face wore a worried look. She was very guarded; finding out anything about her life took a long time.

'How much time do you spend checking?' I wanted to know. 'Oh, not too much.' 'Well, how much is not too much? Do you check things often or for a few hours at a time?' 'It varies a lot.' Working with her was exasperating. No matter what I asked, the answers came back polite but vague. I was used to a certain amount of denial common to most OC patients, but Laura was vague about everything. She paused between words and sentences, during which she stared off vacantly.

I was surprised to learn that she was married and that her husband had taken the day off to come along with her. After we had talked about her marriage for a while, Laura admitted that it was her husband who had got her to come to the clinic. Her checking and washing rituals had to be completed to her satisfaction before she could have anything to do with sex. Their sex life had almost disappeared. Laura talked about this with a vague smile, making me pry to get information. Yet she didn't seem shy so much as preoccupied.

Laura's day was divided equally between checking, counting, and hoarding (like Sal, my first patient, she picked up scraps of paper and took them home). Like so many OCD patients, Laura had to be unusually efficient to go to school, fix meals, and keep up friendships because she had so much less time to do this than the rest of us. But while her husband could tolerate her obsessions and compulsions, he didn't like them, and the sexual problems had got worse during the year they had been married.

The marital stresses weren't surprising; they are common with OCD patients, who are more likely than others never to marry or, if they marry, more likely to divorce. It was her secrecy that seemed extreme – or perhaps 'reserve' was a better word. She kept me at a distance as she stared off into space or turned every question over and over. It took hours to learn anything. This slowness didn't fit with my other clinical experience. I simply didn't know what was going on.

Laura's childhood, to say the least, was not typical. During our third interview, when I was used to the pauses, I asked Laura to tell me about her school days.

'I put myself into the retarded school,' she said. 'I did that when I was eight.'

'What do you mean, "put yourself into retarded school"?'

'That's what I did. I put myself there.'

'Kids don't do that,' I insisted.

'I did, though.' For the first time, Laura cried. At last it felt as if we were in the same room having the same conversation. Her pauses grew shorter.

When Laura was seven she began to exhibit OCD. Her first symptom was hand washing. Within months this soon changed to a compulsion to fill in with a pencil the space in every letter with a closed part that could be filled in – like *o* or *p* or *a*. (Hearing about this reminded me that my college roommate did the same thing. Was it a mild form of disorder or just a doodle?) The most time-consuming ritual of all for Laura was having to count up to fifty in between reading or writing each word. The silent counting had never stopped. Understandably, this made her extraordinarily slow, particularly when she began second grade.

Laura, like all my other patients, hadn't a clue why she had to do these rituals. When she was seven, she had seen a science fiction movie on television about Martians controlling what people on earth did. They were friendly Martians and they were taking over in a peaceful sort of way. She thought that that must be what was happening to her. It certainly wasn't like anything else she ever experienced and, to an eight-year-old's mind, the idea didn't seem so impossible. The thoughts certainly didn't seem like her own, even though they came from inside her head. (I have heard the same story from a dozen OC patients whose OCD started in early childhood. They, too, entertained a science fiction hypothesis about being controlled from outer space because it was the only remotely understandable model they could find.)

'I had this idea,' Laura told me, 'that this was a way for the Martians to make contact with earth. It made me feel important and it was almost worth it some days. Because then there was a reason for it all, and then I was sort of chosen to be special.'

Uppermost in Laura's mind was that *no one* should ever know what she was going through. 'I didn't want everybody to think I was crazy,' she said. There were other children at her school who had learning problems, so when Laura could not finish her tests or show that she had any of the basic skills, she was put in the special class with them.

Because Laura's mother and sister were dyslexic, the school was prepared for Laura to have the same problem. Reading *was* impossible, as she was counting to fifty before continuing when the class was reading out loud. She never really got started before her turn was over. When asked to spell or say letters in class, she had to count in between each word she said so the sentences came out slowly and haltingly. As a result of this behaviour she was put in a special school for mentally handicapped children. Still, Laura didn't tell about the counting.

Perhaps some families might have discovered the truth, but Laura's mother worked two jobs and her father was dead. Grandmother was at home, but Laura now thinks she was demented, though no one realized it at the time. Grandma never seemed to understand what was happening to Laura.

Certainly some school systems would have been suspicious. A clear deterioration in schoolwork is usually a sign of a psychiatric disorder or, rarely, of a neurological condition. But Laura was in a smalltown school in a state that spends little money on its schools. Whatever the reason, Laura just slipped through.

Nights were different. At night when she had finished her rituals, Laura read. Her sister had schoolbooks, and Laura read those. She didn't hide the reading. The rest of the family had other problems and simply didn't pay attention.

What was the worst thing about being in the special school where she didn't belong? 'The worst was being teased by the other kids on the way to class,' she said. 'Kids in the regular school would see the bus go by and they knew where it was going. They'd shout "There go the dummies," and we'd all feel awful. I'd duck my head so my old friends wouldn't see me. At night I'd dream I was back in the old school. But I still was counting, even in my dreams, so I knew it wouldn't work.'

Sometimes the other students scared her. She was bored with the work, but at least the staff left her alone with her ritual counts; no one could stop those. She considered telling a teacher, then thought of the consequences and kept silent. She still did everything with excruciating slowness. No one could help her if she did tell, of this she was sure. At almost all ages, patients quickly catch on that there is little help from even the most sensible people.

Did the teachers ever guess how much she understood? 'Sometimes the teacher stared at me, but I was good at copying the other kids in the class so then teacher left me alone.'

One young teacher, whom the kids called Miss Lucy, almost guessed. She was really interested. Laura almost took her into her confidence. Miss Lucy used to say how Laura 'didn't seem like the others'.

Things straightened out in the peculiar way that can only happen in a second-rate school system. Laura had spent five years in the special school, reading at night, and counting by day. But the special school finished at the eighth grade [around age thirteen] and something had to be done about high school.

The special high school was fifty miles away and it would have been a disaster. Plans were already being made for Laura to live in a foster home for handicapped children. But by some miracle, the compulsions died down for a while. Miss Lucy suggested that Laura be enrolled in the 'slow' class in the local high school for normal children. 'I was so used to counting, I almost didn't know what to do without it. I was even sort of sad for a while that the Martians didn't need me any more. But by then I really knew that it wasn't Martians.'

Laura remembered her first day at the high school: 'I was the only one from the other school ever to go there. I was so scared.' The rest of the class had heard rumours about her and everyone seemed to be whispering. But Laura wasn't the sort of girl to keep anyone's attention for long. 'I sort of faded into the woodwork,' she recalled. To everyone's except Laura's surprise, she did well. During the next few years she was moved to the main stream, although the teachers encouraged her to take practical nonacademic courses.

'What did your family think of this?' I wanted to know. 'Weren't they proud of you being at the high school?' Laura didn't remember anyone saying anything.

Her grandmother had died. Her mother still worked at two jobs. By the time I met her, Laura had almost finished at her local community college (where she met her husband) and was working part time keeping books in a local paper mill. She likes the work, and except when the counting is very bad, is able to get it all done.

What had it meant to her, being in the 'wrong' school? Laura looked wistful. 'I don't know how much was my compulsions. I am more used than anyone I know to just thinking alone.'

Laura was a partial success. Clomipramine helped her compulsions, but not her sex life. Behaviour therapy is working, slowly, with some benefit for both.

Laura's story is about a particularly unusual way in which OCD was hidden. If the newest statistics are correct, and there really are as many as five million people in America (which would mean over one million in the UK) with OCD, we'll be learning of even more curious and painful ways of hiding it. To complicate matters even further, there may be a real association between learning problems and OCD, particularly in young boys. Laura did not have any learning problem, but at the clinic we see more children with both problems than we should by chance, perhaps another clue that some crucial brain connections are 'miswired' from the start.

Others with childhood OCD have trouble with schoolwork through slowness or perfectionism that prevents them from finishing tests at school or homework after school. Teachers could easily be trained to recognize telltale signs of OCD, such as over-erased homework papers – often so that there are holes in the paper – or to spot the child who won't give up his paper because he must check it 'just one more time'. If we added rough, chapped hands (with severe washing symptoms, it can look like the child has eczema), teachers would be able to spot some cases that everyone else has missed. Their help could save years of grief.

20

Love Story

Robert's obsessive–compulsive behaviour has permeated every corner of his life. I was fascinated by this tall, earnest, unmarried physicist who, at forty-five, was most attractive in a shyly seductive way. The other female physician interviewing him with me said when he left, 'If he gets better, what a catch he'll be!'

But the day he met us, love was the last thing on Robert's mind. His life had been dominated by compulsions; even his earliest memory in life was a compulsive event. 'At about age two, when I was still in a stroller, my mother was pushing me down a street in New York City and all of a sudden I felt compelled to hold my breath until we got to the end of the block. Of course, I wasn't able to do it, but I remember that it was terribly disturbing that I had to do this, even though it was unpleasant and I didn't want to do it. Little did I realize that this was the beginning of the hellish nightmare that would poison my whole life.'

Robert spoke easily about this. He had had four years of psychoanalytic therapy and had worked on his symptoms with his kind and compassionate therapist for over one thousand hours.

He painted a bleak picture of a lonely life. Whether male or female, his friends were pushed out by the meaningless compulsive tasks he would set himself. If the radio had just played three songs, he would say to himself, 'What were the three songs the radio played?' He could do nothing else until he found out, even if it meant calling the radio station. This information was useless, but as Robert put it: 'It felt like a matter of survival. The force of these crazy thoughts was so intense – it was as if nothing else could matter.' He had to have privacy to carry out these absurd rituals. All his remaining energy went into schoolwork.

Even after hearing so many similar stories about peculiar demands that could rule a life, it seemed unreal when I heard such an intelligent, attractive, and above all rational adult describe the meaningless rituals that dominated his days and nights.

I could picture Robert at his Catholic grammar school where his compulsions took the form of religious excess, forcing him to memorize religious passages and the lives of the saints. He spent his nights reading and rereading the same pages over and over again until he could pronounce every word exactly.

But his most humiliating ritual appeared when Robert was at high school. He had to check his trouser zip over and over again. The checking called attention to his preoccupation and he became the butt of the other boys' jokes. Girls avoided him. The habit remained strong for almost ten years before fading. He remembers those years as perhaps the loneliest time of his life.

There was one bright spot. Teachers would praise his scholarship. It was the only thing he had going for himself, and Robert remembers the relief of escape into maths or physics. 'But the more I pursued my studies, the more isolated from the real world I became.' He needed time to complete all the rituals and avoiding people was easier than being found out for the mental cripple he felt himself to be.

Early on in graduate school, something extraordinary happened. Robert fell in love with another graduate student. 'It was the most wonderful and the most terrible event,' he told us. 'I had never been in love before; we really cared for each other. But no one else had ever known about my problem. I didn't dare let her know.' The relationship lasted for years. Robert would seem to ignore her while he was actually carrying out rituals. 'What were the rituals then?' I asked. 'They were trivial, stupid to admit. Suppose I had seen one of the TV chat shows the night before. I *had* to remember who the guests were. Until I got it right, looked it up in the paper, called the studio, or blessedly sometimes just remembered, I could do nothing else.'

'And she never knew?' I asked.

'She thought I was bored or angry or both. Still, I couldn't tell her.'

There it was: the same story I had heard from husbands, wives, and children – the need to keep the rituals secret from the most intimate, most important person in their lives. 'I thought I was crazy. I didn't understand it myself,' Robert explained.

They finally separated. It had been ten years since Robert had seen her. He was successful professionally, but his one-man consulting firm, which allowed him time to carry out rituals when necessary, was also terribly lonely. His reluctant conclusion was that, 'I will never have the character and discipline to beat this. Every day I would start out with determination to beat it, and every day I would fail. It was agony. I just kept asking myself "What is the matter with me?" '

Robert had phoned us after watching the '20/20' programme on Obsessive–Compulsive Disorder. He knew he had this problem and like most of the thousands who phoned in after the programme, he was correct. Once you see another person with this same problem, there is no confusion. Unfortunately, most people never know of anyone else with the rituals and obsessions because of the secrecy surrounding OCD.

Robert decided to keep a record of his compulsions, the number of rituals or thoughts per hour. Such a record came naturally to him because his work involved frequency analysis.

Soon after he started on clomipramine, the number of compulsions decreased dramatically, and those that remained lost their force. Robert wrote: 'My theory is that some thoughts, usually trivial, get trapped in a primitive centre of the brain such as a survival centre, if there is such a thing. There is some internal communication that doesn't work and these idiotic thoughts become mixed up with survival. The brain has no perspective and so the thought goes off on its own within this centre and becomes a matter of the highest importance to complete so there is no room for anything else.'

Robert's battle with OCD has a storybook ending. After six months on the drug, Robert began to believe he might stay better. He traced his old girlfriend through a mutual friend. She had never married. When he called, she told him she had never stopped dreaming about him. They are back together. The last time I heard from Robert he told me: 'It is the best it has ever been. We are living in a honeymoon atmosphere and talking about marriage, children, and a family, something we were never able to discuss before. Now the world is bright and exciting with a vision of the future that is nothing less than beautiful. As we say, it is just unbelievable.'

Robert was lucky. Patients with Obsessive–Compulsive Disorder are almost twice as likely never to marry as the general population. If they do get married, they are more likely to divorce. The rituals and ruminations eat up their time and energy, while secrecy prevents them from sharing what's left over. Will the new treatments change this? I'll have to wait and see.

21

AIDS: The New Obsession

Acquired Immune-Deficiency Syndrome is the national health obsession of the 1980s and for good reason. In addition to what I see and read about it in the papers and on the evening news, I hear about AIDS from a unique perspective: it is the new focus of washing and checking compulsions. In the past the 'dirt' washed off was germs, faeces, or bugs. Sometimes it was sweat, semen, or any other body fluid; now it is AIDS.

For example, AIDS now keeps Alan preoccupied. He is not gay, does not do drugs, has never worked in a hospital and doesn't think he knows anyone in a 'high-risk' group. But as an obsessive–compulsive patient who has spent the last fifteen years worrying about contamination, AIDS has become for Alan the most feared contamination, replacing all others.

A 'washer' during all his school years, Alan and his mother came to my office together when he was struggling to get through high school. Alan's mother, a short, heavyset dynamo, keeps the whole family moving. Alan had problems reading and was older than the other kids. Having repeated some grades twice, his mother 'read him through school' and kept after their county school to get Alan the special educational services he needed. She had to stay on top of things just to keep Alan on the go. Until his new obsession with AIDS, his worst problems had developed when he turned into a checker. He checked doors, windows, and worst of all, the papers on the family truck that delivers the *Washington Post*. Delivering papers is the family business.

Alan checked to see that the advertising inserts had been put inside each paper. He only worked his way through the piles already put together; he never got new ones started. His brothers stopped going out on the paper delivery truck with him. He didn't pull his share. Alan's mother went out on the truck with him until even she couldn't get the job done. Alan didn't permit a paper to be delivered until he checked it 'one more time'. After spending eight hours on a three-hour route, his mother had to give up, and Alan was out of the family delivery business.

After the newspaper round ended, I began meeting with Alan and his mother as he lost one job after another. Adding up the time it took him to shower, lock the door, get out of the car, lock the car, and begin the job – many hours on a bad day – Alan couldn't make an 8 a.m. or even 9 a.m. appointment. So Alan lost his jobs. But then his compulsions took a more ominous turn.

Now Alan's problem is AIDS. He doesn't have AIDS, but he was tossed off his last job after a brawl about it.

Alan had found a construction job that finally seemed to be working out. The digging and carrying was more relaxing than the newspaper round and Alan liked the other guys on that job. Some were friends from high school. For the first time in months, Alan was swapping jokes and kidding around on the job. One day on a lunch break, Bill, a man who happened to be sitting next to Alan, put his black thermos down on the wall next to Alan's black thermos. Alan took a swig. It was coffee, not milk, and he knew he had drunk from the wrong one.

The thought flashed through Alan's mind: 'What if Bill has AIDS?' He tried to push the thought away; Alan wasn't stupid. This was going to be trouble. But the thought left room for no other. 'Bill,' he blurted out, 'you gotta get an AIDS test.' Bill didn't think it was funny. Alan got agitated. 'Please, Bill, I won't be able to sleep. I drank from your thermos.'

'Leave me alone! Are you saying I got AIDS?' Bill screamed. A free-for-all followed.

After that, the guys never stopped kidding Alan. 'You got AIDS yet?' they'd call out when he got to work. He tried to cope but gave up and now stays at home. He hardly checks or washes. He just can't get AIDS off his mind. (I should have realized this would happen. The year before, he had had an obsessive preoccupation with rabies for a month after passing a frothing dog. That passed, but the AIDS terror stuck.)

Almost one-third of our obsessive–compulsive patients have incorporated AIDS into their rituals and beliefs. The washing came first. Making a fear of AIDS the cause of the washing came later. Man is a rational being: when he finds himself doing something that looks purposeful – for example, repeated washing – his logical mind has to find a reason. That's the best explanation I can find for those obsessed by AIDS. Some *never* know why they wash but they suffer an awful feeling of discomfort if they don't. And obsessive–compulsive patients, sensing a danger that they can't see, feel, or understand, fixate on AIDS; it's an illness made to order for OC victims. And it doesn't matter how sophisticated you are. The AIDS obsession takes over anywhere.

Claude is a successful surgeon, happily married with two children. Ten years ago, on an impulse, Claude answered an ad and had a brief homosexual encounter. After three meetings, Claude stopped. This was long before the AIDS scare; Claude just didn't feel like continuing. Around the time of Rock Hudson's death, he began to appear at friends' offices worrying constantly about AIDS. Because he is a physician, Claude has convinced his colleagues to carry out every known test for the disease. He has had innocent skin rashes biopsied, every antibody measured, the Western Blot (the most sophisticated test for AIDS antibodies in the blood), and has had his blood cultured.

The result is the same every time. Claude comes anxiously to his friends' offices when the results are back. 'Good news,' his colleagues say, 'you can stop worrying now. Everything is fine.' They share the inevitably negative results with him. For a minute Claude looks relieved, then the worried look returns. 'It could take a while longer to get positive,' he will say. Or 'I read of a new kind of lab error last week. The tests could be wrong. It could have been someone else's test!'

I asked his wife if he had ever done anything like this before. 'You know,' she said, 'I had forgotten. His mother once told me about something that happened when Claude was at high school. He had to borrow a team mate's underwear when his own got misplaced after a game. After that, he started worrying whether he had syphilis.' 'Did the other boy have syphilis?' I asked. 'No, of course not. He was fine. But Claude didn't stop worrying for months.'

For my patients, the washing, the sense of danger to be washed off, comes first. The explanation, if there is one, changes, and will always change, with the times. AIDS is a judgement, suggesting sexual transgression, and illegal and immoral acts. It causes hideous shame and discrimination. It is so terrifying, so irrational that it could have been the creation of an obsessive–compulsive's worst fantasy. One of my young patients now cannot go on with her chosen college training as a medical technician. When she was a small child, she was washing without comprehending its purpose. Then came the AIDS epidemic. Now AIDS is the reason she washes. She told me: 'I think I knew about AIDS before it happened. In a crazy way, it's what I was waiting for. It's what anyone with OCD was waiting for. We just didn't know it.'

22
The Hair-Pulling Women

Jackie P. sat in the waiting room, wearing a wide-brimmed straw hat that hid her face, and oversized mirrored sunglasses that made her look oddly glamorous. The rest of her appearance quickly dispelled this illusion, however, for she was really a slightly dumpy woman in a pastel trouser-suit.

In the examination room, she took off her glasses, tilted the hat back and exhibited other touches of incongruous sophistication. Her eyebrows were pencilled arches worthy of Marlene Dietrich, her eyelashes jet black and enormously long. The whole effect was exotic, overdone, and curiously disconcerting.

Jackie's manner was straightforward and earnest. 'I'm so glad to be here,' she told me. 'When I saw the programme on television, my husband and I couldn't believe our eyes. We always thought I was the only one with this problem.'

'What is your problem?' I asked. 'Well, oh boy, do I *hate* to do this, but it's easier to show you,' she said, taking off her hat.

Jackie began to unmask. First she took out a Kleenex and wiped off her eyebrow pencil, then she peeled off the artificial eyelashes, and finally she removed her wig. The result was startling: there was absolutely no hair on her head and no hair on her face. The skin where her eyebrows should have been was white and blotchy. The unbroken pink span of skull and face stared at me like an undressed shop mannequin. But its eyes, Jackie's eyes, were red and teary.

'This is really embarrassing,' she said, 'but you wouldn't understand if I didn't show you. Only my husband and parents have ever seen me like this. Even the kids don't know.' She rubbed her hands over her face. 'Maybe it's like Grandma said, I was breech-birthed and that meant life would be rough. I was like anyone else until I was thirteen. People admired my green eyes and long lashes. My grandma said I started to pull out my eyelashes to get Mum's attention; the house was always so full of Mum's friends. Maybe I didn't like it; I don't know. The next thing I remember is how I started to pull out my hair and eat the roots. I do know I wanted to stop. Can someone be an eyelash and hair *junkie*?

'I tried all sorts of things to stop,' Jackie went on. 'I wore gloves, cut the ends of my fingers, cut my nails so short that they would bleed. Finally my mother took me to a psychiatrist who asked me if I masturbated! What a question! He certainly didn't help.

'The worst part,' Jackie added, 'is that I couldn't do any of the fun things like swimming, riding in a roller coaster, being in the wind. I was always afraid my wig would blow the wrong way and someone would see I was bald, or my eyelashes would come off. It was a crazy, awful adolescence.'

'You did get married,' I said.

'When I went out with my husband the second time I liked him so much that I told him about what I did. He took it as if it were an everyday occurrence. He didn't care. God was good to me when he sent Jerry my way.'

'When I went to our fifteenth high school reunion some of the guys got drunk and came up to me and asked if I still did crazy things like pulling out my eyelashes. I thought, God, that's how people remember me from school! That is the last reunion I'll ever go to.'

Jackie had three children, nice clothes, a good husband and a nice home but she continued to pull her hair out even though, as she put it, 'You would think that would be enough in my life to keep me from pulling but it isn't.' Her prayers to be healed hadn't worked and she still didn't know why she did what she did. When she saw the programme on '20/20' about Obsessive–Compulsive Disorder Jackie was sure that her problem was one form of compulsion. The television studio wasn't so sure, but she wouldn't take no for an answer. She called the television studio until they promised to contact us.

We treated Jackie with clomipramine. The results surprised both of us. We weren't actually sure whether Jackie was right in her conviction that she belonged in our clinic. But she wouldn't take no for an answer from us either. She was very convincing. 'I know it's crazy to pull out my hair. And I can't help doing it. I started when I was a kid. I kept it secret. You've got to let me be in your study.'

We decided, maybe 'rationalized' is the word, to include Jackie because she did have one really obsessional symptom: when she was pulling out her hair, she had to make it even. If she picked one from the left she had to pick out one from the right to even it up, if she picked three from the left, she had to do three from the right and so on. So we tried to treat Jackie.

Within a few weeks of taking clomipramine, Jackie had a curious experience. She still had a desire to pick out hairs. But for the first time since she was thirteen she was able to resist that feeling. Two months later, she came in without her glasses – she had eyelashes and eyebrows. We were all excited. Her hair is taking longer to grow, but at least it's there. The next time she's due for a visit, she promises to give up the wig. Jackie is a new person; she bubbles.

'I've gone on a roller coaster,' she told me. 'I've got wet, and even rode in a convertible. I wish my mother had lived long enough to see this, I hope she knows.'

Jackie P. is one of ten people with trichotillomania – a compulsion to pull out one's hair – who pushed themselves into our clinic. All are female, and all, like Jackie, began when they were teenagers. Except for the embarrassment and occasional depression, except for rare complications such as infections or eye abrasions, all are managing to cope. Yet as soon as they recognized themselves on the '20/20' programme about compulsions, these women went to a lot of trouble to come for help. We had not planned to include trichotillomanics in our study, but these patients taught us that we should.

The term for a hair-pulling compulsion, trichotillomania, was coined by Hallopeau, a French physician, in 1889. He felt that these patients were otherwise sane. Most of the early medical reports about this puzzling problem have been by derma-tologists, but during the past twenty years psychiatrists have become more aware of its existence. It was once thought to be very rare (like OCD), but now series of twenty or thirty cases have been described in reports from some behaviour therapy treatment centres. Trichotillomania does occur with other disorders, but our small group of subjects has convinced us that it is a form of Obsessive–Compulsive Disorder. Most intriguing from a genetic point of view is that several have family members with typical OCD. As in OCD, the victims are otherwise normal or depressed, wish they could stop, but continue in spite of their shame. Like obsessives, these patients go to great lengths to keep the problem secret.

One woman moaned about how much her arms ached from hours of sitting and pulling out her hair. Yet she couldn't stop. Jackie knows her hair-pulling is unnecessary and painful, but she is compelled by an irresistible urge to pull hair anyway. The puzzling part of trichotillomania is that these women usually have not had other obsessive or compulsive symptoms. None of them washes or checks, now or in the past. They don't come up with thoughts or fantasies the way obsessives do. When I asked Jackie what would happen if she didn't have to pull out her hair, she just smiled and said, 'It would be wonderful.'

A major difference from the usual obsessive–compulsive is that almost all trichotillomanics are female. As with Obsessive–Compulsive Disorder, a common complication of hair-pulling is depression. Talking to these women, all so amazingly alike, gave me the eerie sense that a primitive behaviour pattern has come loose. An innate, atavistic urge to groom, to preen that can't be suppressed. The dramatic response of these hair-pullers to clomipramine (and their lack of response to other drugs) forges another link between this odd problem and obsessions and compulsions.

In classic psychoanalytic literature, hair has multiple symbolic meanings. It is a symbol of beauty, virility, and physical prowess. It is also a bisexual symbol and sexual conflicts are said to be displaced to the hair. Hair-cutting or plucking is felt to symbolize castration.

A psychoanalytic essay by Edith Buxbaum on the fairy tale Rapunzel suggested that the cutting of Rapunzel's hair represents separation and loss of the mother. In various Hindu cultures, shaving the scalp is associated with mourning. In a particular community in India, hair is plucked before a person enters a life of penance, and there is a long tradition of shaving one's hair in the Christian monastic life.

What none of these theories tells us is *why* people develop trichotillomania. How does the identical pattern, almost always in women, emerge apparently out of nowhere? Do we turn again to the brain to solve this puzzle? Are there biological models? There are some animal models: e.g. cats often swallow their dead fur. Unfortunately, psychotherapy, behaviour therapy, and, until now, drug treatment didn't help. Fortunately, most of the women seem able to cope, to live with loved ones, and to work their lives around their bizarre and painful habit.

Still, too many puzzles remain. Why are these subjects almost always female? (We have seen only two boys with this problem. They had other OC symptoms as well, but they would spend hours plucking out their hair just like the girls.) Why are trichotillomanics so single minded while our other patients move from symptom to symptom? Like most of our findings, this raises as many questions as it answers.

But our news is exciting. We have compared clomipramine and desipramine, our comparison antidepressant, in all ten of these hair-pullers. The results are very convincing. Nine of them got no help from desipramine and got much better on clomipramine. We now officially view trichotillomania as another form of OCD.

Are other 'dumb' habits in otherwise normal people odd forms of OCD? What about nail-biting? Should that be treated with clomipramine? We may have to take a fresh look at these habits that we thought we understood. If they respond so specifically to one particular drug, what does this mean? Could nail-biting too represent an ancient grooming pattern that for some unknown reason some of us still exhibit? Are these habits all odd quirks in the functioning of our brains?

23

Innocent Sinners

I first heard about scrupulosity through Sally's aunt Leora, who didn't know what it was either. Leora was a college friend I hadn't heard from in years. She telephoned me out of the blue for advice about her favourite niece. My friend, a suggestible sort, had just seen *The Exorcist*. 'My niece is acting like she's possessed,' she told me.

'You don't believe that stuff, do you?' I asked.

'Well not really, but it is weird. All of a sudden this happy-go-lucky little girl talks about sin and asks for punishments. She uses words like blasphemy and says an evil force is inside her. It's not natural. Where *could* it be coming from?'

Whatever was happening to Sally, her aunt was really worried. And the story she told *was* curious.

Sally, a bright, blonde eleven-year-old, had looked forward to her Confirmation. Getting a new dress and having her aunt so proud of her outweighed all the hard work. But a few weeks before the big day she started having crying spells, couldn't sleep, and lost ten pounds. It all began suddenly, when Sally was doing a class punishment assignment. She thought that she wasn't doing it properly, that she was 'sinning'. I'm always doing something wrong, she felt. The feeling stayed with her.

Each day her symptoms became more intense. 'If I touch the table, I'm really offending God,' she whispered. She folded her arms and withdrew into deep thought. Sally was terror-struck that she might have offended God by touching her hands. Did that mean that she was striking God? she wondered, retreating further into herself.

Always self-reliant, Sally now began to follow her mother around the house, kissing her, holding on to her. She felt she had 'less chance of sinning' if her mother was at home.

In school, when Sally's teaching Sister returned from an errand, she asked the class how many times the girls had talked. Sally 'confessed' to have spoken twelve times! This was for 'breathing noises' which her classmates hadn't even heard. She volunteered to do punishments which she felt were unfair, but she felt better for having done them. The Sister, a strict but fair teacher, was at a loss. Sally felt as if an evil inner force hovered over her constantly.

Sally asked herself if she perhaps *wanted* to sin. She said she was offending God by writing sloppily. If she didn't write properly, if the words were written below the line, it was a mortal sin. Soon it got worse. She started to ruminate. 'Did I take a false oath? Did I lie?' She had thoughts of 'selling my soul to the devil'. It was at that point that my friend Leora had telephoned and I agreed to see Sally.

The interview with Sally was a script from a bizarre morality play. She was agonized, frantic, rocking and pacing. 'How have I sinned? Tell me what my punishments should be? Will that make it better? I am sure I am sinning!' The questions were repeated over and over. She didn't listen for answers. Her stomach hurt; she cried. My answers didn't help any more than her aunt's.

'I don't see what you did wrong,' I said. The effect was disastrous.

'Don't say that,' she screamed. 'It's bad enough without you making things worse. I need to have my punishment. That's the only thing that would help.'

'What or where *is* the bad part?'

'I just know it's in me, that's all. I have these terrible thoughts.'

Two priests had already seen Sally. The first had said she had a psychological problem and she shouldn't pray more than five minutes a day. Reasonable sounding advice, but it didn't work.

For her next confession Sally went to a priest with a reputation for strictness. He did add prayers, and it felt better. But only for a day, and then the cycle began again. The second priest saw he was in over his head and backed off.

I was stuck too. In a sense, Sally *was* 'possessed'. The force behind her questions had a direction of its own; she wasn't really asking the questions and she ignored the answers. Her words didn't sound like a little girl's. The effect was eerie. I had been bored thoroughly by *The Exorcist*, and here I was acting it out!

I lost track of Sally at this point but later learned that somehow she got through her Confirmation. The symptoms faded afterwards. Two years later, I met her aunt again. Sally was now a busy teenager, only moderately observant, and unconcerned. Sally was my first contact with scrupulosity; we were both in the dark then about what was happening.

That was twenty years ago. The bursts of scrupulosity weren't rare in old-fashioned, private Roman Catholic schools. A 1927

church-conducted survey claimed that 4 per cent gave answers
that were considered scrupulous. Those who did so indulged in
excessive prayer, unreasonable doubting, and extreme fastidiousness (some also washed their hands excessively). I could find
no more recent survey for scrupulosity, perhaps because the
Catholic Church has long since recognized this as a form of
Obsessive–Compulsive Disorder. But within a religious context,
the name is scrupulosity.

Sally recovered in time and with a little help from her family.
But the next patient I saw with scrupulosity was harder.

During my residency training at Boston, I was assigned
Audrey as a clinic patient. A thin nervous woman of twenty-
eight, with hair pulled back in a bun, Audrey was preoccupied
with prayer and confession. Her daily absences from her two
little girls to attend dozens of weekly confessions just added to
her guilt. A force, she explained, was filling her mind with
fleeting but terrible thoughts.

'What sort of thoughts?' I asked.

'Oh, terrible thoughts. Terrible. I am afraid to even say.'

The 'terrible thoughts' weren't so terrible and Audrey knew
it. They were mildly disrespectful perhaps. Like being bored in
church. Like thinking the priest was attractive. What *was* terrible
was the force behind them and the need for ritual penance.

Audrey and I got on well. We met weekly and talked about her
marriage, her parents, her children, and her strict parochial
school upbringing. She readily aired her insecurities, and her
anger at the sternness of the Sisters when she was small. But
only after she was really at ease with me did I learn her worst
fear. Audrey believed that Satan was putting sinful thoughts in
her head. She had had ideas like this before but never with such
a terrible intensity. As the year wore on, I watched Audrey
become more and more preoccupied. I needed help to help
Audrey. She needed more than my interest and reassurance.
My case supervisor was increasingly puzzled and worried. Both
Audrey and I turned to the authority of the church for guidance.
My tolerance upset her.

'It's not your fault, Dr Rapoport,' she'd say soothingly, 'but
you could lead me off the right path. The Devil could still be in
me.' Audrey had run through several priests and finally found

one familiar with this problem. Father John turned out to be a wonderful co-therapist. A priest with extensive experience in lay counselling, he knew about scrupulosity, and he had an ideal mix of patience and authority.

His training in the Roman Catholic Church's treatment of scrupulosity was more sensible than contemporary psychiatry's treatment of OCD. For psychiatric treatment of OCD in those days focused on exploring the unconscious symbolic determinants of compulsive behaviours or of obsessive thoughts. I had been doing that, under my psychiatric supervisor's guidance, without any effect. In contrast, the church stressed the importance of full and absolute obedience to an 'enlightened spiritual director', most usually a priest, to help the overscrupulous decrease their excessive religiosity as quickly as possible. And so Father John spent hours with Audrey going over how much time she devoted to these thoughts and fears and prayers in detail. Ultimately, he took the position that her prayers were not useful to the church or herself.

Father John's treatment was not unlike behaviour therapy. (At the time, however, behaviour therapy was not a well-recognized treatment for OCD and was practised only by a very small group of psychologists; it was neither familiar nor available to Audrey or myself.) First Father John formed a trusting relationship. Then he learned about her problems in great detail. Finally he gradually limited and reduced her excessive piety. Audrey was first 'exposed' to the dreaded experience by saying her thoughts out loud, and then he prevented her from making her excessive response to them by not praying or going to confession. Most important, he won her agreement to limit the excessive ritual and prayer.

Audrey and Sally were obsessive–compulsives. I was astonished at the transformation of these two disparate personalities into people 'possessed'. Scrupulosity isn't in the psychiatric handbooks, but under that name the Catholic Church was treating OCD long before any doctors were.

I have now achieved a novel historical perspective on scrupulosity. I find it a compelling image: Audrey and Sally as compliant victims in a Salem witch trial. In those days the guidelines for distinguishing 'good' and 'evil' scruples were hardly clear. There are, it is known, major social determinants for religious and personal persecution that lead to witch trials. But my patients provide a possible contributing note.

Sally would have confessed to any sin to gain relief from her 'planted' thoughts. Audrey was already confessing to Satanism – her best way to account for the astonishing, intense, foreign yet inner force. She didn't need prompting. If in Puritan New England two out of every one hundred persons, as we know is true today, actually *had* Obsessive–Compulsive Disorder, can you blame the judges if they were sure they were on the right path? Had the flames of the Inquisition been heightened by such victims as well?

Obsessions and compulsions are found in persons of every religious faith, but the Catholics have written most about it. The disease is not more frequent in Catholics; perhaps, though, a form of religious expression with greater emphasis on ritual penance and purification serves particularly well as a vehicle for compulsions. (There is more detail on the Catholic perspective on OCD in the Appendix.)

24

A Thousand Commitments to God

My colleague Dr Xavier Charles came to our NIMH clinic to talk to us about behaviour therapy for Obsessive–Compulsive Disorder. Xavier didn't want to bore us with theory; that's not his style. Instead he told us about his treatment of Daniel, one of his most unusual patients. Daniel's story was unique in two ways: first, because Daniel's obsessions and compulsions were so numerous and complex that behaviour therapy for his OCD was an extraordinary challenge. Second, because of the role played by Daniel's rabbi. It is the only instance I know in which a Jewish religious ceremony was invoked in the treatment of OCD.

Behaviour therapy can be lengthy and tedious. It means

spending many hours with a patient counting how often and just when, where, and how each and every ritual occurs. Next it means helping the patient face the 'trigger' situations and not ritualize. Sometimes a companion is there to lend courage. That is a thumbnail sketch of behaviour therapy: rational, often effective, but just as often too cut and dried – not quite how real life turns out. I know of too many complex cases for whom behaviour therapy failed; the *real* patient fell between the cracks in the neat structure of behaviourist principles. But when Xavier talks about his work with Daniel, the process comes alive, dramatic and convincing as a powerful tool for treating OCD.

Xavier and Daniel had worked together since 1986. Beginning in his first year at high school, Daniel had been making thousands of 'commitments to God' that limited his every possible choice, action, or thought. This bizarre state could never have been predicted from the events and style of Daniel's earlier life. In brief, this is the background Xavier gave us:

At grade school, Daniel was seen by family and friends as a bright, thoughtful, friendly child who had grown into a 'good kid' and B student. He was popular throughout grade and middle school. For a very brief period while in seventh grade [aged about twelve], Daniel had worried about germs and would 'blow germs away' when anyone near him sneezed or coughed. This somewhat odd behaviour passed during that year and would have been forgotten except that in his first year of high school, [when he was about fourteen], those close to Daniel remembered it as the first of the unsettling patterns that eventually made his parents seek professional help.

Tenth grade was when things really got difficult. Daniel changed schools and his grandfather died from cancer a month before school started. Daniel's fear of germs returned and to 'prevent potential illness' he would wash his hands up to thirty times each day. Scrutinizing all silverware, dishes, and glasses for specks of dirt or food, he would even wash all money he received from any source. In addition, Daniel's parents watched the 'piles of clothes, books, and papers accumulate on the floor and furniture of his room that he was unwilling to move'.

As the school year progressed, Daniel decided to 'become

kosher', though his family only loosely observed Jewish rituals and practices. He severely limited the varieties of food he was willing to eat, going far beyond the requirements of keeping kosher.

Greatly disturbed by his behaviour, his parents had him examined at the children's hospital, where he was diagnosed as having Obsessive–Compulsive Disorder and was referred to a psychiatrist for treatment. After six months of 'verbal psycho-therapy', Daniel, his parents, and the psychiatrist agreed that no progress had been made and a second psychiatrist began treatment. Daniel seemed to 'open up' to this person more and confided that much of his problem stemmed from chronic fears that he was 'doing something wrong'. His rituals, he said, were attempts to ward off punishment by God for the wrongs he had done. The psychiatrist proposed to work with Daniel to help with these concerns. The psychiatrist tried a few behavioural techniques with some good results. It turned out to be too good to be true. Within a month after systematic exposure to dirty hands, unwashed money, and the like, Daniel seemed 'cured' of his problem. His hand washing was returned to appropriate levels, his diet was greatly expanded in variety (though he remained kosher for a while thereafter), and he handled and used unwashed money.

For a while, at least, Daniel seemed 'almost normal' to his hopeful parents. But a short time later his problems escalated to alarming proportions and took even more bizarre turns. His parents were mystified and disturbed by some of Daniel's behaviour during the summer before the eleventh grade. While walking he would incorporate 'silly steps' into his movement. He refused to watch most of his favourite television shows and wouldn't go to films or almost anywhere else with friends. He would repeatedly walk in and out of rooms in a 'very odd' manner. He would return to places he had just left to see if he had 'done everything right'. Daniel would do other odd things: for example, he washed the family car wearing only a bath towel. Worst of all, from his parents' perspective, was that Daniel, who had always been an open and communicative child, seemed to be 'turning inwards'. He refused to explain his behaviour and appeared to be emotionally distancing himself from his parents.

Daniel's psychiatrist understood that Daniel had a fear that he 'had displeased God by doing things wrong' and that, in Daniel's mind, the probability of being punished by God was somehow lessened by performing these rituals. He described Daniel to his parents as a 'classic example of an obsessive'. The therapist provided emotional support, through his relationship with the boy, and urged Daniel to try to be more normal by resisting his impulses.

But Daniel could not resist, and though he survived his final two years of high school, disaster was imminent. His academic work began to suffer. His writing, once fluent and logical, began to seem childlike. By twelfth grade his sentences were stilted and primitive, his papers almost incomprehensible, with words and phrases endlessly crossed out and rewritten. But somehow he passed his twelfth-grade courses and graduated from high school. By this time, however, no sphere of life was untouched by his disorder. His efforts at going out with girls were doomed to failure by his bizarre behaviour and unwillingness to engage in many 'normal' teenage activities. He had friends, but they had to tolerate his 'weirdness'; to their credit, a few stuck by him.

On the basis of his previously strong academic record, Daniel was admitted to a local college to which he would commute beginning in the autumn. That summer seemed quieter for him. His parents had become used to the many manifestations of his disorder and were hopeful that he would either 'grow out of it', respond to his psychotherapy, or benefit from imipramine that he began taking in late summer.

By November their hopes were dashed. Daniel seemed stranger than ever, making unusual repetitive movements with head, arms, and legs. He would walk in and out of rooms of his house in 'mechanical ways' and still refused to give any explanations. He was failing every one of his courses and had yet to receive anything but an F on any paper or test. Imipramine had not worked and he had found the side effects, of drowsiness and dry mouth, extremely unpleasant. It was time to try something new, and because Daniel was reluctant to try any other medication (clomipramine was considered) he agreed to try behaviour therapy in 'stronger doses', which involved a much greater commitment to this approach.

This is when he began his sessions with Dr Xavier Charles, who found Daniel 'responsive and personable from the outset'. The remainder of the story is taken from Xavier's own notes.

Daniel is a pleasant-looking, polite, and well-spoken young man, of average to above-average intelligence. As we spoke, I saw his 'strange' hand and head movements. I told Daniel that he could tell me as little or as much as he wished about his problem at this session, but that if I was to help him, he eventually would have to tell me everything. This made sense to him and he asked me if I knew where obsessive–compulsive disorders came from. I explained that while I certainly didn't know enough about his situation right now, I was confident that given enough information to work with, I would understand his problem well enough to explain it to him in ways that would help him understand it on the basis of known psychological principles. He would understand not only where these disorders came from, I explained, but he would understand what we must do to overcome them.

He seemed interested and wanted to know more. I said it would be necessary for him to provide me with more information about the specifics of the problem so that I wouldn't have to speak in generalities. Daniel began his account by saying that there would be many things he couldn't tell me about now, but that he would try to find ways of telling me these things in the future. I accepted that.

As Daniel told his story, he described how hundreds of times each day he would 'get a feeling' that he had 'done something wrong' and that it displeased God. To avoid possible punishment for these 'wrongdoings' at God's hands, he would punish himself in some way, thus reducing his concern about some more awful punishment occurring at some later time. He would also avoid any actions or thoughts that had accompanied these feelings. This led to the development of complex rules which, in Daniel's mind, placed prohibitions on his behaviour and thinking in virtually every situation of his life. His account was absorbing as he described the multitude of things he must do, or could not do, or must do in certain ways or in a certain order. He spoke of thoughts he could not think, of memories and information he could not retrieve, of things he could not say or had to say in certain ways, using or not using certain words. He described a system that was so complex, so convoluted, so pervasive that I wondered how he was able to function at all within the rigid guidelines of his unforgiving system.

Daniel asked, 'Did I give you enough to get you started?' and we both had a good laugh. (Humour is useful with OCD patients, not to make 'fun of' but to show appreciation of some of the 'absurd' aspects of the disorder.) As he left my office, with some self-monitoring forms in hand, I marvelled at the spirit of this boy that enabled him to go on despite the 'oppressive weight' of his obsessive–compulsive disorder. He would need to rally all that spirit if he was to regain his ability to function in this world.

The second session began with Daniel handing me his self-monitoring forms. The forms required him to self-monitor three aspects of his problems during a 24-hour period: (a) repeating something; (b) stopping himself from doing something he wished to do; and (c) walking out of and back into a room. He would note when any of these events occurred, the activity or thought that evoked the ritual, the distress he felt based on a scale of zero to one hundred, and the number of minutes spent on the ritual.

The page was literally covered with tiny notations, many crossed out and rewritten on the form's back and front, in its margins, between its lines, wherever a coded entry could fit in. He noted his actions minute by minute, hour by hour while walking, sitting, writing, eating, watching TV, brushing teeth, washing, attempting homework, driving, going to sleep, sleeping (he even ritualized in his dreams!). The record sheet was unintelligible, but at least we had something of a baseline to work with. Because monitoring is essential in behavioural treatment, I was glad we had some kind, any kind, of a start.

Just sorting through the myriad of prohibitions was a daunting task. Daniel listed hundreds. We organized them into things he couldn't eat or drink, places he couldn't go, things he couldn't use, clothes he couldn't wear, activities he couldn't be involved in, things he couldn't think about or talk about, things he couldn't buy, things he couldn't write down or say. No mundane detail of everyday life seemed too insignificant to go unregulated in Daniel's private world. Even when there was no outright prohibition, he had developed special ways that they had to be done. Usually this involved the 'order' in which activities were carried out, or seemingly meaningless repetitions of insignificant movements. Getting to a class was a major accomplishment: getting dressed and out of the house, driving to the campus, parking the car, walking to the building, getting through the door and seated all involved multitudes of separate instances of avoiding repetition and ordering. Even in class all was not well because Daniel's problem prevented him from listening to certain information, taking notes, sometimes even opening his notebook. Any occurrence, at any moment, could and was likely to be an antecedent for Daniel's avoidance and ritualizing. At no time was he free of his preoccupations about following rules and 'doing the right things'.

'What would happen if you simply did things like everyone else did them?' I asked. Daniel said that while his thinking 'usually doesn't go that far any more' he firmly believed that he would be punished by God if he did not follow the dictates of his beliefs and feelings. The probability of punishment he truly believed to be 'at or near 100 per cent' and no exhortation by parents, friends, or therapists had been able to dissuade him from his unique way of going about things. (It is always essential to know how strongly the obsessive believes his fear is realistic. The stronger such a belief, the more likely for behaviour therapy to fail.) Daniel acknowledged that he, in fact, was suffering from Obsessive–Compulsive Disorder because 'everyone says that'. But in his own mind, it was necessary that he avoid and ritualize in what had become his usual manner.

But I had made a commitment to provide Daniel with a perspective on his problems that involved no supernatural forces, no mysterious and unpredictable internal signals of wrongdoing. Instead, there would be a new scheme, one based upon principles of conditioning and learning, one that I hoped would motivate him to co-operate in the demanding phase of therapy. To be effective, it would require him to face his fears and relinquish the short-term comfort he got from his rituals in favour of the hope of a life free from the constraints he had imposed on himself.

We embarked on a co-operative fact-finding mission into the earliest beginnings of the problem. While this was going on, Daniel's academic predicament went from dismal to hopeless. A letter to his Academic Dean produced a leave of absence with a promise of re-admittance for the spring term or whenever some assurance could be offered that his prospects were improved substantially. The spring term was two months away.

I was very pleased with the relationship that had developed between us. Daniel wanted badly to believe the explanations I gave him about the development of his current thoughts and actions. He knew we were inexorably moving towards his direct confrontation with his fears and rituals. He listened intently as I described mechanisms of conditioning, reinforcement and the like. I tried to weave his own personal history in with the theory and show him how he could have gone from a fully functioning happy kid to an incapacitated, preoccupied, dysfunctional adolescent in just a few years, under the watchful eyes of loving parents and skilled therapists. We spent an unusual amount of time on this because it was especially important to Daniel's acceptance of the confrontational part of the treatment.

In four sessions, we finished our account and Daniel was pleased. He asked that we commit to a 'chart' so he could keep it with him and study it. It made sense to him; it was logical and scientific and explained the twists and turns his problems took in the evolution of his disorder.

Daniel's chart summed up his story as I had come to know it. He remembered his childhood as a happy one, filled with friends and relatives, free of problems. He acknowledged some 'minor' worries that passed quickly (like fearing toilets would overflow if he flushed them) but dismissed them as childhood 'silliness'.

During middle school (in his early teens) his home life erupted into a series of crises. One of his older sisters began to use drugs and had got into some trouble with the school authorities. Daniel remembered much yelling and arguments in the family, often between his parents, about how to handle his sister and he worried about the breakup of his home. His 'nerves were on edge' and he prayed to God that things would get back to normal. At the same time, his grandfather was dying a slow and painful death.

Daniel recalled the first time that he had 'that feeling'. It was in December of the tenth grade [when he was about fifteen] as he sat in the synagogue during a long service at his grandfather's funeral. He remembered it was hot and he was not feeling very well. When the thought crossed his mind that he really didn't want to be there, he suddenly felt a strong 'twinge' of guilt. He thought it was wrong to think like that; it was 'against religion' to think about being elsewhere at a time like that, and that God would punish him for having such thoughts during a holy service. He sat there wondering how he could make amends, but he couldn't undo the thoughts. His fear and discomfort increased until he left the service.

Shortly after that, another episode strengthened the link in Daniel's mind between the fear of God's punishment and his sense of personal wrongdoing. While he was masturbating late at night in his room, the television was on in the background. To Daniel's horror he became aware that the television was tuned to a religious programme. In his view, he had been masturbating 'in the presence of religion and God'. He deserved to be punished. Since then, when he masturbated, he couldn't rid his mind of thoughts about God. He even fantasized about his masturbating before holy objects. His fear of punishment grew, and every thought about God or religion triggered strong and lingering feelings of anxiety and guilt. Daniel began to worry more than ever before and he began to look for ways to 'prove himself to God' to escape almost certain punishment.

Anything associated with religion would set off Daniel's new pattern of thinking: driving past a church, hearing someone say 'Goddamn', seeing things that looked like a cross, even crossing 't's' as he wrote.

He made more and more rules for himself and grew increasingly preoccupied with a concern to do what was 'right'. But he couldn't control what he thought about. He started to punish himself to square things with God so that God wouldn't need to punish him later. During this phase he began to deprive himself of pleasurable activities: he would not drink Coke or Pepsi, or watch his favourite shows, or go out to films or bowling. He would not eat certain kinds of sweets or chew certain flavours of gum or even think about pleasant memories. Finally to punish himself, he would allow himself to appear 'foolish' in front of friends and strangers. He would walk in 'silly steps'. He would dress peculiarly, he would say ridiculous things, all without explanation. Daniel also did things the 'hard way', such as taking long routes to places instead of short ones.

This worked a little for a short while. But it created new problems. His actions *were* embarrassing and he couldn't explain them. Relief was always temporary and it was becoming impossible to follow all of his own rules.

One night, while watching 'Hill Street Blues', a pivotal incident occurred. A character in the story died of AIDS and was revealed to be gay. What an awful punishment! The thought flashed through Daniel's mind: if he were to be stricken with AIDS, the disease would be bad enough, but the humiliation of having family, friends, and acquaintances thinking he was gay would be the worst punishment God could inflict that he could imagine. And so Daniel became a 'washer' during the last few months of the tenth grade.

Washing was in many ways easier for him than following so many difficult rules. In fact, his preoccupation with cleanliness distracted him from thoughts that had been more disturbing.

When his previous therapist 'broke him' of his contamination fears and washing rituals by exposing him to dirt and not letting him wash – the standard behavioural techniques – it was then, as Daniel put it, his problems 'really got bad'. The fear of AIDS had been under control. Now the thoughts were all-pervasive.

When the behaviour therapy stopped the washing, Daniel told me the rituals 'went inside my head'. The hundreds, no thousands, of commitments to God were back. He had to cope with the likelihood that at any given moment he was, in fact, breaking a promise to God he had made earlier that year. It was too much to follow any more. Daniel refers to this new phase as 'pure rituals'.

When he started seeing me, he performed pervasive rituals that had lost all logical meaning. He couldn't keep up with his elaborate bookkeeping of guilt and punishment. Somehow, in some way, just repeating some of the gestures and motions that earlier had been connected so logically to particular trans-gressions against God now achieved some protective value in themselves.

By ritualizing continually, Daniel felt more assured that he had done as much as possible to protect against violating any rule. Each repetition, usually of a movement but sometimes of a thought, resulted in temporary relief from his emotional dilemma. If he were writing and the feeling came, words, phrases, or even whole lines had to be crossed out and re-written, often with entirely different words. If the feeling occurred during conversation, Daniel had to go back to what he had said last and say it again before he could go on. If he was doing nothing special when the feeling came, he would repeat whatever movement he could remember that he had just made.

He tried to disguise these manoeuvres when others were around. But if the movements were 'too subtle' they felt inadequately done. Daniel's system was in shambles and he knew it.

My new 'learning-based' explanation gave him an under-standable scheme to think about. It gave him hope, a framework without God, sin, or religion. Did Daniel want to 'buy' this view? Well, yes and no.

Daniel carried his charts and books back and forth like talismans. He consulted them frequently and would review them at bedtime. We would fit incidents, old and new, into the scheme, sometimes modifying the charts. He began to describe his problems of daily life in language that would warm the hearts of the behavioural-oriented everywhere. Yes, he believed that there was great promise in this new conceptualization. For the first time he felt his problem was understood by someone else, and it made sense to him as well. He began to confide in me more. His parents said he seemed more relaxed and spoke hopefully about therapy working.

But he could not yet fully discount his beliefs about the fundamental validity of his own views about the 'true nature' of his difficulties, though his confidence in this view was weakened. (He now thought the probability of being punished by God if he broke rules was about fifty-fifty.)

At this point help came in the form of a visit to his rabbi. Daniel and I discovered at this meeting that in ancient times, Hebrew sages had not been ignorant of Obsessive–Compulsive Disorder. In fact, during the Middle Ages a religious ceremony had been developed that seemed to be an uncanny match to the present circumstances. The rabbi scheduled the religious ceremony for a morning later that week.

The ceremony was held in the rabbi's study. The rabbi and two of the older men in the congregation sat at one end of the room. Daniel stood before these 'judges'; I looked on as Daniel read from a copy of an ancient text.

Before three rabbis serving as judges I ask release from every vow or oath or prohibition or restriction . . . even a prohibition to derive enjoyment that I imposed upon myself . . . that escaped my mouth or that I vowed in my heart . . . both regarding vows that are known to me and those that I have already forgotten . . . it is impossible to specify them because there are so many . . .

Daniel of course was released and the ceremony had provisions for release from any future vows, declaring them all 'totally null and void, without effect and without validity'.

Daniel walked out of the rabbi's study with a lighter step. He even smiled a little as we parted. We both sensed we had reached a turning point. But there was a long road ahead. It was time to get on with the treatment we had agreed upon.

Of course treatment had long since *been* underway. There had been twelve sessions up to this point, usually three times a week. But 'the treatment' meant that Daniel had to violate systematically every existing rule and taboo that could be specified. He knew this was crucial if he were to free himself. But where to begin and how to proceed? We were dealing with a powerful, long-entrenched system.

All our preparation for this moment, including the religious ceremony, and a later 'booster session' with the rabbi, provided confidence and motivation. Now Daniel had to confront the forbidden actions and thoughts. It would take all his courage to go about doing exactly what his deeply entrenched feelings told him he must not do.

Daniel now rated the probability that he would be punished

by God if he broke his rules as less than 30 per cent. He was now willing to tackle the rules head on and I felt satisfied he would have a fighting chance.

Because most of the rule breaking would have to be done by Daniel alone as 'homework' assignments, he carried a card in his wallet which listed four guidelines from the religious ceremony. In a 'weak moment' Daniel was to consult them. They were:

1. It is proper to enjoy God-given gifts of life and improper to deny oneself life's everyday pleasures.
2. No thought is inherently evil or sinful. We don't have complete control of our thoughts, and thoughts help discharge tensions.
3. Self-imposed vows, promises, rules, etc., are invalid and unacceptable unless they are grounded in accepted religious principles or practices and even then are valid only if they are reasonable, i.e., ones we can be expected to follow.
4. We are urged to refrain from engaging in 'self-conceived false religious practices', and rituals should be viewed in this way when they are done for religious purposes.

I warned Daniel it would be a long hard job before systematic exposure to taboos would 'evaporate' the rituals, a concept he understood better than I.

We made a careful plan of attack. First we worked on the avoidance. By not avoiding taboo situations, Daniel would have to violate them.

Life for Daniel was as hard as it ever had been. He was getting Fs on his papers and tests. He was being bombarded constantly with 'spontaneous feelings' and 'pure rituals' that he couldn't link to taboos.

We started with 'imagining work' in my office. We developed categories of all the rules that Daniel had set for himself. He had rules for choosing food and drink, how to dress and groom, how to carry out household chores, how to drive, walk, write, remember, talk, make a purchase, and so on.

In each of these categories, we made lists of specific taboo activities from the least anxiety provoking to the most. We both could see from the beginning that this would work. Daniel dredged up in his imagination the mildest, least frightening ones to think about. It got easier and easier to do this. He would imagine telling me a 'taboo' memory, then he would actually *tell* me one. He came to tell me *every* 'forbidden' memory.

His homework was practising what we did in the office in his home. It was harder without me around, but he managed.

His life began opening up in substantial ways. Saturdays were scheduled for work in settings that triggered particularly strong feelings. I accompanied Daniel as he drove to campus along 'forbidden' roads, parked in various 'taboo' spaces in different 'prohibited' parking lots, walked to buildings along 'unacceptable' pathways and went through 'verboten' doors. He did all this with very little difficulty.

It is now the end of May. Daniel has not solved all of his problems. He still has what we call 'spontaneous feelings' and we are trying to solve those. Daniel is so encouraged that he will not accept his current status even though he is better than he has been in years. There are many ways to tackle the symptoms that are left. The biggest problem is having the patience to give each step in therapy enough chance to work.

Daniel is looking for a flat with some college friends, but will keep working with me in the autumn.

Daniel is not the sort of case that behaviour therapists hope will walk through their doors. It was clear from the first that Daniel was not going to be easy. People write about behaviour therapy for OCD as if you can just 'flood' the patients with whatever they fear or avoid the most and 'prevent them from ritualizing'. But anyone who has worked with more than a couple of OCD patients knows how complicated it can be to translate this formula into something that really works. In the end, good therapy is first about people reaching people, and then about a technique.

Daniel was doubly blessed. He had the amazing good fortune not only to work with an extraordinary therapist, but also to have a rabbi who uncovered a ceremony which is the Jewish counterpart to the Roman Catholic treatment of scrupulosity.

There is no long-term follow-up as yet on Daniel. But as of the autumn of 1987, he and Xavier are still working together with slow but steady progress. (More information on Judaism and OCD is found in the Appendix.)

IV
ON THE BOUNDARIES

There are several subjects that lie beyond the usual clinical questions raised by Obsessive–Compulsive Disorder, but which are just as interesting and important. Our new perspective and understanding of this illness touches on at least three far-reaching and diverse aspects of our everyday life. First consider our superstitions (I touch wood) and our housekeeping habits (I can't stand dirty dishes in the sink). Where do these stop and OCD begin? Second, I am impressed by the resemblance of my patients' compulsive rituals to the fixed behaviours of some animal species. This resemblance makes me wonder what studies of innate animal behaviours can offer the student of OCD. Third, I am always being asked: Is love an obsession?

Since the late 1970s, I have pondered the philosophical implications of Obsessive–Compulsive Disorder. Two of these questions hold my particular interest: Do compulsive patients lack 'free will'? Will understanding the 'doubting disease' lead to a biology of certainty – a biology of knowledge?

25

The Obsessionality of Everyday Life

The more I learn about OCD, the less sure I am about where true disorder ends and the spectrum of 'compulsive' styles, habits, and predilections begins. Obsessive character is harder to describe, and sometimes just as devastating as Obsessive–Compulsive Disorder. It's also almost impossible to change.

De Maupassant's story, 'The Piece of String' is a splendid introduction to a 'classic' compulsive personality. The compulsion of Maître Hauchecorne of Bréauté seems a trivial event:

> He had just arrived at Goderville, and he was directing his steps towards the public square, when he perceived upon the ground a little piece of string. Maître Hauchecorne, economical like a true Norman, thought that everything useful ought to be picked up, and he bent painfully, for he suffered from rheumatism. He took the bit of thin cord from the ground and began to roll it carefully . . .

As this elegant, sparse tale continues, Hauchecorne is observed by Maître Malandain, the harness-maker with whom he is on bad terms, 'both being good haters'. Maître Hauchecorne is falsely accused of having picked up a stolen purse, instead of the piece of string, and finally acquitted. But *he cannot leave it alone.* He persists in discussing his innocence to such a single-minded degree that this preoccupation in itself becomes ridiculed. He dies an early death, it is implied, due to this disgrace and humiliation, still muttering 'it was only a piece of string'. He becomes the town laughingstock, never understanding how they could smile about his piece of string dispute. The sketch of a 'trivial' habit, of a rigid personality capable of deeply held grudges, and single-minded preoccupation with right is a classic study of the obsessional temperament. Obsessional personalities are cold, rigid, and righteous. And often very neat.

I began this book with the disclaimer that everyday 'obsessionality' has little to do with what my patients suffer. I overstated the point. I have not resolved in my own mind where the obsessionality of everyday life leaves off and OCD begins. Take being neat or messy. What does it mean if you couldn't stand life with your sloppy roommate because the room was such a mess? Why is neatness in co-workers, flatmates, and employees so important to some of us and so irrelevant to others? Some see these attitudes as very mild forms of OCD, to others they are unrelated. The evidence is mixed.

One way that everyday habits are *very* much like obsessive disorder is that both are very hard to change. Because people don't, or can't, change these habits, even if they have a lot to gain by being less fussy or by neatening up, the 'neats' and the 'slobs' are at constant war.

When the communes of the 1960s were breaking up, the sociologist Andrew Rigby observed in his book, *Alternative Realities*, that everyday issues of neatness were a major source of conflict. Very often, it was different standards of cleanliness and hygiene that gave rise to conflict within a commune.

A poll of the disadvantages of communal living gave this issue as the *most common* source of dissatisfaction. Untidiness in the kitchen and bathroom, and sharing the washing machine (which tended to break) were the most common complaints. Together with the economic and spiritual issues that broke up the commune ideal were the realities of dealing with one another's habits. It turned out to be easier to agree on the big issues than to agree on whether the newspaper should be picked up or the clothes put away. Emotions ran strong on this issue: one commune in Rigby's poll described a member as a 'fascist housekeeper'.

The concept of 'dirt', or the definition of 'dirt', is a complex blend of care for hygiene and respect for conventions. When the Western housewife spring-cleans her home, she is obeying much more than the rules of hygiene. It is a statement of social belonging, a claim for group acceptance and conformity. Like many human activities, cleaning is a symbolic act by which we remodel our environment, making it conform with an idea. The anthropologist Mary Douglas has argued that dirt is removed because it is matter *out of place* and flouts the ideal order of our lives.

The mess and disarray of the commune to some meant an open free community without boundaries. Sharing unwashed dishes meant friendship to others, like Thomas Hardy's shepherd, Gabriel, who refused a clean mug for his cider: 'I never fuss about dirt in its pure state and when I know what sort it is . . . I wouldn't think of giving such trouble to neighbours in washing up when there's so much work to be done in the world already.'

In contrast to Hardy's rather lovable shepherd is Mrs Craig, the central character of George Kelly's popular 1925 play *Craig's Wife*. Continually watchful for specks of dirt, footprints on the rug, or furniture out of place, Mrs Craig drives off her family, her husband Walter's friends, and Walter himself.

Mazie, the maid, tells the housekeeper: 'There's plenty like her – I've worked for three of them; you'd think their houses were God Almighty.'

Mrs Craig's aunt, Miss Austen, moves out after telling her hostess: 'I've been practically a recluse in that room of mine upstairs just to avoid scratching that holy stairway, or leaving a footprint on one of these sacred rugs. I'm not accustomed to that kind of stupidity. I'm accustomed to *living* in rooms.'

'Craig's Wife' became a catchword term for a woman who exerts fanatic control through household management. Craig's wives still exist in today's world. House-proud housewives are common topics for marriage counsellors.

Joan and Steve fought because she was 'too compulsive' about the house. Joan had never thought she was one of those 'neatness freaks', the kind who emptied ashtrays before the guests left. Until she got married, Joan hadn't thought about her neatness much at all.

Joan and Steve had lived together before they married. Why hadn't this happened then? Well, they were never at home, and most of their things were still at their parents'. Now settled into a routine of married life, at home more often, their clothes, books, and paper piles filled up their flat. Joan was appalled at the chaos of socks, shoes, newspapers, and all the unread manuscripts (Steve edited a magazine) surrounding the bed – and the dirty shirts and underwear.

Joan's solution was mechanical, but it worked. She told me: 'I bought this big Mexican basket and I throw all the mess in it.' In return, she doesn't bug Steve. Peace, of sorts. It worked, more or less, but filling the basket was a fixed chore. It didn't take much time but there was always something to go in that basket. If she didn't, for her it was like sitting in a room when a picture is crooked. Some people don't notice – Joan would have to straighten it.

'I don't want to be like this,' she told me, 'I know it gets him angry. But I just can't help it. If I don't pick up all that junk, I feel too uncomfortable to sit down and read or do anything in that room. Do you know anyone who ever changed that sort of thing? I don't. I'm just like my father. I know I could never stop feeling this way.'

Steve never seemed to see the shirts, the socks, the old newspapers on the floor. He could always fish out the unread manuscripts. Every sock, unread manuscript, every scrap of paper was in that basket. Steve didn't care about where things were when he wasn't using them; these were irrelevant details. Everything important to him, everything that really needed to get done, sooner or later got done. Hadn't he lived alone all those years without losing anything important? Had he ever lost a manuscript? Hadn't his bills always got paid sooner or later? His telephone and gas had never been cut off, he had never even paid interest on his credit card. 'So why, tell me why,' he complained to me, 'does it matter to Joan? Besides, it's my business. Not hers.'

Trivial? Of course! But for this couple relatively manageable because Steve's easygoing nature helped. Two Joans living together would have been a disaster. Easily remediable? Not at all.

Bring up this topic with any married couple and you get knowing smiles. The most self-contained pair will have something to say about their differences concerning neatness, the ability to throw things away, a desire for order. He lets the bills he pays pile up for five weeks. She pays hers every Sunday. Is this Obsessive–Compulsive Disorder? Probably not. But it is remarkable how fixed these habits are and, for some marriages, how important the solutions.

The best solution is to agree to disagree and not try reforming each other. I pay the bills (rather promptly) while my husband does the taxes (always late). It has worked out much better with these 'separate but equal' chores.

Any experienced marital counsellor will challenge the spouse who says 'It's simple, if only he/she would just not leave things around that way' or 'I can't understand why he/she finds it so difficult to . . .' The counsellor knows that this is a truly important issue, one with ramifications affecting other aspects of their relationship, and more often effectively 'absorbed' and non-responded to than decisively altered. Usually it's a matter of coming to terms with 'temperamental differences' (like who needs to sleep more and who needs to sleep less) rather than something that could be decisively altered (like driving on the right even if you learned to drive on the left). As one skilled therapist told me: 'There are two approaches for the neat partner. Hide the mess or clean it up yourself. I tell my patients, "That's what doors are for." Nothing else is going to work.'

Everyday neatness, good handwriting, clean desks, hanging up clothes, paying bills weekly – do these routine, mundane matters have anything to do with what OCD patients suffer? Is it a milder form of the disorder? The penalties and rewards these everyday habits can bring, starting early, astonish me. A study of experienced and novice grade-school teachers showed that even when instructed to grade essays on content alone, neat essays got higher marks.

Does neatness always win? No, in some settings the messy desk or the informal type of classroom were rated as having more creative leadership. But being messy or neat affects all our other perceptions.

Messy or neat, people don't change. In my clinic, I know which patients to call up if they are ten minutes late; when one of these patients is ten minutes late and doesn't telephone, it *has* to mean that they forgot.

In subtle and not so subtle ways, this obsessionality of everyday life determines our living styles. A friend and I joke about a mutual friend whose holiday planning takes up more time than the rest of us spend on the planning and the trip *combined*.

As the 'OCD expert', I have become a repository of people's 'habits', curious acts that come from nowhere. My friend Wally counts in threes by clicking his fingernails together as he walks down the street. Leda likes to touch walls or bushes, 'just to touch them' as she walks. If someone is watching, she won't do it. But if alone, she finds this oddly comforting. My hairdresser counts his steps when going up or down stairs. Are these mini-compulsions? No one knows.

In the extreme, there is what psychiatrists label Compulsive Personality Disorder. This is considered a different diagnosis from Obsessive–Compulsive Disorder. When severe, the person is so rigid about their daily routine that they are just as stuck as any of the patients in this book. Compulsive personalities don't usually come for treatment for their habits; their complaints are about everyone else. When I think about Compulsive Personality Disorder, I always think of Terry.

A former patient, Terry is a total treatment failure. It was his wife who got him in to see me. He had temper tantrums when she accidentally got his shoes out of line on the cupboard floor. Terry could tell from an unaligned shoelace that someone had 'messed up' his cupboard. Terry didn't want a psychiatric consultation; it was others who were out of line. Only his wife's threat to leave had brought him in at all. He'd arrive at our appointments livid: 'How can she be so careless. I've told her so often I like things neat.'

Cupboards were just the beginning. As soon as dinner dishes were washed, and washed they were right after dinner, the table was set for breakfast. 'Just so it's ready.' Anything moved out of place, even an ashtray, was put right back. Terry's fanatical neatness and rigidity discomforted guests and gradual social isolation added to the household tensions.

Terry made lists. When Sunday began as a day for pleasure, he converted it to a list of tasks. An interesting lecture or sculpture could become a tiresome list of exercises and proscriptions. Terry's projects became dreaded obligations.

Friendships were also coloured by what I call Terry's 'demand sensitivity', a common feature of compulsive personalities. If Terry felt that someone, even a good friend, was asking something of him, he had an automatic, unpleasant reaction – the urge to say no. It was not that he avoided responsibility, quite the contrary. As he explained to me, for someone else a promise or reassurance was just small talk. For him it was a weighty contract. He was very serious about what people expected of him.

Terry's wife had heard about our drug treatment for obsessions, and wanted me to get her husband to try clomipramine.

'Life with him is absolute hell,' she said. 'He's got worse and worse. You've got to do something.'

I was sympathetic, but we couldn't help. Terry's diagnosis was

Compulsive Personality. He didn't want to change; he was not tormented. Terry had always had rigid patterns of behaviour and didn't see them as his problem. He knew that the world was full of problems, but they were inefficient employees, messy service people, people who didn't understand how to do things the right way (*his* way!) No one knows yet whether clomipramine would work for compulsive personalities; it is a fascinating question that should be studied. In Terry's case the subject of treatment was moot; Terry wasn't having any. So we never tried, and life at home got harder.

Terry's divorce was no surprise. At work, his inability to delegate held up his promotion. His boss wrote on his performance rating: 'Mr B is so busy polishing his glasses that he never looks through them.'

Even though he would never become acutely ill, never reach the helpless misery of our severely sick obsessive–compulsive patients, Terry was as much a prisoner of his constricting habits as any patient with Obsessive–Compulsive Disorder. In some ways he was worse off, because he never could see that anything was wrong and try to work it out.

This rigidity is one reason why so many of my obsessional patients – those with extreme Compulsive Personality Disorder as well as Obsessive–Compulsive Disorder – end up divorced or never married. Loneliness may be a big price to pay but giving up the habits to accommodate others, even those they love the most, is so uncomfortable, so distressing that my patients insist they don't have a choice.

This is no diatribe against routine. Routines are helpful; they make busy lives efficient and easier. As we get older, it may be routines that will keep many of us, the normally forgetful elderly, out of nursing homes. Establish certain routines, always check the gas, make sure you have your key, put your purse down in the same place every time you come into the house, make lists, and always put the list in the same place.

Following these routines won't save you if you begin to suffer from severe memory loss, but for the usual absent-mindedness that most elderly get, these routines can make the difference between independence and dependence, especially for the elderly person who lives alone.

But, true as this observation may be, following routines is not always helpful. They can become totally inflexible. *No one* has yet found a way to change a person who tosses car keys onto any convenient surface into one who always hangs them on the kitchen nail. A substance that could do that would be truly labelled a 'miracle' drug.

26

Touch Wood

Whenever I walk in a London street,
I'm ever so careful to watch my feet;
  And I keep in the squares,
  And the masses of bears,
Who wait at the corners all ready to eat
The sillies who tread on the lines of the street,
  Go back to their lairs,
  And I say to them, 'Bears,
Just look how I'm walking in all the squares!'

A.A. MILNE
'Lines and Squares'

As a child growing up in the city I avoided (at least for several years) stepping on the pavement cracks. There were many superstitions about avoiding cracks between stones and cracks in pavement. 'Step on a crack, break your mother's back' was one of them. In hopscotch, you avoided the lines. I still touch wood after mentioning a piece of good fortune or a boast. Why do I do that? I don't know anyone else who does. And what do these superstitions have to do with obsessions and compulsions? Not very much, I think.

What compulsions and superstitions *do* have in common is magical thinking. Words and gestures assume powers that common sense denies. They both deal also with protection from harm. But the resemblance stops there. There is no real or valid relationship between these common superstitions and what my patients suffer.

In the first place, obsessive–compulsive patients are not likely to have been particularly superstitious before they became ill. We conducted a poll of all our patients and found they weren't. Moreover, my patients tell me that the few superstitions they might have had before they became ill, didn't 'feel' at all the same. They were weak, transient, easily ignored, without the grip of OCD. More striking is how different the nameless contents of common superstitions are from the debilitating symptoms of Obsessive–Compulsive Disorder.

Common superstitions include touching wood, avoiding ladders, spilling salt, avoiding the number 13, and so on. They are simple, brief gestures performed to avoid bad luck or bring on good. They have little force or urgency.

Superstition seems part of the human condition. Few clues exist to tell us why someone is more superstitious than another. Education, sex, or occupation don't predict it. Spinoza said that we would never be superstitious if we controlled our fate or were always favoured by fortune:

'. . . but being frequently driven into straits where rules are useless, and being often kept fluctuating pitiably between hope and fear by the uncertainty of fortune's greedily coveted favours, they are consequently, for the most part, very prone to credulity.'

Obsessions and compulsions are idiosyncratic, consuming, intense, and complex behaviours. The great majority are washing or checking rituals, or thoughts of harm that go beyond all superstitious belief. My patients focus on specific fears, and above all on dirt and germs. There is no common folklore to which my patients conform, for many of them no ungoverned menace of fate. So it is clear how little superstitions have in common with OCD.

Stretching mightily, I found a pale analogue for compulsions in the superstitions of athletes. Only sports rituals come close in quality and content to true compulsions; perhaps the stress of performance anxiety creates a similar, if temporary, level of tension. Religious ritual and superstitious behaviours are very common – almost universal – in competitive sports.

In addition to team prayers, team cheers, and hand slaps before a game, individual players commonly practise private rites. A basketball player, for example, will always wear the same pair of socks or a special hat. There are rituals centred around dressing (one side of the body must be dressed first), lucky drinks to have before the game, and even special cups or glasses from which to drink. These superstitions give some feeling of control during tense anticipation of a game, where the outcome is uncertain. Indeed, the greater the stress, the more likely we are to find well-established rituals.

Our patients' rituals, though, are far more elaborate than athletes' simple good luck gestures. Amy, a ten-year-old, had a special order in which her teeth were brushed, face washed, bed made, and breakfast eaten. Her mother had to kiss her in threes, three on the right and then three on the left cheek. She said: 'Bye Mum, bye Dad, put on your seat belt and drive carefully,' and she had to say this three times. If there was any interruption in this entire routine, the entire sequence had to be repeated.

When our patients' compulsive rituals occur during sports, they interfere with the game the same way they interfere with the rest of their lives. One boy had to run down the soccer field using special steps. He moved too slowly to keep up and missed the ball because his mind was on his feet. He had to leave the team.

Over the years I've learned never to tell a patient with compulsions that 'everybody does that', or 'I know just how you feel'. *They* don't and *you* don't. Everyday superstitions and normal developmental rituals, such as the bedtime rituals of very young children, have a pattern, intensity, and a 'feel' different from the rituals of this mysterious disorder. Why are washing and checking such common rituals? We have to look elsewhere for our answer and the place we do might surprise you.

27

Grooming and Nesting

I filmed David, aged twelve, plucking lint off his underwear. Meticulously, slowly, he studied each section of the cloth and assembled a midget pyramid of white thread. David always sets about his plucking in the same way. And he always does a perfect job of it, his fingers moving in fine pincer movements. David's undershirt, like several of its predecessors, is about to fall apart. He has, in a sense, picked it 'clean'.

Under David's bed is his entire lint collection, the result of three years of thread-pulling. It resembles a grey cloud spreading out from underneath the mattress. This collection remains undisturbed because David's family cannot deal with David's hysteria when it is touched. Just seeing his white shirt or trousers sets him off. If his mother were to dress him and set him off on a busy routine, he would stop plucking for hours.

David has no explanation for what he does, but he can remember when he began collecting. One day, suddenly, these bits of cloth that he had never particularly noticed before simply assumed a new importance. He started noticing them and they gripped his attention. He could not simply pass them by. At first, he tried to avoid seeing the lint, but gradually the effect of even a glimpse of lint strengthened. David had never heard of anyone else doing this and had never tried to understand it. By age eleven, he had accepted this as 'how I must be'. David's only model for himself was the squirrel in his garden: 'I'm like that too,' he told me, 'I have to collect things.' After three months in a psychiatric hospital, David said he still felt that the 'squirrels I watched out of the window were the ones who understood'.

David's 'squirrelling' habits, and the habits of most of our compulsive patients, remind me of many aspects of animal behaviour. Their perfectly executed, meticulously deliberate collections look like the nest-building of birds, the hoarding of squirrels. Was my first patient, Sal, the involuntary yet fanatic trash collector, building a nest? At one level that is an absurd thought. But I had begun to see a complex behaviour pattern develop in an identical fashion among many unrelated people. Its source had to be located somewhere in the brain. Could I find a model to explain this behaviour? I have come to believe that ethology might be a source.

Ethology, founded by Charles Whitman and Oskar Heinroth in the late nineteenth century, and brought to recognition by Konrad Lorenz in the 1930s, is the study and comparison of animal behaviours. Konrad Lorenz dubbed himself and other ethologists as 'starers-at-animals'. In ethology and its offspring, neuro-ethology, I find a model, a beginning for understanding the fixed patterns I see in our washers (read groomers), ritualizers (read ritual displays), and collectors (read as nesters and hoarders). Neuro-ethologists study the role of the brain in developing these behaviours and in keeping them intact.

Ethologists study inborn behaviour patterns. Like our patients' behaviours, these patterns, once again, continue to the end whether or not they are appropriate. My collie dog, for example, turns in circles to prepare his bed before lying down. Historically it may have been necessary for some of his ancestors to trample tall grasses or to chase off snakes or insects. But my collie circles the same way whether he is preparing to sleep outside my camping tent in the Shenandoah or on my living room carpet.

The squirrel's ritual of food storage is also what an ethologist would call a 'fixed action pattern'. Squirrels with extra food, even those in cages, will look for places to 'hide' those extra nuts, and go through covering and tamping down movements. The behaviour is a 'programme' that 'runs' once started.

Nesting, like hoarding, is another highly ritualized behaviour. The animal has to locate, collect, and bring into a shelter the necessary building materials. Then the materials are formed into the nest shape, and finally the animal settles in.

Nesting can be started by hormonal change in a pregnant mouse (progesterone is released during pregnancy), and nesting can be started in a non-pregnant mouse by the injection of progesterone. There are fascinating hints of endocrine disturbances in OCD: male children with OCD outnumber females two to one; OCD occurs as a complication of childbirth; and drugs that are anti-androgens are used to treat OCD. Another link between OCD and ethology.

In the introduction I told the story of Sal, who felt compelled to pick up every bit of paper and trash and never knew why. The pleas of his wife and the threats of his boss were not enough to silence the urgent inner voice in Sal that told him that every scrap he saw must be hoarded. The intensity of the urge is of course the hallmark of OCD. But the highly selective nature of OCD behaviours is just as remarkable. Washing, grooming, hoarding – any theory of this disease must account for the incredible selectivity of these behaviours, which could be action patterns from an ethologist's field book. As psychiatrists we need to be field observers much more often than we are.

Shirley was twenty-four when she first told me about her life as a compulsive hoarder. At our first meeting, her words came tumbling out.

'For the past seven years, I have saved virtually everything that has come into my ownership with the exception of Kleenexes, gum wrappers, torn cinema tickets, but not much else. I do, however, save *unused* but worn and crumpled Kleenexes that I have taken out of my pocket, for 'just in case' times that I'll need them.

'I save receipts, even ones for low-cost items, paper bags, boxes, newspapers, magazines, notes and lists to myself, freebie flyers and advertisements, old cinema listings, empty vitamin bottles, shampoo bottles, and jars, old TV guides, catalogues and calendars (for the pictures), clothing I don't wear any more and know I never will, unfinished crafts projects, clippings and articles from newspapers, and very old make-up that I think I am allergic to, but I feel compelled to use it up instead of throwing it out.

'The worst is my mail. For the past seven years, I have kept 99 per cent of all the mail I've received. Most of it I never read, don't even open, because you can see from the envelope that it is junk mail and I can tell at a glance whether it contains a personal letter, a cheque, or a bill. Even after I've read my personal mail, I save it. I save it all! But I am not saving it for sometime in the future, or because I will ever read it again. I'm saving it because I can't help myself. I feel compelled to save everything.

'My bedroom at home is a monumental junk heap of all my collections. Strewn and piled and boxed everywhere in the most disorderly fashion are all the items I mentioned. There is a narrow path from my bedroom door to my bed and even there I walk on mail and newspapers. Aside from this path, there is no other place for me to walk, not even to my wardrobe unless I clear the way. And there are piles of stuff in other parts of the flat too, growing larger and larger every day.'

I asked Shirley if I could visit her home. Surely this poised young woman wasn't living in a paper heap like the Collyer brothers! Those elderly reclusive brothers had lived in their New York Fifth Avenue home until their deaths in 1947. The bizarre contents of their house made headlines for weeks. In order to enter the home, the police had to cart off two lifetimes of junk including numerous packages of newspapers, over 3,000 books, and, most peculiarly, fourteen grand pianos and a model-T Ford. The police removed 120 tons of junk before pronouncing the house cleared. Was I about to see such a scene? (Did the Collyer brothers have OCD?)

I had to see Shirley's place for myself. The following week, I drove out to the pleasant suburb in which Shirley lived. Nothing about her apartment complex, certainly not its neat external appearance, prepared me for what was inside. She answered the door timidly. 'No one but my mother has been here in years,' she said. 'Well, here goes.' She let me in.

The flat presented an unusual sight. Not as bad as the Collyers', but getting there. There were piles of paper everywhere. These were about six feet tall, stacked neatly above eye level. In order to move about, paths had been kept between rows of paper stacks. It was a little like moving through a warehouse, or a peculiar sort of library. Shirley kept up her chatter, nervous at my presence. The scene wasn't quite as disorderly as Shirley had suggested. It was cavelike and protective, a paper burrow. But Shirley's desperation didn't leave room for dispassionate ethology.

'I am ruining my life by holding onto this horrendous *mess*! Two-thirds of the contents of this flat should be thrown out.' (I thought, closer to 95 per cent!) 'What stops you?' I asked.

'I just haven't been able to do it. Cleaning up my room and the rest of this flat has been foremost on my mind all these years and yet I have barely done anything about it. I get this intense anxiety whenever I think about doing it. I just don't want to face what I think will be the agonizing process of sorting through everything – what to keep and what to throw out.'

She pointed to the stacks closing around her and started crying. 'I won't accept any dates, I don't see friends, because they would have to come and see this. I don't know why I do it.'

We talked for a while longer. She calmed down. 'Would it help if we started together right now?' I asked.

'I tried that,' she said. 'A psychologist, a behaviour therapist, worked with me for a while. Each day we would try throwing out some things together.'

'And?'

'It just didn't work. I got too upset. I tell you I couldn't do it. I got scared.'

'About what?'

'I don't know. I really don't.'

We puzzled this over and over together. Shirley is held captive by an incredibly powerful force, one she doesn't understand. Like Sal and other hoarders, the force is irresistible and she doesn't know why she obeys it. She knows only the discomfort of trying to resist it. Like Sal, Shirley described her collection with absolute clarity. She knows her behaviour is odd, but it comes from some part of her she doesn't recognize or understand, and she wants so badly not to want to go on hoarding and hoarding. (Why didn't behaviour therapy work for her? It often does work for others like her. Candidly, I can't explain why it hadn't helped.) Shirley couldn't tolerate even the lowest dose of clomipramine, and so far has not been helped.

Konrad Lorenz described innate patterns of behaviour as the 'back side of a mirror'. Lorenz chose this metaphor to stress that we do not simply reflect what is outside ourselves in the real world the way a mirror does. The human mind contains built-in drives, and skills which are transmitted within each species. These genetically determined patterns behind the mirror are 'stored knowledge', determining what we see and how we react to it.

Life itself is a process of acquiring knowledge, said Lorenz, and the innate patterns – which he described so brilliantly, and for which he won a Nobel Prize in 1973 – were these pieces of information about how to deal with the world.

I have come to see the rituals of Obsessive–Compulsive Disorder as fixed action patterns, innate behaviours which in our patients for some reason and in some way have been released inappropriately. The obsessive–compulsive patient checks whether the coffee pot is unplugged: he can check this thirty or forty times. Each subsequent checking episode is identical to the first. Rituals often include arranging one part of personal space, which then must be guarded. One boy who joined our study last year had slept outside his bedroom door for years so that the room inside would remain 'perfect'. It became difficult for him even to enter the room to rearrange it.

On a more familiar level, Ginger, at twenty-eight, has a lonely existence, wiping, dusting, cleaning, and straightening her two-bedroom flat. When not at work at her receptionist job, Ginger counts the towels in the cupboard, arranges the pillows on her couch, and sets out the breakfast things. Cereal is placed in the bowl with sugar on it, ready to pour milk on the next day. Shoelaces are untied and ready, vitamins placed out. All of this straightening is wasteful, unnecessary, and exhausting. Ginger described herself as a 'nervous wreck' twenty-four hours a day.

At one time, I might have dismissed Ginger as an extreme sort of American housewife, brainwashed by television commercials. Not any more. Not since I learned the pattern. Obsessive–compulsive patients do the same thing in Sweden, China, England, the Sudan, or in India. Comparisons of obsessive–compulsive patients across these very different countries show them to be remarkably alike. This cross-cultural pattern means that we have to look within ourselves at a more elemental level to find some model for such absurd rearranging and collecting.

But back to the key questions: Why and how are these behaviours released? What is their functional significance? I have no answers, only hints. The behaviours in OCD resemble misplaced grooming and/or protective rituals. OCD can occur in association with disease of the basal ganglia, the 'old' part of the brain (evolutionarily speaking) known to control reactions to, and anticipation of response to, information from our senses. But any explanation must account for the remarkable similarity of one patient to the other. At this time, I see OCD patients as victims of evolutionarily meaningful but personally horrific 'orders from the brain'.

It can be argued (and will be) that the idea of 'innate' stimulus patterns that set off fixed behaviours is fine for animals, but is there any reason to think that humans or even the other higher primates – say, monkeys – have mental mechanisms anything like this? There haven't been many studies of this subject, but a few done with rhesus monkeys suggest a yes to this question.

I have found some examples that move me to think more about such 'pre-wired' behaviour patterns in primates like ourselves. In one study, monkeys, raised in complete social isolation, were given control of a slide machine and could choose whether they looked at pictures of scenery or of other monkeys. They chose the other monkeys and vocalized to them. When the face of a threatening adult monkey was shown, the older monkeys began to withdraw and act afraid. The point of this study was that recognition of one's own species and display of a specific emotion can occur without learning.

A recent study done by Susan Mineka at the University of Texas in Austin is even more convincing. Her study showed that there might be some innate basis for the development of *particular* fears. Working with rhesus monkeys, Dr Mineka was studying how fears develop.

Monkeys who grow up in the wild all fear snakes. Monkeys who are raised in the laboratory, where they never see snakes, will show no fear of a snake the first time they see it and will even reach out to play with it. Dr Mineka studied how her laboratory-reared animals learned fears. All of her monkeys had been brought up in laboratory cages, so they had never seen the outside world, had never seen snakes. They also had never seen flowers. Dr Mineka tried to teach them to be afraid of snakes. This she could do easily: they acted afraid of snakes after watching a field-reared monkey with a snake, or even after seeing a short video film of another monkey being terrified of a snake. But she could *not* teach the monkey to be afraid of a flower! Even when a (spliced) film of a monkey looking as if it were terrified by a flower was shown.

What does this mean? Why should we care if you can make a monkey afraid of a flower or not? This, in fact, was a tremendously important experiment. It tells us that in primates like ourselves there are certain inborn ('hard-wired', in modern computer terms) neuronal patterns in the brain that will react to only some stimuli (for example, snakes, spiders) but not to others (in this case, flowers).

Phobias emerge in humans after only a single unpleasant experience and they are very hard to cure. Remarkably, the most common phobias concern mankind's most ancient dangers: closed spaces, heights, snakes and spiders. People are rarely phobic about the really dangerous objects in modern life: automobiles, guns and knives. This ability to easily 'learn' a selected pattern of fears is also present, then, in ourselves.

Some would call these preferences and reactions innate patterns of knowledge. Whatever you call it, this sensitivity, or preparedness to react to some stimuli and not others, might explain the patterns of obsessive–compulsive patients. The release of innate behaviours in animals may be 'out of date' responses to signals that were appropriate thousands of years earlier. Some behavioural patterns in disturbed humans might be interpreted similarly. For example, why do most obsessional patients have such identical patterns of washing and grooming and of rituals in doorways?

Grooming behaviours are particularly interesting to me because washing and rituals of dress are by far the most common of all the obsessive–compulsive patterns. Almost all of our youngest patients who start out counting and checking spend some months or years as washers before their teenage years are over. And once the washing ritual appears, it seldom leaves.

Washing is ritualized and specific. Each of our washers has his own routine which is followed precisely for every episode. In an attempt to 'just stare' as Lorenz had done, I have had our washing patients demonstrate their showering rituals for me, explaining the minutiae of their routines. In the shower, Brendan strokes the right side of his head eight times, applies shampoo, then strokes another eight times, rinses eight times, and strokes eight times more. He repeats this for the top of his head, the left side, and the back, in that order. Next on to the face, neck, and the rest of his body. Susan's rituals involve the 'right way' to turn on the water, continuing after the showering is over, to the 'right way' to hang up the towel.

Rats normally spend about a third of their waking lives grooming. The grooming lets them regulate temperature (evaporation of saliva) and influences their sexual behaviour (different odours in male saliva). But grooming also takes place during frustration or conflict, and at such times rats groom even more. Under any circumstances, the rat has a fixed pattern to his grooming as elaborate as that of any of our patients. The washing always proceeds from head to tail. Scratching and tail sniffing end the ritual.

In the laboratory, grooming can be 'turned on' with eerie predictability by a number of chemicals, hormones, and certain lesions of the brain. If ACTH (adrenocorticotropic hormone) from the pituitary is injected into the brain, a rat starts grooming exactly like it does in the natural state. There are also a host of drugs that *stop* the rat's grooming. Probably, ACTH is released naturally in the brain when the rat faces what researchers term a novel or a conflict situation and sets its grooming programme off.

Do some animals indulge in 'super grooming' under natural conditions? Lab technicians at the National Institute of Mental Health have got used to such a sight when they flick on the lights in the morning at the Animal Genetics Center. Among the cages for the twenty thousand or so mice kept at the centre for scientific experiments are some in which all the mice have had their hair and whiskers clipped.

All, that is, except for one mouse who is clearly responsible for the mass haircuts of his cage mates. Because of their enthusiasm, these mice are called 'barber mice'. Aside from the fact that there is only one barber to a cage, and that the cutting takes place in the dark, not much is known about this behaviour. One theory, advanced in *The Mouse in Biomedical Research*, a work devoted mainly to more serious problems, is 'exaggerated grooming behaviour', a compunction for cleanliness run wild. It is not certain if this behaviour happens among uncaged mice. Interpretation of these rituals is as complex in the mouse as it is in our patients. Grooming another mouse is part of the surprisingly complex rodent social life. But it is one possible model for our washer subjects. Sometimes the behaviour of our subjects seems like models for *animal* behaviours.

Two of the youngest boys in our study spend three or four hours each day licking their hands. Each finger gets licked in its turn, the order doesn't change. The atavistic patterns set loose in these children will probably be replaced as they grow older with more 'ordinary' washing rituals.

Self-grooming is just one particularly striking animal model for my patients' excessive cleaning. But throughout the zoological hierarchy are examples of innate patterns of cleaning the nest, removing faeces from the nest or burrow, defecating away from home base. These habits are so basic to survival that they are part of almost every mammalian repertoire.

There is something about thresholds that call forth ceremonies. Our patients leap and gesture, posture and gesticulate at gates, arches, doorways – any sort of entrance. Paul got stuck in doorways for hours. When John would arrive home in the family car, he was compelled to roll the window down and up. He would open the door and then shut it, open it again, and get out of the car. He would then walk to the mail-box and around the oak tree. At last he could enter the house.

John used to try to trick his ritual. He would drive into the garage and try to enter the house through the garage door. But he was always caught at this deception. He would have to return first to the car, and then to the front entrance to begin his ritual entry. John's entry rituals were mere distractions compared to those of another young patient. When she came home, the sight of her front door called forth a time-consuming and, if observed, humiliating entrance ritual. She had to roll around on the grass and then touch each of the trees in her backyard. Horrified, she avoided leaving her home, remaining upstairs for years, a princess trapped in a tower, with threshold rituals for locks.

Do animals have inappropriately released action patterns similar to those our patients go through? There are stories from the ethologists about a dog that performs a 'mouse jump' every time he approaches a machine shed where he had first scared a mouse. Another scientist tells of having to unload and reload her old pack horse every time she came to a place where they had frequently camped or else the horse would not go on.

But the most appealing, the most scientifically suggestive story, is about a goose. Konrad Lorenz kept his greylag geese in the house with him. One of these geese had got used to walking in a special way when she would return home:

'At first she always walked past the bottom of the staircase towards a window in the hallway before returning to the steps, which she then ascended to get into the room on the upper floor. Gradually she shortened this detour, but still kept on heading a little way towards the window before turning around and heading up the stairs.'

One day, Lorenz forgot to let his goose into the house at the usual time. It was beginning to get dark, and the goose was very eager to get home. She ran in the door and hurried straight away towards the stairs and began to climb up. Lorenz continues:

'Upon this, something shattering happened: arriving at the fifth step, she suddenly stopped, made a long neck, in geese a sign of fear, and spread her wings as for flight. Then she uttered a warning cry and nearly took off. Now she hesitated a moment, turned around, ran hurriedly down the five steps and set forth resolutely, like someone on a very important mission, on her original path to the window and back.

'This time, she mounted the steps according to her former custom from the left side. On the fifth step she stopped again, looked around, shook herself, and performed a greeting behaviour regularly seen in greylags when anxious tension has given place to relief! I hardly believed my eyes. The habit had become a custom which the goose could not break without being stricken by fear.'

Is it possible then, that the obsessions and compulsions of my patients are manifestations of our inborn knowledge? Could it be that the patterns of grooming, nesting, ritual displays are kept encoded, that they are not evident in normal human lives but only reveal themselves in this odd and debilitating disease? It's as if the useful everyday functions, of checking one's surroundings and appearance, run wild.

The parallel between OCD and animal behaviours is compelling. The built-in patterns document some stored knowledge that serves an ancient purpose. Cleaning, avoiding, checking, and repeating relate to the most basic preoccupations of cleanliness, safety, aggression and sex. When they are carried out out of context, they make no sense. The most convincing evidence will come when we find key 'releasers' of these behaviours, analogous to the hormones that typically set off such patterns in animals.

In *The Naked Ape*, Desmond Morris argued how our zoological heritage controls many of our seemingly 'spontaneous' activities. Grooming is a major part of this legacy. Morris points out: 'The place where the environment comes into direct contact with an animal – its body surface – receives a great deal of rough treatment during the course of its life. It is astonishing that it survives the wear and tear and lasts so well. It manages to do so because of its wonderful system of tissue replacement and also because animals have evolved a variety of special comfort movements to help keep it clean.' Compared with patterns of feeding, fighting, and mating, these behaviours may at first seem trivial. But without them the body could not function efficiently.

All mammals engage in a good deal of grooming, licking, nibbling, scratching, and rubbing. In the wild state, monkeys and apes can frequently be seen to groom themselves, systematically working through their fur, picking out pieces of dead skin, insects, or other foreign substances.

My thesis simply is an extension of that notion – that there may be complex behaviour patterns programmed into human brains, of which modern man is ordinarily unaware. With our fur long gone, is washing a primitive ritual that still remains with us? Compulsions such as washing, arranging, and pulling hair may give us a window into this zoological heritage; in my patients, a heritage deranged, gone berserk.

28

I Can't Get You Out of My Mind

In the 1985 film *Desperately Seeking Susan*, Roberta Glass, a bored housewife in suburban New Jersey, becomes completely preoccupied with a mysterious Manhattan woman who makes her dates through the personal columns. The pages of Roberta's diary become filled with fantasies about Susan; the offbeat style and adventures of Susan's life. Roberta first spies on Susan, then eventually enters her world. This is a secret passion; Roberta's husband never knows about it. The energy and time Roberta spends following Susan's life, the zany punk world of new values and behaviours, the often dangerous secrecy – might all this be called Roberta's Obsession? Several film critics used the word. One of the most common uses of the word 'obsession', in fact, is when we describe someone's excessive preoccupation with another.

Can an intense, totally preoccupying fascination with another, bordering on monomania, be considered an obsession? Is it a form of illness? I think usually not, but the theme fascinates and entertains. The fanatic, almost crazed pursuit might be a hunt. In *Les Miserables*, the inspector of police, Javert, hunts Jean Valjean for thirty years. This pursuit brings about Javert's own humiliation, ruin, and ultimately his death by suicide. Javert couldn't reconcile life's complexities with his rigid and bizarre determination to punish a trivial crime.

What characterizes these fanatic pursuers? Intensity and an unrelenting quest. Life is lived in absolutes, in rigid demands. Romance may be what draws us to the stories, but the obsessional rules are what ruin the protagonists. Inspector Javert is as uncompromising with himself as with Jean Valjean. When he believes he has falsely accused Mayor Madeleine, Javert tries, albeit unsuccessfully, to have *himself* dismissed! Victor Hugo calls Javert desperate and resolute, oddly honest, whimsical, but above all, a fanatic.

In the 1979 novel *Endless Love*, Scott Spencer writes about

David's obsession with his high school love, Jade. The novel has the quality of a case study. For David, nothing that isn't connected to Jade is real. Only through contact with Jade or her family does he feel as if he actually, legitimately exists. David's persistence, his indifference to proprieties and to the needs of his own family, destroy his life, and Jade's family. The intensity of their passion provokes equally intense responses – longing, envy, anger – in Jade's and David's parents, indirectly causing their separations and the deaths of both fathers.

David's obsession with Jade is frightening. He ends up in a psychiatric hospital. The book jacket uses the word 'obsession' three times. Throughout the novel David is told that he has an obsession. David is beyond the tolerated, delusional, irrational state of being in love. But does he have a disease? If so, which one? I don't call David's passions OCD. They are something else, though I'm not sure what.

Have I personally seen Robertas and Davids as patients? Only once. And when I did, nobody knew what to call him. Or what to do. You can't take love out of the mind. I still think about Sebastian, whom I haven't seen in twenty-seven years.

The court ordered a ten-day examination of Sebastian at the Boston Psychopathic Hospital in 1960, when I was training there. This was the third time in two years that the court had asked for psychiatric help with him. He had been arrested again in front of Dotty's Donuts shop on Washington Street in downtown Boston after complaints from the shop owner had failed to discourage his regular, and indeed extraordinary, presence around the shop. He had been arrested outside where he was waiting to see Sandra, the counter girl, when she got off from work. Sebastian was fifty-one, and had been separated from his wife for many years.

Sandra, a widow of fifty, had been the waitress at Dotty's Donuts for ten years and was a favourite with the regulars. She always had a smile, never failed to ask a customer how they were today, and always noticed if they had been away from the breakfast counter for a while.

For several years, Sebastian had worked as a dishwasher at Dotty's Donuts and, as he put it, had fallen in 'unrequited love' with Sandra. At first he was content just to work near her. Then he had started to linger longer, to leave notes for Sandra, and to bring presents.

Sebastian was a small, self-effacing man, but the intensity, the fixity of his behaviour frightened Sandra. The notes, written painfully in his broken English, announced his love, his unshakable devotion to her. But his love note included the phrase 'If I can't have you in life, I'll have you in death,' and this frightened Sandra even more. When she started to go out with a man, Sebastian let all the air out of the fellow's tyres. He was always polite and never tried to touch Sandra but he stared at her, always trying to catch her eye. She got angry and asked him to please leave her alone. The manager fired Sebastian. For a year, he found work in other restaurants. They all had to be on the same block as Dotty's Donuts.

His longing grew stronger. He had stolen a pair of shoes that Sandra kept as 'extras' at the shop. He just wanted to sleep touching something that was hers. After a time, he appeared at the shop to tell Sandra that he had had them bronzed. This was too much. The police were called again.

Sebastian was given a six-month suspended sentence and told to stay away from Dotty's Donuts. Within two weeks he had broken parole and was arrested once more.

Sebastian had been, as usual, polite and deferential to the officer who stopped him outside the donut shop's door. But he insisted that his love for Sandra would sooner or later be requited, and he could never contain his desire to see her.

In the hospital record, his physician, Dr Alan Hobson, recorded:

'Sebastian had been living on Tremont Street, reclusive and slightly alcoholic, obsessed with thoughts of Mrs S. but for the most part in control of his strong desire to see her. During his life before moving to Boston, he had held a series of jobs as gardener, handyman, and even grave digging. When in his room, he plays recordings of famous operatic arias and drinks beer to console himself. He was desperate about having been ordered out of the donut shop and felt ''in jail on the pavement''. Finally he began to wait outside the donut shop if only to see her arrive and leave. Following attempts to speak with her, she re-entered charges.'

Sebastian had good character references from employers and

co-workers. Everyone who knew him described him as gentle. He had been born on a farm in Newburyport, his mother's home, and remained there until his mother was committed to Danvers state hospital. His mother, aged seventy-four, was still there. His father had deserted the family, and Sebastian was raised by a foster family who he said 'used me nice'. His brother had been in a state hospital for ten years. His maternal grandmother, who had lived with them on the farm, was called 'mentally unstable' and was found dead in a swamp.

Sebastian's landlord, Mr Brown, came into the hospital to see him and see the doctors. He wanted the staff to know that he would do anything to help Mr Sebastian, that he was keeping his room for him. He thought Sebastian was a 'great guy'. 'Please help him out,' said Mr Brown, 'we miss him.'

Sebastian, his last boss said, was a good guy to have around. He was willing, got along with everyone, and was reliable. Yes, they would be glad to have him back.

Sebastian had completed eight grades of school. In the 1930s he had been happily married for a while to a woman who worked on a neighbouring farm and they had three children. Then something changed. In the 1940s he became infatuated with the wife of a neighbouring farmer, and would go away for long weekends with her, which led to the break-up of his marriage.

The hospital staff considered various diagnoses but were not satisfied by any. Sebastian was odd and certainly unrealistic about Sandra, but he did not have the thought disorder present in schizophrenia. He had periods of agitation and was depressed away from his love, but was not like patients who are called manic depressive. His love for Sandra is called his obsession throughout the hospital record, but Sebastian was not obsessive in the way I use the word in this book. The hospital formulation states:

'This middle-aged man's chief symptom is an obsessive affection for a woman who has never returned his feeling. His life history is one of early deprivation of almost certainly inadequate parents and his family is disturbed, with illness or hospitalization in every known member. He has always been somewhat childish and irresponsible, naïve, fanciful, and credulous if dutiful to those whom he admired. This atypical picture defies satisfactory diagnosis.'

Sebastian was very fond of his doctor, Dr Hobson, but his need to see Sandra was too strong. He 'eloped' from the hospital, but continued to write his doctor notes describing his miserable hunted life with only stolen glimpses of Sandra to keep him going.

During this period of elopement from the hospital, Sebastian went to Hartford, Connecticut, to see Dr Francis Braceland, a famous psychiatrist, whom he had learned of from another patient while in the Boston hospital. She had told him that Dr Braceland was the most helpful doctor she had ever met. So Sebastian took off and somehow found his way into Dr Braceland's office. According to Sebastian, and there are no other records of this visit, Dr Braceland told him 'I cannot help you. Your problem is love.' About this visit Sebastian wrote to Dr Hobson (on a postcard with no return address), 'I begged Dr Braceland to take my memories away. But Dr Braceland told me there is no cure for love.'

Sebastian surfaced only once more. On that occasion, he tried to serenade Sandra with his harmonica; she promptly called the police but Sebastian got away. Sebastian wouldn't give up his freedom, but missed Dr Hobson. He solved this by correspondence. 'I miss talking with you, Doctor, I know I need help. But I don't want to be put back in the hospital, so I better lay low. Nearly seven months have gone by since I was in that hospital, and I'm not worth more than when I left there. I work fifty hours a week to try to forget. But I am sick inside. I can't bear to live back in the past but each new job I take, she comes to my mind. Oh, I say, she is not in the same building as I. So I quit the job and tell my boss, you will not have to pay me any more.

'I would like to talk with you doctor, but do not know how I can. I hope you have a happy Easter and your future will be happy. Your friend, Sebastian.

'P.S. My address is the same as the one that's lying under the ground at Forest Hills Cemetery, under God's blue skies. Only one big room with no number. So you will not be able to write to me.'

His last letter, sent from another hiding place, said:

'I'm 53 years old, nearly worn out. I spent this Christmas alone in almost complete darkness. I bought a hamburger sandwich for my Christmas dinner. I go in the bar room, where I see married couples, and I can't stay there. It makes me just screech. Only my harmonica don't make me sick. My freedom is no good to me, I am so miserable this way.

'The train she rides on passes me every morning, making it only one minute of seeing one another. I suffer more in the early morning than at any time. I take a job, but I think, she is not in that building so what is the use? I can not make much money in this condition. I am 53, nearly worn, so what is the use? I hope this finds you well and happy.'

In this, his final letter, Sebastian gave his address as: 'Under the stars – No number.'

He captivated me. I found him fascinating because of his sanity. His passion was weird but real.

No one ever heard from Sebastian again.

Are such tireless pursuits examples of Obsessive–Compulsive Disorder? Very probably not. Today Sebastian would probably receive the diagnosis of erotomania, which had long been recognized as a psychiatric disorder in females but has only recently been described in males.

The French psychiatrist Ferdière Clérambault first described a curious erotic pattern in females (published in 1920 and 1921) in which the woman held the delusion that she was loved by a particular man with whom she had actually had little contact. Clérambault and others noted how the chosen man was usually socially unattainable; that the women afflicted with erotomania (or Clérambault's Syndrome as it came to be known) were convinced that their idol protected them, and remained 'faithful' to, and utterly preoccupied with, their love.

In the past fifteen years a number of reports of erotomania in males have appeared. The men are isolated individuals, who came into contact with the law because of their aggressive and annoying romantic pursuits; their families often contain several relatives who are schizophrenic, and they themselves – if their clinical picture alters – may become psychotic. But most do not exhibit signs of schizophrenia and, like Sebastian, hold responsible jobs, working satisfactorily between episodes, and are sad and lonely when away from their loved one.

But whether in the clinic or fiction, such bizarre pre-occupations with another are usually doomed. Sebastian was hospitalized. David burned down Jade's house and was hospitalized. Roberta lost her past life (she comes out the best). At the end, as Victor Hugo tells it, Javert lost *himself*:

'All the axioms which had been the supports of his whole life crumbled away before this man . . . Javert felt something horrible was penetrating his soul, admiration for a convict. Respect for a galley slave, can that be possible? It was useless to struggle, he was reduced to confess before his own inner tribunal the sublimity of this wretch. That was hateful.' With this realization, Javert kills himself.

How do such fanatical preoccupations begin? What was Inspector Javert like as a child? Is it possible that he began with an obsession of the sort my patients have, and then convinced himself that this was quite the right way to be? Is there a turning point where one decides it's better to be a self-declared fanatic than an obsessional patient in pain? Why does a habit torture one man and form the passion of the next?

29

Free Will and the Uncertainty of Knowing

My patients' complaints have made me think about problems that have not concerned me so deeply since college philosophy courses. Their disabling symptoms are about 'will' and about their 'knowledge'. I am certainly not the first to observe this.

The great child psychoanalyst Louise Despert described one of her patients, a six-year-old girl with severe compulsions and obsessions to touch and count. During an attack, the girl would run to her mother saying: 'Mummy, Mummy, my other mind is back. Tell it how silly it is. Can you tell it to stop being silly?'

The certain sense that the obsessions are an intimate part of one's conscious intent, *and yet that they are senseless*, is so much the essence of the disorder, even for a six-year-old, that this state of mind is used to define it. The *American Psychiatric Association's Diagnostic Manual*, the official book of definition of psychiatric disorders, cites the sense of being compelled, of being forced from within, to carry out senseless acts or think senseless thoughts as the definitive feature of the illness. Does this mean that my OCD patients have lost their 'free will'?

In no other disorder do patients so clearly stress the importance and the power of will to carry out their peculiar acts or thoughts. A patient with a tic will say 'my arm jumps' or 'my eye twitches'. But an obsessive patient says, 'For some reason, I *have to*, I *must* move my arm over and over again.' This is what confuses them, particularly the children. They are prisoners; they *want* these rituals for the moments of peace they can offer, but they really *want not to want* them.

And this is the key point. The philosopher Daniel Dennett points out in *Brainstorms* that humans may be unique in having two kinds of intentions, what he calls first and second order desires. The first order of desires or intentions – for example, to wash – we share with animals. But our second order intentions, our desires *about* our desires, are most likely a unique feature of the human mind.

Young Murray, a boy with severe washing rituals, told us how his obsessions 'drove him crazy'. He *knew* he didn't *want* to wash, but he felt he *had* to. Being psychologically oriented, after a period of time he would occasionally wonder if maybe he really did want to wash, since he was washing so much. Obsessive-compulsives, particularly those in psychotherapy, are sometimes temporarily convinced that they want to do something, or they 'must have a need for' something because they act as if they do.

But I think it is clear they don't truly want to wash, check or count. Not only do the rituals come first, and the explanations much later, or not at all, but my patients say: 'Treat my problem, I want to stop wanting.' They fully retain their second, higher order 'will' that doesn't want to want.

So my patients are still free – they can want not to want. They come to the clinic for therapy, or to take the new drug in order to stop 'wanting'.

There is, though, a more difficult question that remains. Where do compulsive personalities fit in? As far as I can tell, they seem to want to want the rigid rules they live by. Are they free? Or, in a very real way, are they trapped in an even more rigid, imprisoned world than the obsessive–compulsives? A hard question to pose and one without an easy answer.

'Nothing is certain,' Pyrrhon concluded, and on his death bed he urged his pupils who loved him not to grieve for him, since they could not be sure he was dead.

ALICE

Alice's father called from Chicago. His voice rang with the self-confidence and bravado of the self-made millionaire. He owned a large clothing factory and ran that and an even larger business almost effortlessly. Mr B. wasn't used to finding problems he couldn't solve or couldn't hire the right person to solve. But he had one now.

Alice, his sixteen-year-old, fought with them all the time, or more exactly with her mother all the time, and her father when he was at home. 'She keeps asking questions,' her father told us. 'She doesn't agree with anything we tell her; nothing we say seems right.'

That didn't sound so desperate to me. All bright kids ask a lot of questions. And a lot of teenage girls fight with their parents. Mothers and daughters particularly. I told Mr B. as much. There must be someone in Chicago to consult on this, why come to Bethesda?

'But she gets in shouting matches with her mother. They scream and pull hair. Alice won't stop asking questions.'

'They pull hair?' I repeated.

'Well, yes, her mother gets so mad, she fights back,' Mr B. told me miserably.

'Does she do it with anyone else?' I wanted to know.

'Not out of the house,' Alice's father said. 'She's popular at school and the teachers like her. She's not a great student, but she passes everything fine. The school doesn't know what we're talking about. We have taken her to three different psychologists and psychiatrists. They all say the same thing, that Alice has problems with us, is jealous of her beautiful mother, but is otherwise fine. But it has got to be more than that; we haven't had a normal family life since Alice was three.

'There have been some years that weren't so bad. But now it's the worst it ever has been. Right now it's terrible, Alice says we can't answer any questions right. She says we just confuse her.'

I started to pontificate on generation gaps, mother–daughter rivalry, respecting teenagers' autonomy, and the like.

'But no other children I know ask questions like these,' he persisted.

'What sort does she ask?'

'Well, her most recent question is "Is the sky blue?" ' said her father. 'But before that it was the leaves.'

'The leaves?'

'Yes. She asked, "Are the leaves green?" For months she asked about the leaves.'

'What did you say then?'

'Well, of course I'd say "Yes the leaves *are* green." And then she'd ask "Are they dark green or light green?" So I'd say "Well some are dark green and others light." But that doesn't satisfy her. She points to a particular tree and a particular leaf on it, and wants to know exactly what colour green that leaf is. When I can't answer just right, she gets upset and starts screaming.'

'So you're still talking about leaves at home now, or have you refused to answer?'

'Right now, the worst is her hair.'

'What about her hair?'

'She asks if her hair is blonde or dirty blonde or brown. Well, my wife started to say how her hair is all different, that it's blonde on top, and medium blonde in places, and brown at the back. Just trying to be accurate because by now she's afraid of what is coming, and as usual, Alice went wild. She screamed, she just shouted, over and over, 'What colour *is* it?" '

I met Alice soon after. Her hair was a streaky blonde, and she would have been pretty if she weren't so sullen. She sat across from her parents while we all met, giving us angry looks and not saying much. The two of us went off to talk while others stayed with her parents.

'Alice,' I asked, 'what is the problem about?'

'I have fights with my parents, they drive me nuts,' she told me.

'What do you fight about?'

'They mix me up. They can't give me a straight answer.'

'Give me an example.'

'Well, like Mum will see a show. And she said to me she loved it. Then later, I'll hear her talking to someone on the phone and say she liked it a lot. Well, you see what I mean. Did she "love" or did she just "like it a lot"? Mum confuses me. She can't make up her mind!'

'That doesn't seem so difficult to me, Alice.'

'It seems terrible to me. How can I tell what she's talking about?' Alice pouted.

'Can you give me another example?'

'Well, I asked her if she thought Sue, my best friend, was pretty.'

'What did she say?'

'First she said she thought Sue was quite pretty. Later I asked her again. She said she thought she was really pretty. Then again, that she was very pretty.' While she told the story, Alice looked embarrassed; she was watching me carefully for any sign of ridicule.

'You know this doesn't really make sense, don't you, Alice?'

She nodded. She was crying.

Unlike other obsessive–compulsives with their symmetry, checking, straightening, or erasing, Alice, I soon discovered, had to have an exactness and consistency in labelling with words. She did indeed have OCD (as her referring doctor had considered) but it took the form of a compulsive need for exactness of speech that none of us would be able to satisfy. But it was only at home that she 'had to get it right'. Why? Why there and nowhere else?

Alice admitted that when she was at home, 'that feeling' was there, at other times it was in the background, but it could be suppressed. The words her family said weren't just words; they stirred up this feeling of having to have the words exactly right, more so than anything any English teacher's grammar lesson had ever demanded. And when Alice felt that way, *nothing* sounded right enough. What was clear and ordinary language for someone else was different for Alice; it created an intolerable confusion.

'Why does this just happen at home?' I asked.

'It sort of happens at school, but I can control it there. When I washed my hands a lot, I only did that at home, too,' Alice pointed out. And I realized that this, like other OCD symptoms, was malleable, and, as with other forms of the disease, could only show itself at home.

I spent hours putting all of this together. Alice's parents and I went over every detail of her childhood. Looking back, she and her mother had been fighting for years. She fought with her dad too, but that wasn't so bad. Even before the questions began, there were other clues. When Alice was three, she would wear the same polo shirt every single day of the week. It had to be washed at night while she slept. Alice and her mother fought over this. New clothes hung in the wardrobe, many with the price tags still on them. Winter was a big problem because the winter jacket was a new item and Alice was rigid about what she would wear. When snow came, the jacket was forced on her.

Friends and family chalked this up to a 'mother–daughter' problem. Were her beautiful ex-model mother and Alice really competing? Perhaps Alice didn't like the way her mother dressed her? Her handsome, very successful father may have acted seductively with her? In short, was this a family triangle played out in other arenas? The first psychologist had suggested it. They worked on the problem from that point of view and the dressing ritual got better over time.

But when Alice was six, another problem began: she started to wash her hands an hour a day. That too eventually got better.

When she reached ten there was yet another battleground – her hair. She couldn't stand having her mother do her hair. Again, on first hearing, it sounded like another classic mother–daughter struggle; that is, until you listened for the details. This really wasn't just another argument over style or length or knots. The problem was more subtle and one impossible for her mother to fix. Alice's hair never 'felt right' to her and her mother had to do it over and over again. It started with her feeling too 'tight'.

'It doesn't feel right,' the little girl would whine. So her mother made the plait looser.

'It *still* doesn't feel right.' And so on. The same with two plaits, then a new problem got added.

'They aren't even.'

'They look even to me, Alice.' And a shouting match would start between the miserably unhappy little girl and her bewildered mother. Hair clips were tried and quickly thrown out because they were never even. Alice spent so much time checking their symmetry that she stopped playing with friends.

'I can't tell you what it is like to live with Alice,' her mother said. 'My heart pounds when I'm with her, I have had more headaches than you could imagine. Alice never passed me without starting a fight.'

Alice's mother had badly wanted a daughter. She had loved it when her own mother had fixed her hair when she was little. Helping her daughter look pretty should have been the fun part of raising a little girl, but instead it was a nightmare.

Alice's mother had looked forward to marriage and a family. Except for a brief period as a model, raising children and running her home were her goals. Instead, her tortured relationship with her daughter had reduced her to a 'screaming, hair-pulling, hitting bitch', as she called herself. She had become someone she didn't recognize any more. And she had had sixteen years of it!

I explained to Alice and her parents that Alice's problem seemed to be a form of OCD. The diagnosis was made easier, of course, by knowledge of earlier episodes in Alice's childhood. Some children need to get their homework perfect, I told Alice, and rub out and rub out even though it was as good as it could be in the first place. This time, it was how words had to be for her: exact, precise, consistently dependable.

Because counselling and some behaviour therapy had already been tried and hadn't helped, we tried clomipramine. The clomipramine effect seemed and still seems too good to be true.

For the first three days nothing happened, and Alice complained about the dry mouth. When I called, I heard her voice in the background shouting 'Is the sky blue?' and I thought perhaps we were all wasting our time.

In the second half of the week, Alice's mother called to say that she couldn't believe it, but 'it' had all gone away. She had just come back from a bus ride with Alice and she couldn't get over what fun it had been. Alice had said things like: 'Look, Mum, isn't that pretty?' Her mother waited for a scene but nothing happened. Alice didn't even expect an answer!

Next week, Alice's father called. 'There is a sort of calm surrounding our home. All of a sudden no one is yelling. My throat doesn't hurt. Doors aren't slamming. We walk around in disbelief. We are happy being together.'

There are very few experiences in psychiatry like this, and few indeed anywhere in medicine. Alice came in to see us when she had taken the drug for three weeks. The symptoms had all gone away.

This story does not have a simple happy ending, however. Alice needed a very high dose of the drug to keep her idiosyncratic need for exactness away. With a high dose of clomipramine, Alice would be drowsy, dizzy if she stood up suddenly, and felt weak and sometimes nauseated. She and her mother still prefer to have the drug than to be without it, but Alice can only take enough to remove perhaps two-thirds of the problem. We are working with other drugs that make clomipramine more potent, but it's still too early to tell if they will work. We are still far from a good answer to the enigma of OCD.

KIM AND WILLIAM: HOW DO I KNOW?

Kim, the first young girl I met with Obsessive–Compulsive Disorder, had only one symptom: the thought that she had caused someone's death. Sixteen years old, beautiful, blonde, and slim, Kim sat at the nurse's station weeping over her destructive power. Hours of staff time went into reassuring her that she was not a killer, but it didn't seem to help.

'Kim,' they'd say, 'your parents say you'd never hurt a fly. How *could* you have killed anyone?'

'Well, I *might* have looked angry one day and the man who walked by me on the street and saw that look might have got really upset and had a heart attack.'

This was about as much of a story as Kim could put together. An obsessive ruminator, she spent most of her time on the ward talking with the nurses and with me, asking for reassurance about her crime. At our ward rounds, the nurses and I would stress how Kim really must know she didn't do anything; she never went to the police. We felt that not going indicated that she really knew it was her obsessive *thoughts* that made her feel guilty. One day one of my patients actually went to the police; they were not amused.

William, a graduate student in English literature, had been brought in by his mother, who asked, 'Can't you reason with him, Dr Rapoport? He keeps saying he *might* have *murdered* someone!'

I talked with William briefly on other subjects. He spoke lucidly and with enthusiasm about his thesis on modern American poetry.

'Now what is this about your doing harm to someone,' I asked. The interview changed; I had set it off. William got a worried look and then began a repetitive monologue:

'Do you think I killed someone, Dr Rapoport? How do I *know* if I killed someone?'

I said some sensible, to him meaningless, things that didn't interest him, couldn't hold his attention, and didn't help. His weekend proved dramatic and eventful.

At six that Sunday morning, William turned himself in at the local police station saying, 'I confess. Who do I see? I've murdered someone.' After a very short interrogation, William's story came apart.

'Where is the body?'

'I'm not sure.'

'How was the murder committed?'

'Well, I *might* have pushed someone off the Calvert Street bridge.'

'When did this happen?'

'I think it was last night.'

William had had a terrible night. The thought 'I have murdered' was stronger than it had ever been. Television hadn't broken through and relaxed him and a half a bottle of gin hadn't weakened the inner voice that accused him over and over again.

By dawn, the burden and the doubting were too much. The station was slow. The sergeant offered him coffee and listened.

Soon it was William who was asking the questions. 'Sergeant, *did* I kill anyone? *Have* there been any bodies reported near the Calvert Street bridge? Tell me, Sergeant, *how do I know if I killed someone?*'

The sergeant saw that William was *not* in his office to confess. He was there *to find out if he was a murderer!*

The sergeant told me later, 'Doctor, I've seen strange things happen at this station. But the craziest part of this story was that the guy didn't seem crazy.'

William was asking a bizarre question, but he wasn't on drugs, was not really drunk, and hadn't been injured. This wasn't like the practical jokes or fraternity stunts that hit the sergeant's station a few times each year. William was genuinely upset. After the sergeant had called to verify that William was a patient of mine, he asked me a few questions of his own: 'How can anyone not know something like that? What's the matter with this guy?'

Talking helped William pull himself together, or maybe the 'attack' had just stopped. He admitted to the sergeant that he had had these doubts on and off for years and didn't know why they had got so bad that particular night. William left the station a free man. But the sergeant had seen something new and kept asking, 'What does he mean, ''How do you know if you killed someone?'' That's weird, really weird.'

Kim and William face two bizarre and deeply troubling problems. One is their preoccupation with their danger to others. The other is that they can't be sure if they know something. Their memory and their perceptions are fine by every test we can devise, but they just don't 'sink in' the way memories and perceptions usually do. My severe doubters keep saying, 'How do I know?'

Obsessive–compulsives don't have trouble 'knowing' most things. The doubting disease is highly selective – only certain things are doubted. The doubts leave no room for anything else. There is no problem with memory; Kim and William could describe every step they took on the days of their 'murders'. A much more complex cognitive or perceptual process has gone wrong. If Alice met Kim or William, she wouldn't have understood their preoccupation with murder. But if she heard them ask 'How do I know?' *that* would be familiar!

Doubts of the most simple observations may be the most fascinating side of OCD. The French called Obsessive–Compulsive Disorder *folie pourquoi* and *folie de doute*, literally the doubting disease. Something in the mind – in the brain – goes wrong. I think we all have unreasonable doubts more frequently than we even notice. Is some mental filter working well for the rest of us that isn't working for them?

Perhaps underlying the dramatic content of doubts – for which there are a number of explanations, all unsatisfactory – is an even more basic problem: that of *knowing*. Something gets stuck. Most of us don't plan how to decide if the door is locked, we just know it is after we lock it and try the knob. Our normal checking habits are so ingrained it is hard to break them down into steps. But my patients are caught in endless loops of trying to be sure of the obvious.

Obsessive–compulsive patients must ceaselessly check or wash, or they must ruminate over the threatened danger. A classic battle of sensation versus reason is represented by these two kinds of patients.

The checkers are in a kind of Berkeleyan nightmare, doubting what they do not see, needing continually to see and re-see, to look and look, again and again and again. My checking patients appear to say 'knowledge comes from the senses only'; therefore, the test of their truth will be in what they can hear, see, and touch. Hence the door knob must be turned again and again; the light switched on and off, on and off. These acts bring immediate information, yet it doesn't *get through*. They can't say, 'Yes, I have checked this out and now I *know* that the door is locked.'

Those who aren't satisfied that knowledge can depend on the senses are our 'ruminators'. These idealists are indifferent to what their senses tell them. They turn *ideas* over and over, trying to *think* their way to a good answer. A Humean nightmare!

When William asks how he could 'know' if he killed someone, he is not asking for someone to look and see. He is asking to get back his ability to 'just know'. Alice wants to 'know' what blue is again.

My patients are painfully aware that they are not thinking right. Kim, who felt sure she might have caused someone harm, was not asking for us to tell her: 'It's okay, you didn't kill anyone.' Of course we did that. And, of course, she answered patiently, tolerantly, 'Doctor, *everyone* tells me that. But it doesn't help.' We couldn't bring back the glue that made good reasons stick so that her mind could accept them and the doubts would cease.

Pragmatism isn't needed. None of our patients wants the practical answer. Alice wasn't appeased by learning that everyone thinks the bush is light green. Forget the sensible approach; they don't care what the answer is in that sense. That is why the boy who couldn't stop washing rolled his eyes in exasperation when told he was clean, and said, '*Everyone* tells me that!'

This inability to dispel doubts turns my patients into the ultimate sceptics who, like the ancient Greek philosopher Parmenides, feel that 'Most mortals have nothing in their fallible intellects that did not come in through their fallible senses.' They trust neither experience nor intelligence. This doubting disease is truly well-named.

What does get through? Why do they stop checking or doubting sometimes? They say that something sometimes just 'happens' so that if feels 'right', and for a little while they can 'know' it is all right. Sometimes they can 'borrow' a friend's judgement, ask a friend to lock the door, turn off the gas, and so forth, just the way a blind man might ask someone to see if it is clear to cross the street. Sometimes they can borrow 'knowing' successfully. And sometimes they can get by on what they have managed to 'know' on their own. Compulsive washers and checkers cherish the moments when they can say, 'I just know I am clean enough', or 'I just know the door is locked'. For a little while, at least, it seems just that simple; until the ability to 'just know' turns off again.

Does it do a patient any good to muse about the philosophical implication of Obsessive–Compulsive Disorder? Not much. But it can be valuable to know that he or she *won't get help from asking the same questions over and over*! Children in particular need to be told that this doesn't work.

The situation resembles that of the old joke about the psychiatrist and the patient who insisted that he was dead. The psychiatrist first had the man memorize the sentence, 'Dead men don't bleed.' Then the psychiatrist stuck his subject with a pin, producing a drop of blood. 'Well, what do you know!' the patient exclaimed. 'Dead men *do* bleed!' The point of which is that if you want to be of help, you need to deal with the assumption, not the question.

Obsessive–compulsive patients must be told that not knowing, not being able to know, about danger, locks, cleanliness, and so on, is part of the problem. They must be told that the sense of compulsion is part of the problem and that you *know* they want not to want.

At least they'll feel that someone understands. And that eases their pain and anxiety somewhat.

How does all this tie in with our new biology of OCD? I've said it is a genetic disease connected with neurological illnesses, often of the basal ganglia. I've said this part of the brain may function differently in OCD. Where does 'knowing' fit in?

I think the new biology of Obsessive–Compulsive Disorder lets us go on where Professors von Economo and Janet left off. We may really be describing a 'biology of knowing'. Parts of the brain check sensory information (what comes through all of our senses) and checks this input against action and expectations. The basal ganglia deep within the brain are considered to be both modulators of movements and integrators of sensory information. When my patients ask me 'How can I know?' I see them as people who have lost a special function: the ability to know *if they know* something.

We're just beginning to define brain circuits that control this special sense of knowing – of knowledge. These circuits control basic dimensions of behaviour: safety, grooming, attack. Within this context of ancient concerns arises the fascinating possibility of a biological basis for that highest of functions – man's sense of his own knowledge.

Great thinkers, from the philosophers Immanuel Kant and David Hume to the ethologist Konrad Lorenz, have assumed that there is an innate brain pattern that generates hypotheses about the reality of our world. The very selective and specific problem that Kim and William have may mean that the circuits that ordinarily give us our built-in, pre-set sense of 'knowing' no longer work for them. Presumably, these programmes which process certain crucial pieces of information about our safety malfunction in OCD.

Until now, the best examples of innate ritualized behaviours have come from studies of animals. These patterns of animal behaviour can be thought of as inborn knowledge. The animal born 'knowing' how to build a nest can be assumed to have some sort of knowledge and expectations about the world and how to cope in it.

Will there ever be an animal model for this quest to be certain of what one knows? Sadly, I doubt it. Animal models have been crucial to our understanding of many important diseases of man, but nothing provides an insight into the complexity of the obsessive–compulsives' struggle to know except understanding them. When we learn more about the function gone wrong in Obsessive–Compulsive Disorder, we will also learn more about the most mysterious secrets of the nature of man.

V
DO YOU HAVE
OBSESSIVE-COMPULSIVE DISORDER?

30

Making the Diagnosis

Lists of symptoms and rating scales in this section will help to make a diagnosis of Obsessive–Compulsive Disorder. But no general list can do it. You should consult your physician or a psychologist to be sure. Other disorders, such as depression or anxiety, can cause some of the same problems. So just because you or someone you know has some of these symptoms does not necessarily mean it is Obsessive–Compulsive Disorder.

Furthermore, no list of symptoms can take the place of common sense. If someone is living his or her life in psychological comfort, and their habits do not disrupt their work or their personal lives, then it does not matter what their 'score' is on any scale – they do not have OCD. On the other hand, a person can have just one habit – for instance, washing or checking – that can be a severe problem, wasting hours of each day. Therefore the most important question you should ask at this point is: Do habits or thoughts get in the way of your work life, social life, or private life? Do you have a friend or a loved one who might be affected in this way? If so, read on.

OBSESSIONS AND COMPULSIONS CHECKLIST*

The following list of the most common obsessions and compulsions contains many common habits that from time to time occur in most people's lives. A thought or a habit is only considered an obsession or compulsion if a person cannot stop it, if it gets in the way of their life in an important way, or if a great deal of time and energy is spent fighting the thought or habit.

Clinically, obsessions and compulsions range from mildly interfering to extremely incapacitating.

* Adapted from the Yale-Brown Obsessive–Compulsive Scale with permission of Dr Wayne Goodman.

AGGRESSIVE OBSESSIONS

Fear of harming others
Fear of harming self
Violent or horrific images
Fear of blurting out obscenities or insults
Fear of doing something embarrassing
Fear of acting on criminal impulses (e.g., shop-lifting, robbing bank)
Fear of being held responsible for something going wrong
Fear that something terrible might happen (e.g. fire, death of relative or friend)

CONTAMINATION OBSESSIONS

Concern or disgust with body wastes or secretions (urine, faeces, saliva)
Concern with dirt or germs
Excessive concern about chemical or environmental contamination

SEXUAL OBSESSIONS

Forbidden or perverse thoughts or images (involving children, incest, bestiality, homosexuality, etc.)

OBSESSION WITH A NEED FOR SYMMETRY, EXACTNESS, OR ORDER

MISCELLANEOUS OBSESSIONS

Fear of not saying things exactly right
Intrusive (neutral) images, e.g., mental image of cat
Intrusive nonsense sounds, words, or music
Lucky/unlucky numbers
Colours with special significance

SOMATIC OBSESSION-COMPULSION

Preoccupation with part of body, e.g., ears too large

COUNTING COMPULSIONS

Having to count over and over to a certain number

CHECKING COMPULSIONS

Checking doors, locks, brakes, etc.

REPEATING RITUALS

Going in/out doors, up/down from chair, etc.

ORDERING/ARRANGING COMPULSIONS

Packing and unpacking a suitcase, rearranging drawers

HOARDING/COLLECTING COMPULSIONS

Saving old newspapers, mail, string, wrapping paper

MISCELLANEOUS COMPULSIONS

Need to tell, ask, or confess
Need to touch, measure

If the answer is *yes* to any of the obsessions or compulsions on this list, then they should be further scored with the following scale according to how much time they occupy, how much distress they cause, how hard it is to resist them, and how much control they have over someone's thoughts and actions.

1. TIME OCCUPIED BY OBSESSIVE THOUGHTS OR
   COMPULSIVE RITUALS

   0–None
   1–Mild: less than 1 hour/day, or occasional intrusion
   2–Moderate: 1 to 3 hours/day, or frequent intrusion
   3–Severe: 3 to 8 hours/day, or very frequent intrusion
   4–Extreme: almost all waking hours, near constant intrusion

2. INTERFERENCE DUE TO OBSESSIVE THOUGHTS OR COMPULSIVE RITUALS

0–None
1–Mild: slight interference but overall life not impaired
2–Mild to moderate interference
3–Moderate: definite interference with work or social performance but still manageable
4–Extreme: incapacitating every aspect of life

3. DISTRESS ASSOCIATED WITH OBSESSIVE THOUGHTS OR COMPULSIVE RITUALS

0–None
1–Mild: infrequent, and not too disturbing
2–Moderate: definite distress from thoughts or rituals
3–Severe: frequent thoughts or marked increase in anxiety if compulsions prevented
4–Extreme: near constant distress from thoughts or rituals

4. RESISTANCE TO OBSESSIVE THOUGHTS OR COMPULSIVE RITUALS

0–Always makes effort to resist, or thoughts so minimal no resistance needed
1–Tries to resist most of the time
2–Makes some effort to resist
3–Yields completely to thoughts or rituals

If your answer is 3 or 4 to any of the above then it is worth consulting a psychologist or psychiatrist for a diagnosis of and, most important, treatment for this problem.

Global Obsessive–Compulsive Scale

The following is a rating scale of overall severity of OCD as it is usually rated at clinics. It is used to follow improvement with treatment, as individual symptoms may change over time.

1–3 *Minimal*: Person spends little time resisting symptoms. Almost no interference in daily activity.

4-6 *Subclinical obsessive-compulsive behaviour*: Mild symptoms, noticeable to the person and to an observer, which cause mild interference in patient's life and which may be resisted for a minimal period of time. Symptoms easily tolerated by others.

7-9 *Clinical obsessive-compulsive behaviour*: Symptoms cause significant interference with normal life. Person spends a great deal of energy resisting and requires some help from others to function in daily activity.

10-12 *Severe obsessive-compulsive behaviour*: Symptoms crippling and interfering. Daily activity is 'an active struggle'. Person may spend all of the time resisting symptoms and requires much help from others to function.

13-15 *Very severe obsessive-compulsive behaviour*: Symptoms completely crippling. Person requires close supervision over eating, sleeping, etc. Even very minor decision making or minimal activity requires staff support. This is as severe as OCD can get.

If you rated yourself at 7 or above on this scale, it would be worth your while to obtain a consultation from a psychologist or psychiatrist. But even if you are successfully concealing your symptoms, a consultation may help you improve the quality of your life by getting rid of repetitive thoughts or rituals that take up so much of your time, and drain so much of your energy.

COMPULSIVE PERSONALITY DISORDER

The essence of a Compulsive Personality Disorder is found in a restricted, undemonstrative person, one who is perfectionist to a degree that demands that others submit to his or her way of doing things. A compulsive personality is also often indecisive and excessively devoted to work to the exclusion of pleasure. When pleasure *is* considered, it is something to be planned and worked for. Pleasurable activities are usually postponed and sometimes never even enjoyed.

People with compulsive personalities tend to be excessively moralistic, and judgemental of themselves and others.

The American Psychiatric Association's *Diagnostic and Statistical Manual of Mental Disorders* requires at least five of the following symptoms to be characteristic of the person's functioning. In addition, the symptoms must cause some problems with personal or work life.

1. Restricted ability to express warm and tender emotions.
2. Perfectionism that interferes with overall ability to see the needs of a situation.
3. Insistence that others submit to the person's way of doing things without awareness of how this makes others feel.
4. Excessive devotion to work to the exclusion of pleasure.
5. Indecisiveness to the point where decisions are postponed, avoided, or protracted (perhaps because of a great fear of making a mistake). Assignments may not get done on time because of ruminating about priorities.
6. Preoccupation with details, rules, lists or schedules to the extent that the major point of the activity is lost.
7. Overconscientiousness, scrupulousness, and inflexibility about moral or ethical matters.
8. Lack of generosity in giving time, money or gifts.
9. Inability to discard worn out or worthless objects.

31

What To Do If You Have Obsessive–Compulsive Disorder

There is an organization called Phobic Action which provides information and support for OCD sufferers. There are about fifty groups scattered around the country under a variety of names, but the central office is: Phobic Action, Greater London House, 547–551 High Road, Leytonstone, London E11 4PR. They will send their newsletter with information about OCD and the regional support group nearest you in return for a large SAE. If you wish, they may be able to put you in touch with others with the same problem. If you need to talk to somebody, ring the Helpline on 01 558 6012.

BEHAVIOUR THERAPY

Behaviour therapists are often, although not necessarily always, psychologists. Most psychologists are not behaviour therapists so it is important to know the training of the psychologist you consult. Your GP should be able to help put you in touch with a suitable behaviour therapist.

If you consult a behaviour therapist you should ask if he or she has worked with obsessive–compulsive patients before. There is a specialization within the field of behaviour therapy, and you would not want to work with a therapist whose work has been primarily with weight reduction, for example, or with people trying to stop smoking. Unfortunately, there are as yet very few speciality clinics for Obsessive–Compulsive Disorder. But many centres that call themselves phobia clinics are now beginning to treat as many (if not more) patients with OCD. If there is a phobia clinic in your area, it would be a good place to call. Check your phone book.

Some behaviour therapists feel that only patients with habits (compulsions like washing or walking in a certain way, or rituals to avoid contamination) will benefit from behaviour therapy and not people with obsessive thoughts. So even if you consult a well-trained behaviour therapist who has worked with obsessive patients, he or she may suggest a treatment different from behaviour therapy.

Behaviour therapists are usually specific about their treatment plan. They will tell you approximately how many visits you will need (anywhere from five to fifty) and how long these sessions will be. The first few sessions are used for recording your habits in great detail. The therapist will note the particular habits you have, when and where you practise them, and for how long. You will probably also be asked to keep a detailed record between appointments. As with all therapies, you should feel comfortable with the therapist and be able to trust the person. The treatment is a true partnership; there is no such thing as therapy being *done* for you.

As the therapy continues, you and the therapist construct a plan that usually involves exposing you gradually to the situations most likely to bring out your rituals or habits. The plan also includes techniques for helping you stop yourself from thinking or doing these thoughts or habits.

For example, one woman who had to wash for hours after touching anyone was treated (after extensive preparation) by going around the poorer areas of Philadelphia and shaking hands with 'street people'. She wasn't allowed to wash her hands until late that night. This is called 'exposure with response prevention' and probably is the approach that works the best.

After the first series of sessions, the therapist will want to see you for a 'booster' session some time later. As with any psychological treatment, each person's experience will be different.

DRUG TREATMENT: CLOMIPRAMINE

The best-studied drug, by far, is clomipramine (trade name, Anafranil). It is available by prescription in the UK and 76 other countries, but not in the US, though legal ways are available to obtain the drug.

It is essential that your physician be knowledgeable about and comfortable with the use of psychiatric drugs. If you don't have a doctor who is, you may get the name of a psychiatrist who is skilled in psychopharmacology from the medical school or university hospital nearest to you.

The side effects of clomipramine range from mild (dry mouth, slight fatigue) to severe. The most common are dry mouth, constipation, and drowsiness. However a tremor, loss of sexual appetite, impotence (temporary until you stop taking the drug), and excessive sweating can be major problems. In doses above 250 mg a day seizures have occurred. These are all side effects common to tricyclic antidepressants – the group of drugs to which clomipramine belongs. Clomipramine is also a good antidepressant. Your doctor will help you deal with the side effects; many go away over time, and most can be controlled by lowering the dose and/or taking the drug at bedtime.

Clomipramine is usually given in doses of 150 to 250 mg a day and comes in 10, 25 or 50 mg capsules. Most patients take a few weeks to respond to the drug, and it can be months before you know how much help you are going to get. Doses can go as high as 250 mg a day for some, although most people who respond need less (150–200 mg a day). If there is no sign of improvement after eight weeks on the drug, it is probably correct to consider another approach.

When the drug works, thoughts and habits gradually seem to lose their intensity. They may not disappear altogether, but they interfere less with your life. About 70 per cent of patients in most of the clinical trials of clomipramine for OCD get at least some help from the drug.

For people who get a partial response to clomipramine, there are reports that other drugs, such as lithium or the amino acid L-tryptophan, may make clomipramine more effective.

OTHER DRUGS

New reports are published each month in medical journals about other medical treatments for obsessions and compulsions. This new interest in drug treatment has led to preliminary studies with two other drugs. Fluoxetine (trade name, Prozac), which Eli Lilly manufactures, has just come on the market for depression, and fluvoxamine, which is manufactured by the pharmaceutical firm Duphar.

Fluoxetine, which is available in 20 mg tablets, appears to have some benefit for obsessions and compulsions, but no controlled trials have yet been published. The available case reports have used up to 80 mg a day and it can be weeks before improvement is seen.

Fluvoxamine is on the market in 12 countries including England (trade name here is Faverin), Germany (Feverin), Switzerland (Floxyfral), and Spain (Dumirox) but not the US. There are now four published controlled trials of fluvoxamine and the evidence suggests that it too could be useful for OCD. The usual dose is 150 mg a day. Information about fluvoxamine can be obtained from Duphar Laboratories Ltd, Gaters Hill, West End, Southampton SO3 3JD.

It is worth trying all of these drugs as one of them may bring improvement even when the others have failed. Even for cases when their therapeutic effect is similar, some patients tolerate the side effects of one drug much better than they do the others.

OTHER APPROACHES

As with other psychiatric problems, patients with OCD have got help just from 'coming out of the OCD cupboard'. Our own studies have introduced patients and their families to each other and these contacts have produced supportive relationships that have lasted in some cases for ten years.

As mentioned previously in this chapter, Phobic Action will help you contact others in your area with the same problem. Parents and spouses seem to me to get the most out of these groups. The teenage patients themselves often prefer to spend time with just one or two particular peers with similar problems. Up until now, little work has been done with the siblings of our patients, and this is a serious omission. OCD so distorts family life that the healthy siblings are resentful and uncomprehending. Informing the well siblings about OCD will probably help both the patient and the entire family to reduce stresses, fears, and resentments.

Just staying informed about research and new treatments as they are developed is one of the most important functions of patient support groups. And with the explosion of new information about OCD it will probably be a major role for Phobic Action and other burgeoning OCD support groups.

Appendix: The Religious Perspective

THE CATHOLIC CHURCH AND OCD

The Catholic perspective of OCD constitutes a vast literature which has remained untapped by mainstream psychiatry. The Catholic concept of scrupulosity dates back at least to the twelfth century. It is derived from the Latin *scrupus*, whose diminutive form *scrupulus* means a small sharp stone. The neutral form, *scrupulum*, means the smallest division of weight, the twenty-fourth part of an ounce. A minute weight could tip the scales of a sensitive balance: the scales of conscience.

Scrupulosity, in the *New Catholic Encyclopedia* (1967) signifies 'habitual and unreasonable hesitation or doubt, coupled with anxiety of the mind, in connection with the making of moral judgements'.

From 1522 to 1523 Ignatius Loyola wrote the *Spiritual Exercises to Conquer Self and Regulate One's Life and to Avoid Coming to a Determination through any Inordinate Affection*. This provided the Catholic Church with its first definition of scrupulosity through a description of Loyola's own obsessive behaviour, and his insight into its irrational yet distressful force.

> After I have trodden upon a cross formed by two straws, or after I have thought, said or done some other thing, there comes to me from 'without' a thought that I have sinned, and on the other hand it seems to me that I have not sinned; nevertheless I feel some uneasiness on the subject, inasmuch as I doubt yet do not doubt.

In 1730, Saint Alphonsus Liguori described scrupulosity as a groundless fear of sinning that rises from 'erroneous ideas'. Since then, a series of theologians provided similar definitions of scrupulosity, most saying it was a condition of the mind that creates futile and unreasonable motives.

Church writers grew increasingly psychologically-minded, and by 1966, scrupulosity was defined by O'Flaherty in almost the same terms as the American Psychiatric Association definition of Obsessive–Compulsive Disorder:

Comparison of scrupulosity with obsessive–compulsive disorder

SCRUPULOSITY	OBSESSIVE-COMPULSIVE DISORDER
1. Persistent concern with thought, word, or deed	1. Persistent intrusive idea, thought, or impulse
2. Thoughts cause uneasiness and distress	2. Ego dystonic (i.e., ritual or thought causes distress, and is seen as alien)
3. Person compelled and obsessional	3. Thoughts or actions performed with subjective compulsion
4. Occurs in healthy person	4. Not due to another mental or physical disorder

Theological writers considered scrupulosity to be *judicium conscientiae erroneae* (an error in practical conscience). In 1660, Jeremy Taylor, a Cambridge-educated clergyman and writer, produced the fascinating religious text *Doctor Dubitantium* in which he gave case materials to show how religious scruples merge into obsessional disorder, and then into madness: 'They repent when they have not sinn'd. [Scruple] is a trouble where the trouble is over, a doubt when doubts are resolved.'

The church writers of Taylor's time felt the presence of these scruples actually *interfered* with an individual's religious development. They usually didn't go on to suggest any supernatural cause.

But theologians did not always agree that scrupulosity was merely a form of fearfulness. Somewhat tortured reasoning argued that God would not cause interior suffering, anxiety, and bad judgement in the afflicted person, but that He might withhold enlightenment to punish sin and promote the victim's spiritual development. God might use obsession as a punishment for 'inclinations of vainness' or as a trial to expiate past faults to bring about a higher degree of sanctity. It's God's way of 'fitting souls for contemplation'.

An alternate cause was Satan. The devil's object was to impede or destroy the victim's health. Scrupulous behaviour was the result when the devil injected his activity 'into the morbid predisposition of our nervous system in order to create a turmoil in our souls'. As late as 1949, both God *and the devil* are listed as causes of scrupulous conscience.

The cause of scruples is the devil. The method adopted by this tireless enemy is to broaden the conscience of evil doers by a rash trust in the divine mercy, and to narrow the conscience of the good by undue fear. He seizes upon their imagination and fills it with dark and chimerical ideas; he kindles in just men apprehensions of sin which, though vain, are terrifying and capable of inspiring the greatest fear; he attacks their sense of humours which usually engender consternation of mind, anguish, bitterness and disturbance so that these poor stiffs become like skiffs exposed to the fury of an angry sea. (From Tesson, 1964)

How to tell which scruples come from where? Saint Laurence Justian proposed that scruples that emanate from hell are 'usually accompanied by a special darkening of the mind and by a notable bitterness of the heart, wherein they seek to engender distrust, lukewarmness, and the cooling of charity.'

On the other hand, scruples deriving from human nature preserve 'a constant pattern, because they are consistent in their manifest effects. Naturally scrupulous people nearly always act in fear and perturbation of mind' (from Tesson, 1964).

To a psychiatrist, the scruples 'from hell' sound as if the victim were also seriously depressed. Those from 'human nature' sound milder and mostly anxious.

Many connections recur between religion and OCD. Ritual purification, order, and danger are related. It is probably no coincidence that the personalities of two great religious leaders were deeply affected by their obsessional thought. John Bunyan, author of *The Pilgrim's Progress*, wrote in *Grace*

Abounding an incomparably vivid account of his obsessions. Blasphemous thoughts were among his chief troubles:

> I could not tell how to speak my words for fear I should misplace them. Oh, how cautiously did I then go in all I did or said! I found myself as in a miry bog that shook if I did but stir. . . . Whole floods of blasphemies were poured upon my spirit to my great Confusion and Astonishment. . . . Instead of lauding and magnifying God the Lord, if I had but heard him spoken of, presently some horrible blasphemous thought or other would bolt out of my heart against him.

Obsessive doubts and impulses also plagued another religious genius, Martin Luther. From 1517, when he first celebrated mass, Luther worried greatly for fear he had carried out some trifling act of omission which would be a sin. Blasphemous thoughts pressed in on him; he wanted to confess several times each day. Eventually his preceptor in the monastery had to discipline him for this.

Note how these obsessive symptoms, even as severe as both these men suffered, were compatible with busy, energetic, and profoundly successful lives. Will modern public figures be more forthcoming about suffering from this particular disorder? If it is as common as we believe, we should expect some revelations as others come out of the OCD cupboard.

The deep and far-reaching religious experiences of men like Bunyan and Luther cannot be dismissed or summarily classified as features of psychiatric illness. But is there a more profound connection between ritual of any sort, compulsions, and worship?

Freud wrote, in 1907: 'I am certainly not the first person to have been struck by the resemblance between what are called obsessive actions in sufferers with nervous affections and the observances by means of which believers give expression to their piety.'

In the 'ceremonials' of his neurotic obsessive–compulsive patients, Freud saw more than a superficial resemblance to the psychological processes in religious life. Obsessions and compulsions were private and often idiosyncratic, however, while religious rites were public and more uniform. In that sense, OCD could be seen as a travesty of religious practice. Freud intended not to disparage religious practices but to emphasize the ultimate meaningfulness of his patients' disturbance. He saw both religious ceremonials and obsessive–compulsive rites as protections against fear, as affirmations of belief. In one, a public, common belief; in the other, a private fear or wish. The important theme was the *symbolic expression* common to both.

At some level so profound that evolution, the brain, and human culture must all be invoked, ritual means safety, purification, and order. Ritual washing affirms integrity and acceptance. In this sense, obsessional neurosis is a pathological counterpart of the formation of a religion, and religion a universal obsessional neurosis.

JUDAISM AND OCD

Little is known about other faiths and OCD. We know the most about the Catholic perspective. In case reports from India, I have seen a passing allusion to Hindu ceremonies in which expiatory rites relieved the symptoms of what sound like obsessive–compulsive subjects but little detail is given. Daniel's case (Chapter 24) is the only one I know in which a rabbi provided important help as a religious figure for an obsessive–compulsive patient. Daniel's remarkable story included a formal religious ceremony which was pivotal for him.

Daniel's rabbi, Martin Halperin of Silver Springs, Maryland, told me how he came to treat Daniel and shared his preparation for it with me. Rabbi Halperin received a degree in rabbinical literature from the Jewish Theological Seminary in New York and had studied psychology as a college undergraduate. In addition to his work as spiritual leader of his congregation, he is also a therapist with individuals and couples. Daniel, therefore, had the good fortune to have a rabbi who was both a scholar of Judaic literature as well as a trained therapist.

In discussing the background for the ceremony he conducted with Daniel, Rabbi Halperin emphasized that mainstream rabbinical tradition was opposed to the making of vows. He cited the following quotations:

'If you forbear to vow, it shall be no sin in this.' (Deuteronomy 23:23)

'The word of the good man should be his oath, firm and unchangeable, founded steadfastly on truth. Therefore vows and oaths should be superfluous. Some men make vows out of wretched hatred of their fellow men, swearing, for example, that they will not admit this man or that man to sit at the same table with them or to come under the same roof. Such men should work to propitiate the mercy of G-d, so that they may find some cure for the disease of the soul.' (Philo)

'Do not form the habit of making vows.' (Babylonian Talmud—Nedarim 20.a)

'He who makes a vow, even though he fulfill it, is called a wicked man.' (16:22)

In general, during the Talmudic period, making vows was considered a sign of bad breeding and affected the honour of one's family. Jewish law stressed that one should strive for the desired end without the aid of vows.

But since the ideal was not always achievable and people did make vows, rabbinical authorities faced a challenge of how one could cope with sacred vows which, for various reasons, could not be fulfilled. For example, in the Book of Numbers, certain exceptions are stated that permit nullification of a vow by an unmarried daughter living in her father's house or a wife in her husband's house.

In the post-biblical period, especially in Talmudic legislation, a great deal of discussion centred around the method of annulling a vow which, due to circumstances beyond the control of the individual, could not be fulfilled.

Some sages took the position that a vow once made could not be withdrawn. In the Babylonian Talmud (Tractate Haggadah) we find the statement: 'The annulment of a vow is like an object fluttering in the air and we have no source upon which to lean.' (10:1)

Many sages, however, took the position that this Jewish law alludes to the possibility of annulment of vows. It was argued that a person might regret a vow and that there should be a remedy for its retraction.

A good deal of discussion centres around a tragic story

recorded in the biblical book of Judges (Chapter 11). Jeptha was a warrior-judge who led his people during a chaotic period in Jewish history. Just prior to an important battle, he invoked God's help by promising to offer as a sacrifice the first living thing that came out to meet him when he returned victorious. To Jeptha's horror he saw his daughter running out to meet him.

The Bible is silent as to the daughter's fate. In the body of collective literature that seeks to interpret the Bible, the Midrash, there are references to the possibility that Jeptha could have annulled his vow by appearing before the recognized sage of his day and expressing regret for a thoughtless vow. One such reference takes the position that Jeptha refused to humble himself before the priest Pinhas, so Pinhas refused to initiate any procedure for him.

Those sages who favoured the annulment of vows succeeded in establishing a methodology for its implementation that became the standard in Jewish law. It is still operative today.

The person who has uttered a vow that cannot be fulfilled may appear before a sage or a quorum of three knowledgeable men, who ask the individual: 'If you had known the consequences of making this vow would you have done it?'

If the person responds, 'I would not have taken the vow,' the sage or the quorum of three individuals pronounces him absolved of his oath. Of course such absolution would not apply if damages or harm to an innocent victim of the vow were involved. In such a case proper restitution must be made first, whether it be an apology or remuneration. A further remedy for the failure to fulfill vows is found in the 'Kol Nidre' ('All Vows') recited at the beginning of the Jewish holiday Yom Kippur, the Day of Atonement.

The twenty-four hour fast is for transgressions and oaths that could not be fulfilled, which one regrets having sworn to:

'All vows, bonds, promises, obligations, and oaths [to God] wherewith we have vowed, sworn, and found ourselves from this Day of Atonement unto the next Day of Atonement. They shall be absolved, released, annulled, made void, and of no effect; they shall not be binding nor shall they have any power. Our vows [to God] shall not be vows; our bonds shall not be bonds.'

But a lesser known ceremony, familiar to the rabbi, focuses more closely on individual vows. It is referred to in Jewish tradition as Hatarat Nedarim, the Annulment of Vows.

The traditional time for this ceremony is just prior to Rosh Hashanah, the New Year. In this ceremony, three or more individuals band together, and take turns in constituting a quasi-ecclesiastical court. Each individual in turn recites a formula whereby he renounces all oaths and promises. Reference in this formula is made to vows and various promises forgotten, as well as vows taken in a dreamlike state, and, of course, vows of which one is still aware.

The effect of this ceremony is intended to be cathartic. The individual can now approach the high holy days free of nagging concern over vows taken or made to God that did not come to fruition.

In Rabbi Halperin's work with Daniel, he emphasized that the use of the annulment procedure did not constitute a cure in itself, but was, rather, a means to an end. Together with therapy, and even repeated when necessary, it could reinforce a determination to reverse the debilitating and terrible system of rules and vows with which Daniel had surrounded himself.

The two rabbinical colleagues who formed the triad for Daniel's ceremony were also scholars of ancient Judaic ceremonies. Rabbi Halperin felt pleased by the visible positive effect that the ceremony of Hatarat Nedarim had on Daniel.

But in addition to the ceremony, the stress was also on Judaism's teaching that enjoyment is a legitimate goal of life. 'I quoted to Daniel,' the rabbi told me, 'from the teaching of Jewish sages, that the biblical Nazirite, one who abstains from drinking wine or cutting his hair, was forbidden to bring an offering after having fulfilled his vows to abstain from drinking wine and cutting his hair. The reason given was that he had prevented himself from enjoying the legitimate pleasures of life. Furthermore, a rabbinical teaching asserts that in the world to come we will be judged for the failure to enjoy those legitimate pleasures provided for us by our Creator for our enjoyment.'

Finally, Rabbi Halperin provided for me the *Formula for Annulment of Vows* as follows:

It is meritorious to annul vows on the day before Rosh Hashanah.

The three 'judges' sit while the petitioner seeking annulment stands before them and states:

Listen please, my master, expert judges: every vow or oath or prohibition, or restriction that I adopted by use of the term *konam* or the term *cherem*, that I vowed or swore while I was awake or in a dream, or that I swore by means of God's Holy Names that it is forbidden to erase, or by means of the name Hashem, Blessed is He; or any form of Naziritism that I accepted upon myself, even the Naziritism of Samson; or any prohibition, even a prohibition to derive enjoyment that I imposed upon myself or upon others by means of any expression of prohibition, whether by specifying the term prohibition or by use of the term *konam* or *cherem* [*konam* means any vow of absinence, *cherem* is any ban]; or any commitment even to perform a *mitzvah* that I accepted upon myself, whether the acceptance was in terms of a vow, a voluntary gift, an oath, Naziritism, or by any means of any other sort of expression, or whether it was made final through a handshake; any form of vow, or any custom that constitutes a good deed to which I have accustomed myself . . .

The petitioner goes on to explain that he is fearful that he will become entrapped in the sin of vows, oaths, prohibitions, and so forth. He expresses regret in taking upon himself a vow instead of having just done these things on occasion without vows. Finally, he states:

Therefore I request annulment for them all. I regret all the aforementioned whether they were matters relating to money, or whether they are matters relating to the soul. Regarding them all, I regret the terminology of vow, oath, Naziritism, prohibition, *cherem*, *konam*, and acceptances of the heart.

Most important, the petitioner does not have to name each vow: 'Please be informed, my masters, it is impossible to specify them because they are so many.'

The judges then repeat three times:

May everything be permitted you, may everything be forgiven you, may everything be allowed you. There does not exist any vow, oath, Naziritism, *cherem*, prohibition, *konam*, ostracism, excommunication, or curse. But there does exist pardon, forgiveness, and atonement. And just as the early court permits them, so may they be permitted in the Heavenly Court.

The ceremony is concluded with the petitioner declaring for the final time that he 'cancels from this time onward all vows and all oaths'. The ceremony is declared proactive so that if an oath is made subsequently and then regretted, it too is declared totally null and void.

References and Suggested Reading

AKHTAR, S.; WIG, N.; VERMA, V.; PERSHAD, D.; AND VERMA, S.K. 'A Phenomenological Analysis of Symptoms in Obsessive–Compulsive Neurosis.' *British Journal of Psychiatry* 127 (1975): 342–48.

AMERICAN PSYCHIATRIC ASSOCIATION. *Diagnostic and Statistical Manual of Mental Disorders.* Washington, D.C.: American Psychiatric Press, 1980.

ANDREASEN, NANCY. *The Broken Brain.* New York: Harper and Row, 1984.

Babylonian Talmud. The Widow and Brothers Romm. Vilna, Lithuania, 1927.

CRITCHLEY, M., AND HENSON, R.S., eds. *Music and the Brain.* Springfield, Ill.: Charles C. Thomas, 1977.

CHURCHLAND, PATRICIA. *Neurophilosophy: Toward a Unified Science of the Mind-Brain.* Cambridge, Mass.: MIT Press, 1987.

DE MAUPASSANT, G. 'The Piece of String.' In *The Best Stories of Guy de Maupassant,* edited by S. Cummins. New York: Modern Library, 1945.

DENNETT, DANIEL C. *Brainstorms: Philosophical Essays on Mind and Psychology.* Cambridge, Mass.: MIT Press, 1981.

—*Elbow Room: The Varieties of Free Will Worth Wanting.* Cambridge, Mass.: MIT Press, 1984.

DOUGLAS, MARY. *Purity and Danger: An Analysis of the Concepts of Pollution and Taboo.* London: Routledge & Kegan Paul, 1966.

EIBL-EIBESFELDT, I. 'Human Ethology: Concepts and Implications for the Sciences of Man.' *Behavioral and Brain Sciences* 2:1–57.

—*Ethology: The Biology of Behavior.* New York: Holt, Rinehart & Winston, 1970.

FODOR, JERRY A. 'The Mind-Body Problem.' *Scientific American* 244 (1981):114–23.

FREUD, SIGMUND. 'Obsessive Actions and Religious Beliefs.' In *The Standard Edition of the Complete Psychological Works of Sigmund Freud,* edited by J. Strachey (1906–1908) vol. 9. London: Hogarth Press, 1958.

—'Notes Upon a Case of Obsessional Neurosis.' In *The Standard Edition of the Complete Psychological Works of Sigmund Freud,* edited by J. Strachey, vol. 10. London: Hogarth Press, 1958.

—'The Disposition to Obsessional Neurosis.' In *The Standard Edition of the Complete Psychological Works of Sigmund Freud*, edited by J. Strachey, vol. 12. London: Hogarth Press, 1958.

GINSBERG, H.L., ed. *Tanakh: A New Translation of the Holy Scriptures.* Philadelphia: Jewish Publication Society, 1985.

HARDY, THOMAS. *Far From the Madding Crowd.* London: Henry Holt, 1874.

KELLY, GEORGE. *Craig's Wife.* In *The Best Plays of 1925–6,* edited by Burns Mantle. New York: Dodd Mead, 1955.

KARNO, M.; GOLDING, J.; SORENSON, S.; AND BURNHAM, M. 'The Epidemiology of Obsessive–Compulsive Disorder in Five U.S. Communities.' Archives of General Psychiatry, In press.

KROEBER, A. *Anthropology: Race, Language, Culture, and Psychological Prehistory.* New York: Harcourt Brace, 1948.

KNOTT, P.; HUTSON, P.; SCRAGGS, R.; AND CURZON, G. 'Electrochemical Recording of Brain Catecholamine and Serotonin Release During Behavioural Changes.' In *Function and Regulation of Monoamine Enzymes: Basic and Clinical Aspects,* edited by E. Usdin, N. Weiner, M.B. Youdin. London: Macmillan, 1981.

LEIGHTON, D.; MACMILLAN, A.; HARDIN, J.; MACKLIN, D.; AND LEIGHTON, A. *The Character of Danger.* New York: Basic Books, 1963.

LORENZ, KONRAD. *Studies in Animal and Human Behavior,* vol. 1. Cambridge, Mass.: Harvard University Press, 1970.

—*Behind the Mirror.* New York: Harcourt Brace Jovanovich, 1973.

MORRIS, DESMOND. *The Naked Ape.* New York: McGraw-Hill, 1967.

MYERS, ROLLO. *Erik Satie.* New York: Dover Publications, 1947.

NEMIAH, J. Foreword. In *New Findings in Obsessive–Compulsive Disorder,* edited by T. Insel. Washington, D.C.: American Psychiatric Press, 1985.

O'FLAHERTY, V.M. *How to Cure Scruples.* Milwaukee: Bruce Publishing Company, 1966.

RACHMAN, S.J., AND HODGSON, R. *Obsessions and Compulsions.* Englewood Cliffs, N.J.: Prentice-Hall, 1980.

'Responsa.' Coordinator: Rabbi Alan Rosenbaum. Cited by RABBIS TICTIN, M.; BEN ADRET, S.; ISSERLES, M. Chicago: Institute for Computers in Jewish Life, 1987.

REYNOLDS, PETER C. *On the Evolution of Human Behavior.* Berkeley: University of California Press, 1981.

RICKABY, J. *The Spiritual Exercises of St. Ignatius Loyola.* New York: Benziger Bros., 1923.

SACKS, OLIVER. *Awakenings.* New York: E.P. Dutton, 1983.

—'Acquired Tourettism in Adult Life.' In: *Gilles de la Tourette Syndrome,* edited by A.J. Friedhoff and T. Chase. New York: Raven Press, 1982.

REFERENCES AND SUGGESTED READING 235

SELIGMAN, MARTIN. 'Phobias and Preparedness.' *Behavior Therapy* 2 (1971): 307–20.

SPENCER, SCOTT. *Endless Love*. New York: Alfred Knopf, 1979.

SARTRE, J.P. *L'Etre et le Néant*. Paris: Gallimard, 1943.

Talmudic Encyclopedia (Hebrew) 'Hatarat Nedarim.' Jerusalem: Talmudic Encyclopedia Institute, 1965.

TAYLOR, J. *Doctor Dubitantium, or The Role of Conscience in All Her General Measures*. London: J. Flesher for R. Royston, 1660.

TAYLOR, P.; MAHENDRA, B.; AND GUNN, J. 'Erotomania in Males.' *Psychological Medicine* 13 (1983): 645–50.

TESSON, F. 'Doctrinal History.' In *Treatment of Scruples*, edited by M.G. Carroll. Illinois: Divine Word Publications, 1964.

VAN BOGAERT, LUDO, AND THEODORIDES, JEAN. *Constantin von Economo: The Man and the Scientist*. Vienna: Verlag der Osterreichishchen Akademie der Wissenschaften, 1979.

WHALEN, J.P., ed. *New Catholic Encyclopedia*. Washington, D.C.: Catholic University of America Publishers, 1967.

Index

ability to function, 27, 53, 84
Acquired Immune-Deficiency
    Syndrome (AIDS), obsession
    with, 139–42, 161
ACTH (adrenocorticotropic
    hormone), 187
action patterns: fixed, 180, 184
    inappropriately released, 188–9
    OCD rituals as, 184–90
actors, OCD victims as, 84–5, 90,
    108
adolescents with OCD, 9, 12, 72–3,
    105–9, 222
    symptoms in, 81
aggression, 25, 190
aggressive obsessions, 214
AIDS see Acquired Immune-
    Deficiency Syndrome
alcohol, 101
Alphonsus Liguori, Saint, 223
Alternative Realities (Rigby), 170
American Psychiatric Association,
    *Diagnostic and Statistical Manual
    of Mental Disorders* (DSM III),
    5–6, 198, 217–18
amino acids, 116
amphetamines, 100, 101–2
Anafranil see clomipramine
angel dust (PCP), 100, 101
anger, 10, 44, 54, 55, 56, 57
animal behaviour: human habits
    reminiscent of, 179–80
    similarity of OCD rituals and,
    168, 180
animal models, 188, 210
    hair pulling, 147
animal studies, 210
annihilation, 79
antidepressants, 59, 99, 220
    clomipramine as, 9, 10
anxiety, 213
    in case histories, 21, 22, 23, 24,
    26
    drugs in treatment of, 97
    relieved through ritualized
    behaviours, 37
arithromania, 87

Asberg, Marie, 9
athletes, supersititions of, 177–8
attack behaviour, 209
Attention-Deficit Disorder, 31, 34,
    41
attention span, 29, 31, 37
avoidance, 84, 130
    out of control, 190

Babylonian Talmud, 228
barbiturates, 100
basal ganglia, 86, 209
    abnormalities in OCD, 14
    connection with obsessions and
    compulsions, 86–9, 91
    OCD and disease of, 184–5
behaviour: biology of, 10, 17
    controlled in brain, 209
    craziness in OCD, 5, 119
    out of control, 25–6, 35, 49, 190
    see also innate behaviour patterns
behaviour patterns: pre-wired,
    185–6
    see also innate behaviour patterns
behaviour therapists, 13, 219–20
behaviour therapy, 11, 13, 15–16,
    40, 96, 104, 151
    in case histories, 66, 70, 78,
    81,130, 135, 155–65, 183, 203
    confrontational part of, 158–9,
    163–4
    with hair-pulling compulsion,
    147
    in treatment of OCD, 152–3, 165,
    219–20
behavioural psychologists, 96
Bible, 228, 229
biological basis of behaviour, 10,
    17
biological basis of OCD, 10, 13–14,
    15, 17, 38, 59, 96, 209–10
biology: of knowledge, 168, 209
    of mental illness, 8, 97, 100
Boston Psychopathic Hospital, 192
Boswell, James, 4
Braceland, Francis, 195

brain, 10, 227
  abnormalities in OCD, 14, 77,
    91, 96, 209
  basal ganglia, 86–9
  hiccup in, 5
  inborn (innate) programmes in,
    6, 16, 180, 209–10
  integration of emotions, sensory
    information, and motor
    behaviours in, 89
  miswired connections in, 135
  role in fixed behaviour patterns,
    180
  short circuits in electrical activity
    of, 5
  study of, 8, 14, 91
  trivial thoughts mixed up with
    survival in (theory), 138–9
  vestigial centres in, activated in
    OCD (theory), 77
brain chemistry, 17
  research in, 10
brain circuits, in knowing, 209
brain disease, OCD as, 85–92,
    184–5
brain function, 3
  quirks in, 147
brain imaging, 14, 15, 91
brain lesions, 187
brain science, 97
brain surgery, 85–6
  see also psychosurgery
brain tumours, 114–15
Brainstorms (Dennett), 198
Bunyan, John, 225–6
  Grace Abounding, 225–6
  The Pilgrim's Progress, 225
Buxbaum, Edith, 146

case histories: Alan, 139–42
  Alice, 199–204, 206–7, 208
  Amy, 178
  Arnie, 67–70
  Arthur, 118–22
  Audrey, 150–2
  Brendan, 186–7
  Charles, 77, 78–82, 96
  Claude, 141–2
  Daniel, 152–66, 227, 230
  Darrel, 82–3
  David, 100–2, 179
  Debby, 107–8
  Dr S., 21–41, 59
  Don, 116–17, 118
  Fred, 106–7, 109
  George, 8
  George K., 115–16, 117
  Gerald, 97–8
  Ginger, 184

Jackie P., 143–5, 146
Jacob, 85–6
Jeffrey, 24, 29–41, 59
John, 92–3, 188
Kim, 204–5, 206–7, 208, 210
Laura, 131–6
Marion, 84
Morris, 70–2
Murray, 110–13, 198
Paul, 63–7, 96, 188
Richard, 92–3
Robert, 136–9
Sal, 7–8, 131, 179, 181, 183
Sally, 147–50, 151–2
Sam, 43–56, 58–9
Sebastian, 192–7
Shirley, 181–3
Stanley, 94–5, 123–6
Steven, 85–6
Terry, 174–5
Tim, 126–30
William, 205–7, 210
Zach, 41–3, 56–60
CAT scans, 14
Catholic Church: and OCD, 223–7
  and scrupulosity, 149–50, 151,
    152
caudate nucleus, 91
cerebral cortex, 89
Charles, Xavier, 152–3, 156–66
checking compulsion, 2–3, 37, 62,
    76, 84, 95, 177, 184, 208, 215
  AIDS and, 139–40
  in case histories, 22–5, 26–7, 59,
    67–70, 108, 124, 131, 137–8,
    140
  doubts in, 207
  normal, 83, 190, 207
chemical treatment, 10–11
children with OCD, 6–7, 9, 11, 16,
    72–3
  case histories, 49–50, 53, 62–73,
    76, 78–82, 131–6
  inability to trust their senses,
    78–82, 83
choreas, 14
CIBA-Geigy Pharmaceutical
    company, 9
cleaning ritual: in case histories,
    128–30
  out of context, 188, 190
cleanliness, 11, 77, 124, 125, 190
  see also neatness/messiness
Clérambault, Ferdière, 196
Clérambault's Syndrome, 196–7
clinics, 219
clomipramine, 8–11, 12, 15–16,
    40–1, 44, 54, 58–9, 96, 104,
    155, 174, 175, 220–1

availability of, 99
in case histories, 39, 58–9, 66,
    70, 72, 81, 98, 112–13, 116,
    120, 121, 122, 123, 130, 135,
    138, 144–5, 183, 203–4
dosage, 220–1
effectiveness of, 98–9
selective positive effect on
    obsessions, 99, 101–2, 118
side effects of, 9, 70, 123, 130,
    204, 220
in treating hair-pulling
    compulsion, 144–5, 146, 147
ways to obtain, 220
as wonder drug, 97–100
cocaine, 100, 101
collectors: fixed behaviour
    patterns in, 180
    see also hoarding compulsion
Collyer brothers, 182
'coming out of the cupboard', 222,
    226
communes, 170–1
compulsions, 1, 2, 6–7
    associated with neurological
        diseases, 13–14
    checklist of, 213–16
    childhood onset of, 6–7
    connection with ritual and
        worship, 226–7
    in control of actions, 26, 49
    differ from superstitions, 176–7
    lack of understanding of cause
        of, 94–5
    neurology of, 89–91
    neutral, 83, 94–5
    not helped by psychoanalytic
        treatment, 13
    rituals/thoughts in, 83–4
    scientific interest in, 5
    and tics, 86–7
    and Tourette's Syndrome, 87–8
    unconscious symbolic
        determinants of, 151
    see also under specific compulsions,
        e.g. counting compulsions
compulsive personality, 15, 92,
    169, 199
    case history, 174–5
Compulsive Personality Disorder,
    174–5, 217–18
    symptoms of, 217–18
concealment see secrecy
contamination obsessions, 77, 214
    in case histories, 41–60, 79, 140,
        141
    protection in, 50
coping, 16, 26
counting compulsions, 76, 125

in case histories, 29, 31, 68,
    100–1, 107–8, 124–5, 131, 132–5
'Craig's Wife' (Kelly), 171
craziness of OCD behaviour, 5,
    119
Cronholm, Börje, 9
cross-cultural comparisons, 77, 184
culture, 227
cures, 12

danger, 11, 225
death thoughts, 125
demand sensitivity, 174
denial, 131
    by parents, 30
    in case histories, 57
Dennett, Daniel, Brainstorms, 198
depression, 10, 66, 146, 213
    in case histories, 55–6, 57, 125
    in children, 6
    complication from OCD, 122
    drugs in treatment of, 97, 221
desipramine, 147
desires about desires, 198
desmethylimipramine (DMI), 99,
    102
Desperately Seeking Susan (film), 191
Despert, Louise, 197
Dexedrine, 34, 37
diagnosis (OCD), 41, 213–18
    in case histories, 35–6, 120
    interviews, 105
diencephalon, 90
dirt, 177
    concept of, 170
    preoccupation with, 84
distress, associated with obsessive
    thoughts/compulsive rituals,
    216
Doctor Dubitantium (Taylor), 224
dogs, 180, 188–9
doorway rituals, 62, 188
    in case histories, 63–7
    of Dr Johnson, 3–4
    identical patterns of, 186
dopamine, 101–2
double-blind trials, 97–8, 99
doubt, doubting: in case histories,
    69, 72, 121, 205–7
    inability to dispel, 206–9
    localization in brain, 91
    pathological, 11, 17
    unreasonable, 150
doubting disease, 17, 83–5, 168,
    206–10
Douglas, Mary, 170
drug abuse, 100–2
drug treatment, 3, 11, 15–16, 17,
    36–7, 38, 40, 76, 96, 117, 220–1

in case histories, 28, 35–7, 39,
    43, 78, 100–2
with hair-pulling compulsion,
    145–6
new, 102
in psychiatry, 8, 96
weakening of symptoms with,
    37
see also clomipramine
drugs: illegal, 100–2
selectivity of effects of, 13, 99,
    101–2, 118
Dumirox see fluvoxamine
Duphar Laboratories, 221

elderly, 175
Eli Lilly (co.), 221
embarrassment, 84
emotional etiology (OCD), in case
    histories, 26, 27–8
emotional problems, 38–9
obsessions as, 94
Encephalitis Lethargica, 87–8
Endless Love (Spencer), 191–2
energy, expanded in rituals, 26–7,
    69, 123–4, 125
epidemiological surveys, 105–9
epidemiology, 105
epilepsy, 14, 85, 86, 89, 90
fugue states in, 114
erotomania, 196–7
ethologists, 16
ethology, 180–1, 189–90
everyday life: interference in due
    to obsessional
    thoughts/compulsive rituals,
    213, 215
obsessionality of, 1, 169–76
evolution, 227
exactness: obsession with need
    for, 214
speech compulsion, 201–2, 203–4
The Exorcist (film), 148, 149
expiatory rites, Hindu, 227
exposure with response
    prevention, 220
exposure to trigger situations, 13,
    153, 164–5

families, 7, 16, 17, 60
effect of OCD on, 79
lack of understanding among, 83
OCD runs in, 11, 21–41, 59
see also father–son OCD
    problems; parents
fantasy, in case histories, 21–2,
    25–6
fastidiousness, 150
see also neatness/messiness

father–son OCD problems, 41
in case histories, 21, 26, 29, 32,
    33, 35, 36, 38, 40, 59
Faverin see fluvoxamine
fears: development of, 185–6
of doing something wrong, 154
of harming others, 82–3
of having killed someone, 21–4
protection against, 227
Feverin see fluvoxamine
finger licking, 188
Floxyfral see fluvoxamine
fluoxetine (Prozac), 102, 221
fluvoxamine (Faverin), 102, 221
Formula for Annulment of Vows,
    230–2
free will, 168
and uncertainty of knowing,
    197–210
Freud, Sigmund, 11, 12
on obsessive-compulsive
    neurosis, 95
'Rat Man' case, 15, 94
on religion, 226–7
friends, 76
in case histories, 80, 107, 155
frontal lobes: abnormalities in
    OCD, 14
see also brain
frustration, 42

genetic disease, OCD as, 11, 38,
    209
germs, 177
fanatic preoccupation with, 5
Grace Abounding (Bunyan), 225–6
greylag geese, 189
grooming behaviours, 77, 179–90,
    209
atavistic urge, 146, 147
encoded patterns of, 189–90
identical patterns of, 186–8
OCD behaviours as misplaced,
    184
selectivity of, 181
guilt, 11
in case histories, 21, 122
parental, 39

habits, 2, 170, 213
in behaviour therapy, 219–20
on continuum with OCD, 173,
    175–6
as forms of OCD, 147
'good', 14–15
hiding, 106, 107, 108
reminiscent of animal behaviour,
    179–80
unbreakable, 5

see also housekeeping habits
hair, symbolic meaning of, 146
hair-pulling compulsion, 143–7,
     190
  case history, 143–5
Hallopeau (physician), 145
hallucinations, 117
haloperidol, 82
Halperin, Martin, 227–8, 230
hand washing, 37
  in case histories, 42, 43, 57
  see also washing compulsion
Hardy, Thomas, 171
Harvard Medical School, 3
Hatarat Nedarim (Annulment of
     Vows), 230–2
Heinroth, Oskar, 180
heredity, OCD, 11, 38, 209
Hindus, 146, 227
  expiatory rites, 227
hoarding compulsion, 7, 179,
     181–2, 215
  in case histories, 131, 181–3
  selectivity of, 181
Hobson, Dr Alan 193, 195
hormones, 187, 190
hospitalization, 38
housekeeping habits, 168, 170–3,
     184
Hudson, Rock, 141
Hughes, Howard, 5
Hugo, Victor, Les Miserables, 191,
     197
Hume, David, 209
humiliation, 137
humour, 157
hyperactivity, 31, 34, 36, 37, 41
  see also Attention-Deficit
     Disorder
hypothalamus, 90
hysteria, 95

Ignatius Loyola, Saint, Spiritual
     Exercises . . ., 223
images in OCD, 115, 117–18
imipramine (Tofranil), 9, 28, 40–1,
     99, 155
  in case histories, 36–7, 39
impulsivity, 10
inborn knowledge, 16, 186,
     189–90, 210
India, 77, 146, 227
innate behaviour patterns, 180,
     183–4
  OCD rituals as, 184–90
  ritualized, 210
innate brain
     pattern(s)/programmes, 209–10
  likelihood in OCD, 16, 180

running wild, 6
Inquisition, 152
intentionality, 89
intentions, first/second order, 198
isolation, 137

Janet, Pierre, 90, 209
Jewish religion, and OCD, 152,
     153–66, 227–32
Jewish Theological Seminary, New
     York, 227
Johnson, Samuel, 3–4
joke-telling compulsion, in case
     histories, 110–13

Kant, Immanuel, 209
Karolinska Hospital, Stockholm,
     8–9
Kelly, George, 'Craig's Wife', 171
knowing, 92, 118–22
  biological basis for, 17
  biology of, 168, 209
  brain circuits in, 209
  in case histories, 83–4
  uncertainty of, 197–210
knowledge: acquisition, 184
  innate patterns of, 186, 189–90,
     210
  stored, 183
Kohler, Wolfgang, 3
'Kol Nidre', 229

L-tryptophan, 39, 59, 116, 221
Laurence Justian, Saint, 225
learning: of fears, 185–6
  learning theory models, OCD,
     96
  problems, 135
  see also knowledge
lithium, 40, 221
lobotomy, 7–8
  see also psychosurgery
logic, in rituals, 50, 53
loneliness, in case histories, 136–7,
     138
Lopez–Ibor, Professor, 8
Lorenz, Konrad, 180, 183–4, 189,
     209
love as obsession, 168, 191–7
LSD, 100, 101, 102, 119, 120, 121
Luther, Martin, 226

magical acts, 2
magical thinking, 47, 53, 176
manic depressive illness, 40
mannerisms, odd, 90
marital relations, 139, 175
  effect of OCD on, 131–2, 135
  neatness issue in, 171–3

Massachusetts Mental Health
    Center, Boston, 7
masturbation, 81, 125, 160
Maudsley Hospital, London, 13
Maupassant, Guy de, 'The Piece
    of String', 169
medical care, 35–6
Medical College of Pennsylvania,
    13
medical literature, OCD cases
    reported in, 6
medical profession, ignorance of
    OCD, 40
mental illness, biology of, 8, 97,
    100
mental images, nature of, 117–18
mental retardation, 131, 132, 133–6
mice, 'barber', 187–8
Midrash, 229
Milne, A.A., 176
mind: hiccups of, 62, 67, 73
    obsession of, 118–22
    problems in doubting disease,
        207
    tics of, 90
    see also brain
Mineka, Susan, 185–6
misdiagnosis, in case histories,
    33–4
Les Misérables (Hugo), 191, 197
modelling theory, OCD, 59
models: animal, 147, 188, 210
    ethology as, 180–1
    psychoanalytic, 15
mood states: in case histories, 33
    psychiatric drugs and, 97
Morris, Desmond: The Mouse in
    Biomedical Research, 187–8
    The Naked Ape, 190
movement disorders, 14
muscle contractions, self-induced,
    in case histories, 29, 30, 31, 34,
    37
music, in case histories, 113–18
musicians, with obsessive tunes,
    117

nail biting, 147
The Naked Ape (Morris), 190
National Hospital for Neurological
    Disease (Queen Square,
    London), 3
National Institute of Mental
    Health (USA), 2
    study of OCD, 7, 9–11, 58, 78,
        84, 97–8, 119, 124
National Institute of Mental
    Health, Animal Genetics
    Center, 187

neatness/messiness, 92–3, 170–3
nest-building, 180
nest cleaning, 130, 188
nesting behaviour, 179–90
neuro-ethology, 180
neurological diseases, 14
    and OCD, 85–92, 209
neurology, of obsessions and
    compulsions, 89–91
neuronal discharge, 90
neurosurgery, 85–6
neurotransmitters, 10, 101
New Catholic Encyclopedia, 223
Nigeria, 77
normality, in combination with
    compulsions, 66, 73, 80
number compulsion, 85, 86
    in case histories, 70, 107
    see also counting compulsion

obsessional neurosis, 227
    see also Obsessive–Compulsive
        Disorder (OCD)
obsessional personality profile, 92
obsessionality of everyday life,
    169–76
obsessions, 1, 2, 6–7
    about doing the unacceptable
        thing, 112
    association with neurological
        diseases, 13–14
    checklist of, 213–16
    childhood onset of, 6
    differ from superstitions, 176–7
    dormant, 90
    lack of understanding of cause
        of, 94–5
    love as, 168, 191–7
    neurology of, 89–91
    neutral, 83, 94–5
    not helped by psychoanalytic
        treatment, 13
    as punishment from God, 224–5
    scientific interest in, 5
    sense that are part of conscious
        intent yet senseless, 37, 43, 76,
        197–8, 201
    term, 76
    and tics, 87
    as tics of the mind, 5
    unconscious symbolic
        determinants of, 151
    'voluntary' aspect of, 27, 93, 202
    see also under specific obsessions
        e.g. aggressive obsessions
obsessive character, 169, 170
    rituals/thoughts of, 83–4
Obsessive–Compulsive Disorder
    (OCD), 1–2

action to take regarding, 218–22
basis for, 17
biology of, 10, 13–14, 15, 17, 38,
    59, 96, 209–10
boundaries of, 14, 17, 110
brain abnormalities in, 14, 77,
    91, 96, 209
as brain disease, 85–92
cause of, 10, 38
childhood onset, 25, 49–50, 53,
    71, 76, 135–6
commonness of (incidence of), 7,
    11–12, 17, 51–2, 66, 108,
    116–17, 135, 226
defined, 198
DSM III definition of, 6
forms of, 66
identical patterns in, 16, 62, 185,
    186–8
literature about, 38
numbers of people with, 1, 12
philosophical implications of,
    168, 208
runs in families, 11, 21–41, 59
scrupulosity compared with, 224
severity rating scale, 216–17
studies of, 6, 9–11, 16, 58, 78, 85,
    97–8, 119, 124
study centres, 12
theories of causation, in case
    histories, 52
obsessive–compulsive neurosis, 95
Obsessive–Compulsive Scale,
    Global, 216–17
O'Flaherty, V.M., 224
order, 6, 52–3, 225
    obsession with need for, 214
ordering/arranging compulsion,
    190, 215
Osler, Sir William, 'On Chorea
    and Choreiform Affections',
    86–7, 91

pain, 66, 126
    in case histories, 21–2, 23, 25,
        26, 28–9
    relief from through ritualizing
        behaviours, 37
parents, 11, 17, 76, 96, 222
    case histories, 19–60
    denial by, 30
    parenting style, 11, 17, 31, 38,
        39, 52, 95
    understanding of OCD, 25, 26
parents with OCD, with children
    with OCD, 21, 26, 29, 32, 33,
    35, 36, 38, 40, 41, 43–4, 50,
    56–7, 58, 59

Parkinson's disease, 87–8, 91
Parmenides, 208
patient-support organizations, 218,
    222
pemoline (Valital), 36
penance: in case histories, 47–9
    need for, 150
    ritualistic, 152
perfectionism, 124, 135–6, 217, 218
personal space, 184
phobia clinics, 219
phobias, 96, 186
Phobic Action, 218, 222
'The Piece of String' (De
    Maupassant), 169
The Pilgrim's Progress (Bunyan),
    225
placebos, 9–10, 28, 97–8, 99
plucking compulsion, 179
Positron Emission Tomography
    (PET scans), 14, 91
prayer: excessive, 149
    secrecy in, 84
    see also religion; religious excess
priests, 6, 149, 150–1
primates, higher, 185–6
primitive behaviour patterns, 77
    OCD symptoms as, 146, 147,
        186, 188, 190
progesterone, 180
protection: from fears, 227
    from harm, 176
protective rituals, OCD behaviour
    as misplaced, 184
Prozac see fluoxetine
psilocybin, 100, 101
psychiatric disorders, childhood
    onset of, 6–7
psychiatric drugs, 97, 220
    see also drug treatment
psychiatric epidemiology, 105
psychiatric treatment, 151
psychiatrists, 6
psychiatry: drug treatment in, 8–9,
    96
    OCD in, 95
psychoanalysis: in case histories,
    53–4, 56, 136
    in treatment of OCD, 12, 15
psychoanalytic training, in
    understanding of OCD, 92–6
psycholepsy, 90
psychological conflict, as cause of
    OCD, 94–5
psychological treatment, 3, 66
psychologists, 219
psychopharmacology, 96, 220
psychosis, 196
psychosurgery, 7, 15

psychotherapy, 198
  in case histories, 78, 122, 154–5
  in hair-pulling compulsion, 147
  in treatment of OCD, 15, 16
punishment: need for, 148–9, 156
  obsession with, 224–5
  self-imposed, 160–1
purification ritual, 77, 152, 225
Puritans, 152

quasi-control, symptoms, 27, 93,
  202
question-asking: in case histories,
  119–204
  repetitive, 29, 31, 36

rabbis, 152, 162–3, 165, 227
'Rat Man' case, 15, 94
rating scales, 213, 216–17
rats, grooming behaviour, 187
reality, innate brain patterns in,
  209–10
reason, sensation versus, 207
reassurance, 17, 208
receptors, brain, 10
religion, 47, 147–66
  perspectives on OCD, 223–32
religious ceremony, in treatment
  of OCD, 152, 163, 165, 230–2
religious excess, 151
rituals as, 137, 177
  see also scrupulosity
remissions, 24, 26, 28, 68, 112
repeating rituals, repetition, 3,
  94–5, 215
  in case histories, 123–6, 158
  out of context, 190
  questions, in case histories, 29,
  31, 36, 199–204
resistance: discomfort in, 183
  to behaviour change, 29
  to compulsions/obsessions, 145,
  216
Reynolds, Frances, 3–4
Rhesus monkeys, 185–6
Rigby, Andrew, Alternate Realities,
  170
rigid personality, 169, 174, 175,
  191, 199
ritual displays, 189–90
ritual penance, 152
  in case histories, 47–9
  need for, 150–1
ritual purification, 77, 152, 225
ritualizers, fixed behaviour
  patterns in, 180
rituals, 1, 2, 3, 5, 10, 177, 178
  behaviour therapy, 13

in case histories, 41–60, 63–7, 79,
  81, 126–30, 137–9
childhood onset of, 6
common, 76
connection with compulsions
  and worship, 226–7
content of, 83–4
developmental, 178
hiding, 128, 135
ideas and fears enacted
  symbolically through, 94–5
as innate behaviour patterns,
  184–90
primitive, 66, 77
protective, 184
religious, 137, 177
repeating, 215
similarity to fixed animal
  behaviours, 168, 181
sports, 177–8
tic-like quality of, 90
to ward off punishment by God,
  154, 155, 156, 158, 160–2,
  163–4
wanting not to want them, 198,
  209
Rosh Hashanah, 230, 231
routines, 175–6
rules, 5
  self-imposed, 49, 53, 156–8,
  160–1, 164
ruminations, 53, 83, 120, 204–5
  doubts in, 207–8
  see also thoughts in OCD

Sacks, Oliver, 89–90
safety, 190, 209
Salem witch trials, 151–2
saliva swallowing compulsion,
  42–3
Sartre, Jean-Paul, 79
Satan, 150, 225
Satanism, 152
Satie, Erik, 117
schizophrenia, 65, 196
  childhood, 6, 33–4
schoolwork, trouble with, 135–6
science-fiction hypothesis, 108,
  132–3, 135
scruples, cause of, 225
scrupulosity, 6, 147–52
  in case histories, 147–52
  Catholic Church and, 223–7
  compared with OCD, 224
  defined, 223, 224–5
  historical perspective, 151–2
secrecy, 1, 6, 7, 12, 16, 59, 60, 117,
  138, 139

in case histories, 24, 26, 27, 51, 64, 132, 146
in hiding habits, 106, 107, 108
inventive forms of, 84
selectivity: of drug effects, 13, 99, 101–2, 118
of hoarding compulsion, 181
in OCD, 181, 206
of symptoms, 66, 93
self-control, 11
self-denial, in ritualizing, 47–9
self-grooming, 188
self-stimulation, 29
self-treatment, 16
sensation, versus reason, 207
senses, inability to trust, 78–82, 83–4
sensory information, 209
serializing, in case histories, 29, 37
serotonin, 39, 116
effect of clomipramine on, 10
level of and effectiveness of clomipramine, 99
serotonin system, effect of drugs on, 101–2
sex, 190
sexual obsessions, 125, 214
shame, in case histories, 42
shyness, 63–4, 72
siblings, 222
in case histories, 58
effect of OCD on, 35
side effects, 59, 220, 221
see also clomipramine
sin, sinning, 148–9
fear of, 223
sleeping sickness, 87–8
somatic obsession–compulsion, 214
Spencer, Scott, Endless Love, 191–2
Spinoza, Baruch, 177
Spiritual Exercises . . . (Ignatius Loyola), 223
sports rituals, 177–8
spouses, 60, 222
in case histories, 26, 27, 54–6
squirrelling habits, 179
squirrels, 179, 180
stimuli, hiding from, 130
street people, case histories, 126–30
stress, 72
string play, in case histories, 29, 30, 31, 32, 33, 34, 36, 37, 39, 59
sugar, in case history, 103–4
super grooming, 187–8
'super normals', 14–15
superstitions, 1, 168, 176–8
support groups, 218, 222

surgery: neurosurgery, 85–6
psychosurgery, 7, 15
Swarthmore College, 3, 6
Sydenham's Chorea, 90
symbolic expression, in religious ceremonials and obsessive-compulsive rituals, 226–7
symmetry, 2, 37, 214
in case histories, 81
symptoms, 14, 84, 177
in case histories, 25, 105–9
change in, over time, 66, 81
of Compulsive Personality Disorder, 217–18
experienced as compulsory, 25, 29, 49, 50, 89, 198
lessening of, with drug treatment, 37, 96, 120, 138
list of, 213–15
monitoring, 13
as primitive behaviour patterns, 146, 147, 186, 188, 190
quasi-control of, 27, 93, 202
removal of, 13
selectivity of, 66, 93
symptom substitution, 95
teachers in detection of, 136
view of, in behavioural therapy, 96
washing as most common, 77

Taylor, Jeremy, 224
Doctor Dubitantium, 224
teachers: in case histories, 38–9, 41, 134
in identification of OCD, 136
teasing, 84, 109
in case histories, 57, 64, 65, 134
Tesson, F., 225
thalamus, 90
therapy, 117
in case histories, 26, 27, 28
see also behavioural therapy; psychotherapy
thoughts, repetitive, 1
childhood onset of, 6
thoughts in OCD, 1, 2, 213
about unacceptable behaviour, 84
blasphemous, 226
in case histories, 67, 68, 69, 71
of harm, 177
tic-like quality of, 90
see also ruminations
tics, 73, 93, 111, 112, 198
and compulsions, 86–7, 90
of the mind, 5
time, occupied by obsessive thoughts/compulsive rituals, 26–7, 69, 125, 213

Tofranil *see* imipramine
toilet training, 11, 38
Tourette, Georges Gilles de la,
    87–8
Tourette's Syndrome, 87–8, 90, 91,
    93, 112, 113
treatment, 7, 11, 12, 15–16, 95–6
    chemical, 10–11
    early, 9
    see also behaviour therapy; drug
        treatment; psychotherapy
trichotillomania, 145–7
trigger situations, behaviour
        therapy, 13
    facing, 153, 164–5
'20/20' (television programme), 12,
    103, 115, 138, 143, 144, 145
twitches, 86, 90

Valital *see* pemoline
valium, 28, 100, 101
viral encephalitis, 87–8
visual images, 115, 116
Von Economo, Constantin, 88–9,
    91, 209
vows, in Judaism, 227–32

warding off evil, in case histories,
    47

washers, 95, 129, 130
    fixed behaviour patterns in, 180
washing compulsion, 2, 5, 8, 62,
    66, 76, 77, 92–3, 177
    and AIDS obsession, 139, 141,
        142
    in case histories, 68, 70–2, 78–82,
        98, 100–1, 127, 128, 130, 132,
        153, 161, 198
    identical patterns of, 186–7
    secrecy in, 84
    selectivity of, 181
    see also hand washing
Whitman, Charles, 180
will, 11
    alteration of in neurological
        disease, 89
    localization of in brain, 91
    see also free will
withdrawal, 122
    in case histories, 72
word compulsions, in case
    histories, 45–6, 48, 52
worship, connection with ritual
    and compulsions, 226–7

Xanax, 121

Yom Kippur, 229